ADVICE

Rabbi Nachman:

ADVICE

(*LIKUTEY ETZOT*)

by Rabbi Nathan of Breslov

Translated by Avraham Greenbaum

PUBLISHED BY
THE BRESLOV RESEARCH INSTITUTE

Library of Congress Catalog Card Number: 83—70202

ISBN 0-930213-04-1

First Edition

For further information:
Breslov Research Institute
POB 5370
Jerusalem, Israel

or:
Breslov Research Institute
POB 587
Monsey, NY 10952-0587

e-mail: info@breslov.org
INTERNET: http//www.breslov.org

Printed in Israel

in loving memory

of our dear parents

Rabbi Zvi Aryeh Benzion

and

Zipporah Rosenfeld

who pioneered the English translations of

the teachings of

Rebbe Nachman of Breslov

and who devoted their lives to the

dissemination of those teachings;

who inspired an awe of God

and a love for *Eretz Yisrael*

in those who knew them.

by their children

Rosenfeld, Kramer and **Maimon families**

ספר קדוש זה הודפס ומוקדש לזכר נשמת

האי גברא רבא ויקירא

גריס באורייתא תדירא

מרבה חכמה יוסיף דעת

גדל החסד כביר המעש

רב הפעלים נודע בשערים

האציל מרוחו לקרובים ולרחוקים

גדר פרץ ועמד בשער

הקים עולה של תורה בכל אתר

הרב צבי אריה בן־ציון ב״ר ישראל אבא רוזנפלד ז״ל

נשיא ישיבת ״חסידי ברסלב״ אור הנעלם

בעיה״ק **ירושלים** תובב״א

נפטר בקרתא קדישא ירושלם

ונטמן בהר הזיתים המקודש

י״א כסליו תשל״ט

Dedicated to my dear wife
A.G.

TABLE OF CONTENTS

Publisher's Preface:

Mayim amukim divrey pi ish, Nachal Novea Mekor CHokhmah.
Deep waters are the words of a man's mouth: a flowing brook, a fountain of wisdom (Proverbs 18:4).
Mayim amukim etzah b'lev ish, v'ish tevunah yidlenah.
Deep water is the counsel in the heart of man, but a man of understanding will draw it out (Proverbs 20:5).

In his comment on the first verse quoted, Rashi remarks that the word for "man" — *ish* — is used throughout the TaNaCh to refer to a person of stature. It was to someone outstanding that King Solomon was referring. Regarding the second verse, Rashi explains that the reason why the counsel of a wise man is compared to deep waters is because the guidance he offers is not necessarily revealed and obvious on the surface. Rather it is hidden within the depths of his wisdom. Therefore it takes a "man of understanding" to draw it out, so that others can have the benefit of it.

The Midrash (*Pirkey DeRebbe Eliezer* 3) relates, God held counsel with the Torah prior to creation whether or not to create the world. When God accepted the Torah's advice, the Torah declared: "In me is counsel and sound wisdom; I am understanding, power is mine" (Proverbs 8:14).Throughout the *Zohar*, the Torah and its six hundred and thirteen mitzvot are described as the "six hundred and thirteen *recommendations.*" The Torah is made up of *etzot* — advice. God looked into the Torah and created the world. The Torah is, then, the blueprint of the world, and it contains guidance and advice for all possible situations in the world, ranging from the most routine domestic, family, educational and business situations to the most bizarre and far-flung possibilities.

At the close of his career Moses warned the Jewish people that they would go into exile, and he told them what would be the cause. "For they are a nation void of counsel, and there is no understanding in them" (Deuteronomy 32:28). The cause of all the exiles and their suffering would be that the Jewish people would ignore the advice of the Torah.

The pain of exile, personal and national, is expressed in King David's cry: "How long, O Lord, will you forget me for ever? How long will You hide Your face from me? How long shall I take counsel in my soul, having sorrow in my heart by day? How long shall my enemy be exalted over me?" (Psalm 13:2,3).

Four cries of "How long?" The *Yalkut* (*Tehillim* 13) tells us that they correspond to the four exiles of the Jewish people. "How long shall I take *counsel* in my soul?" King David understood that the darkness of exile is the result of the doubt, uncertainty and inner conflict which people experience when they lack sound advice. They search their souls for guidance — only to become more bewildered. This cry of King David's corresponds to the exile under Greek dominion, when the Jews were subject to the influence of alien philosophies and patterns of thought. The result was that the wisdom of the Torah was obscured from them.

In the modern era the Jewish people has been confronted with the same crisis — a crisis which was becoming more and more apparent in the lifetime of Rabbi Nachman two hundred years ago. The influence of secularism caused many Jews to weaken their attachment to the Torah.

Rabbi Nachman pointed out that the initial letters of the first verse quoted above spell out his own name: Nachal Noveah Mekor CHochma: the initial letters are an anagram of NaChMaN. As a teacher and Rebbe, Rabbi Nachman devoted himself to the task of guiding the Jewish people out of their exile of thought and ideology and back to the wisdom of Torah. First and foremost he sought to give *advice*: practical guidance about all aspects of life.

Not everyone can understand a blueprint. Normally it takes an expert to do so. It is true that many of Rabbi Nachman's teachings were expressed simply and clearly. But the more elaborate Torah discourses which make up his main work, *Likutey Moharan*, contain both a depth and profundity and a wealth of allusions and references to the entire range of Torah literature, which make them somewhat obcure even to advanced scholars.

It was Rabbi Nathan who played the role of the "man of understanding" who could draw out the implications of Rabbi Nachman's teachings and communicate them to ordinary people. It was Rabbi Nathan, in fact, who wrote down most of Rabbi Nachman's teachings in the first place, and we have Rabbi Nachman's personal testimony that Rabbi Nathan understood them better than anyone else. With Rabbi Nachman's encouragement Rabbi Nathan undertook the task of drawing out from the Rebbe's writings all the practical advice and guidance which they contained. His first approach was to produce an abbreviated version of *Likutey Moharan,* which attempted to present concisely the main practical teachings emerging from each of Rabbi Nachman's Torah discourses. Rabbi Nathan entitled this work the *Kitzur Likutey Moharan* first published in 1812. He realised, however, that even this work was not readily accessible to many people, and he therefore spent nine years expanding and reorganising the work. The end result was *Likutey Etzot* — a handbook of Rabbi Nachman's teachings arranged by subject in alphabetical order.

Yeshivat Chasidei Breslov would like to express its thanks to Avraham Greenbaum for this translation. In many respects *Likutey Etzot* is the most difficult of all Breslov literature to translate. For even when the practical guidance is clear enough, the reader is often left with questions. How? How is this? Why? Why should it be so? All sources have been quoted to enable the reader to uncover for himself the depths of Rabbi Nachman's teachings.

First, however, is to *do*. Understanding, will come later. Thus it is written: "We will do and we will hear" (Exodus 24:7).

May we merit to receive the guidance of the true Tzaddikim, as it is written: "Therefore with joy shall you draw water from the wells of salvation" (Isaiah 12:3). The*Targum Yonathan* (*loc. cit.*) translates the words as: "We will receive new teachings from the choicest of the tzaddikim." By accepting their *ADVICE* may we also merit to see the completion of this prophecy: "And in that day shall you say: 'Give thanks unto the Lord, proclaim His name; declare His doings among the peoples...' Make mention that His name is exalted. Sing unto the Lord for He has done gloriously; This is made known in all the earth. Cry aloud and shout, inhabitant of Zion; for great is the Holy One of Israel in your midst" (Isaiah 12:4-5).

Chaim Kramer
Shevat 5743

Translator's Introduction:

The Midrash tells us that Moses explained the Torah in the seventy languages of the world (See Rashi on Deuteronomy 1:5). On the other hand, the Sages said that when the seventy-two elders translated the Torah into Greek in the days of King Ptolemy, three days of darkness came into the world (*Megillah* 9a).

Translation of Torah is both necessary and dangerous. It is necessary, because the goal of the Creation is that the radiance of Torah should spread everywhere, even to those who do not understand the Holy Tongue. But the danger is that its very radiance will be distorted when expressed in alien languages. The Holy Tongue was the vessel fashioned to contain the light of Torah; no other language is so perfectly designed.

The aim of this translation is to help to make Rabbi Nachman's teachings accessible to English-speaking readers who cannot readily turn to the original Hebrew texts. *Likutey Etzot* (*Advice*) is first and foremost concerned with practical guidance and advice. *Advice* is therefore not intended as a scholarly translation aiming at the faithful reproduction of every nuance of the original with laborious precision. Such a work would most likely be burdensome for many readers. Nor is this translation offered as a "crib" — a literal translation serving to help the student of Hebrew puzzle out the meaning of the original text. This would have been equally difficult to read, and far from attractive to the general reader. The depth and richness of

Rabbi Nachman's teachings called for more explanation than would normally be offered in a literal translation. And there are certain aspects of the style of the compiler of *Likutey Etzot* (each of whose paragraphs is a résumé of a corresponding passage in Rabbi Nachman's own writings) which do not lend themselves to direct translation in English. *Advice* is accordingly a free rendition, which at times expands on the original and at times contracts it. I have tried to convey all the relevant ideas in the original Hebrew text fully and accurately. But I have tried to do so in an English that would be readable and not stilted, in order to avoid stylistic obscurities which could easily become a barrier between the reader and the original idea. I have aimed to convey the ideas and also the spirit of the original, even if it meant altering the sequence of words and sentences.

I hope that this translation will make it easier for my fellow Jews in the English-speaking world to become familiar with Rabbi Nachman's teachings and to follow his guidance in pursuit of their own spiritual fulfillment and the ultimate perfection of the world. "For the main thing is not learning, but doing" (*Avoth* 1:17). Rabbi Nachman's teachings are applicable to the entire range of Torah and to Jews in all places and at all times. As a compendium of Rabbi Nachman's practical guidance, *Likutey Etzot* amounts to a handbook to the life of the Jew. *Advice* is not a book to read through at one go and then leave aside. To attempt to do so could be overwhelming and confusing. It is a book to *work* with steadily and persistently.

One aspect of the spiritual work that is necessary is to work with the concepts presented in the book themselves. Each individual must make an effort to deepen his understanding of these concepts step by step in order to realize them in his own life. What is the fear of heaven? What is the love of God? What is it to know and perceive God? etc. What is his personal understanding of these and other Torah concepts? Is it a true and full understanding, or does he have misconceptions about what they mean? He must identify his misconceptions and discard them, seeking out more authentic meanings and making the effort to live these concepts in practice.

I have become especially aware of the importance of this task because of the challenge posed by translating *Likutey Etzot* to find suitable English words with which to convey the concepts of the original Hebrew. I do not believe that there are ever precise equivalents in English which fully express everything contained in the Hebrew. Not only this, but I believe that even the English words which seem to be the most obvious candidates to translate particular Hebrew words can often be profoundly misleading. Whenever a Jew has been exposed to and absorbed cultural traditions other than Torah, it is perhaps an aspect of his personal *galut*, exile, that he is confronted by an almost unbridgeable gulf between *Lashon Hakodesh*, the Holy Tongue, and the language and traditions which he has imbibed.

No translation could ever adequately bridge this gap. The concepts of Torah are inseparable from the words of the Holy Tongue which convey them. Each word and phrase — and therefore each concept — of the Holy Tongue has a unique character of its own, as can be shown by analyzing the mathematical properties of the word, its relationship with other words as they appear in various places in the sacred literature, etc. Each word and phrase is rich in echoes and overtones from the Bible, the Mishnah, the Talmud, the Midrash, the Kabbalistic writings, etc. Part of the greatness of Rabbi Nachman is to uncover whole treasure-houses of richness in the Holy Tongue.

The languages of the nations are not merely collections of words and phrases, each one corresponding exactly to words and phrases of the Holy Tongue. Each language is inextricably bound up with the culture and world-view of those who speak it. The language both reflects and conditions that culture and world-view. It would be simplistic to assert that there is a single unified culture and world-view prevailing over the entire English-speaking world. After all, this is the age of the ideological free-for-all which sociologists have grandiloquently called pluralism. The fact remains that in many cases the English words which seem to be the nearest equivalents of certain Hebrew concepts in fact carry quite different connotations as a result of the cultural influences dominant in the English-speaking world. There are whole modes of Torah thinking which cannot be readily expressed in English. At times the very structure of the English language seems geared against accommodating certain central concepts and ways of viewing things which seem obvious and simple in Hebrew.

To give some examples: in searching for a way of translating the word *yir'ah,* it might seem that the most obvious English word to use would be "fear" — and indeed this is the word most frequently used. But when the concept is *yir'at shamayim,* there is a terrible inadequacy about "fear of heaven." It turns the relationship with the Creator into a painful, anxiety-ridden experience and easily awakens thoughts of hellfire and brimstone which may have a place in other traditions but not in Judaism. The dangers implicit in such a translation are obvious: tell it to a child and you risk distorting his spiritual life for years. And once it is distorted, the only solution is for him to become aware of the distortion and refine his thinking later on. Another word which could be used for *yir'ah* is "awe." But it is also not satisfactory, besides its not being widely used in current English. There are no other obvious alternatives. Do you give extensive explanations every time the word *yir'ah* appears and end up with an intolerably cumbersome translation?

Another example is the concept of *zechut*. Hebrew speaks of a person being *zocheh* to have a certain experience or attain a certain level. To speak in English of his "succeeding" in having that experience or attaining the level in question gives all the credit to the individual without bringing out the fact that he received Divine help to do so because of his spiritual merit. To speak of his "being helped" would ignore the element of hard work on his part. To say that he "is worthy" of the achievement or "merits it" may convey the idea a little better, but they are hardly colloquial English.

A far more extensive problem arises with regard to the whole system of concepts concerned with the destiny of the Creation and man within it — a system which is the core of the Torah view of things. Among the central concepts of this system are *Malkhut, Malkhut deSitra Achra, kelipot, tikkun, hitgaluth, kavod, le-ha-aloth le-shoresh,* etc., etc. Simple and obvious as these concepts are in Hebrew, there are no straightforward ways of expressing them in English except with cumbersome locutions and extensive explanations. The lack of simple English words and phrases with which to translate them, points to a general lack in this age of scientific materialism, to resolve the evil within and to elevate itself to its source in God.

Finding the best word to translate the concept in question is a problem confronting any translator. But it is a problem which is greatly compounded when trying to translate a religious work into English that will be acceptable to the late twentieth century reader. Even after making the necessary compromise of translating *yir'ah* by "fear," *teshuva* by "repentance," *kavod* by "glory" or "honor" etc., there is still the problem that these words and others like them included in the religious and spiritual vocabulary of English are very likely to have unfavorable connotations in the minds of certain readers because of the cultural shifts of the past sixty years or more. The decadence of English culture has given rise to a widespread cynicism which sees piety as prissiness, goodness as do-goodery and the "straight and narrow path" as archaic and irrelevant. Almost the entire range of traditional religious and spiritual language has been poisoned by the accretion of unfavorable connotations which makes it impossible to use them simply and directly without alienating the reader. It is a sad pointer to the spiritual barrenness of contemporary culture that there are no generally acceptable alternatives. It might be desirable to forge a new religious and spiritual vocabulary in English, and of course many writers and thinkers have tried. But no such vocabulary is used universally at present. To develop one's own would be to speak in a language which no one else understands.

The words and phrases I have chosen in this translation inevitably represent a makeshift solution. There could never be a precise translation. My hope is that *Advice* is less rather than more inexact! I have set out the problems at length in order to make the reader aware of them and to encourage him to work through the text critically: critical of the translation itself — he should know that there is far more beneath the surface than it has been possible to convey in English — and critical of his own conceptions and the inadequacies inherent in them. He must work on his spiritual concepts and discuss them with others in order to separate truth from falsehood and fashion *kelim* — vessels — to receive the light of holiness.

I am all too aware of the deficiencies of this translation, and I am apprehensive that certain parts of it will mislead. I can only pray that no one will stumble because of its shortcomings. I am convinced that the way to advance is to follow the Rebbe's words with simplicity and purity without sophistication. In the merit of the strength of the Tzaddik may we be worthy of witnessing the coming of Mashiach and the rebuilding of the Holy Temple speedily in our days. Amen.

ADVICE

Author's Introduction:

"Who is the man who desires life?" (Psalms 34:13). Who will choose eternal life? Who truly cares about his soul? Who is for the Lord? Attend carefully to what you find in this work.It is small in size but rich in quality. See! Gaze! Wonder! Great things did He do in their days, when awesome and wonderous counsel, pathways old and new were revealed (Psalms 38): founded upon pillars of fine gold, planted by flowing water, gushing from the spring that comes from the House of the Lord. Deep waters are the counsel in the heart of man, waters drawn by a man of understanding (Proverbs 20:5).

Come and see the deeds of God. Pay attention to these words. They are words which stand at the summit of the universe, the words of the Living God, King of the World. They are words to revive all souls, from the smallest to the greatest, from the soul at the peak of all levels to that on the lowest of levels. There is no true guidance or holy counsel which you will not find in this book. Nothing which your soul asks will be withheld. Prick up your ears and hear. Open your eyes and see. Understand and see the absolute truth. Turn away from crookedness of heart, from the paths of mockery and falsehood. Cast away all vain sophistication. Take pity on your soul and direct your understanding and all your thoughts to the truth alone. If you err from the truth, who will you be deceiving? Only yourself.

Take this book, examine it. Do its words contain even a hint of dishonesty, God forbid! Have its footsteps strayed from the path of righteousness and truth that our fathers of old walked? I trusted in God. I shall not be ashamed of these words, not in this world nor in the World to Come. I shall acknowledge the Lord greatly with my lips. Among the multitudes will I praise Him. For He stood by the right hand of one poor as myself, and gave me the strength and courage to gather these precious flowers and the power to bring lasting healing. They are the life of the soul, fountains of living water drawn from the wellsprings of salvation. All that flows from them is founded upon the words of our fathers and teachers, of blessed memory, in the Written Torah and the Oral Torah, in the Scriptures, the Babylonian Talmud, the Jerusalem Talmud, the Midrashim and the books of the Holy Zohar and the ARI, Rabbi Yitzchak Luria of blessed memory. These are the sources for all the teachings set forth in this precious volume. To dwell upon their praises would be to detract from the many curtains that conceal their depth. But anyone who examines them through the eye of truth will see for himself the preciousness of the glory of their greatness.

This volume is an abridged selection of the practical guidance contained in *Likutey Moharan*, which is a collection of the pure and holy teachings of our great and sainted teacher, the concealed light, Rabbi Nachman of Breslov, may his memory be for a blessing. He himself instructed me to prepare this book because the underlying purpose of all the awesome teachings which he revealed to the chosen people was *action.* "For the main thing is not learning but doing" (*Avoth* 1:17). This was clear to all who were privileged to take refuge in the shade of his holiness. His whole longing and desire was to lead men to the ways of righteousness *in practice*: to open the eyes of the blind and let those who were bound, go upright; to say to the captives, go free (paraphrase of Isaiah 43). To come to those imprisioned by desire and trapped in the net of the vanities of this world and teach them the path they should travel and the actions they should follow — "which, if a man will do them, he will *live* through them" (Leviticus 18:5)...live the life of eternity! This was his intention in all his tales, his conversations, his stories and the advice he gave to individuals. This was his only purpose.

This was why he instructed me to collect from his discourses an abridged version of anything which had relevance to practical action and prepare a separate book, in order that we should be worthy of observing, practicing and fulfilling everything that came from his lips. All of his discourses and teachings possess immeasurable breadth and profundity. They are filled with remarkable guidance about how to lead an upright life. There is no wise counsel in the world that is not contained within the words of our holy teacher. They possess a universalism that is incomparable. Anyone who applies himself to his words with intelligence will be able to draw from them sound guidance and wise counsel for everything he needs. Whatever his soul requires, he will lack nothing in the words of the Rebbe, which are deeper and wider than the sea.

But no two faces are alike. Not everyone is able to search by himself and find what he needs. For this reason we shall set forth here the bulk of the practical advice which emerges from the teachings of the Rebbe. We will concern ourselves with the simple meaning of the words... Then anyone who wishes to add to our selection should come forward and do so. For one who attains perfect wisdom can find many more things like this in each discourse contained in the larger book. The words of the book are deep indeed, and every discourse includes many different subjects, explanations etc., as well as being filled with guidance, advice and encouragement in devotion to God. The larger part of the contents of this volume were examined by the Rebbe and found favor in his eyes.

The truth will testify for itself. The Lord God of truth will give truth to Jacob, He will send His light and His truth and ever lead us in the path of truth. He will incline our shoulders to bear the yoke of His service all the days of our lives in truth, and to love peace and truth, until the throne of David will be established and he will sit upon it in truth, speedily in our days. Amen.

Rabbi Nachman was once having a conversation with someone. While they were talking he heard someone else praying the evening service. When the man reached the words "...and direct us aright through Your own good counsel" he said them very hurriedly. The Rebbe commented to the person he was talking to: "Did you notice how he raced over those words? In actual fact we should say them with tremendous emotion and intense concentration. They should come from the very depths of the heart. This is a most precious prayer. We need to *implore* God for mercy and beg of Him to make us worthy of receiving good counsel — good *advice* — from Him as to how we should lead our lives."

(*Sichoth Haran* 238)

TRUTH & FAITH אמת ואמונה

1) In essence, redemption is dependent on faith. The root cause of the exile is simply a lack of faith (*Likutey Moharan* 7:1).
2) Faith, prayer, miracles and the Land of Israel are all one concept. They are all dependent upon each other (*Ibid.*).
3) There are people who attempt to give natural explanations for all the miracles which take place. They are atheists who have no faith in miracles. When all such people have disappeared and faith will have spread throughout the world, then the Mashiach will come. Because the redemption depends upon faith (*Ibid.*).
4) The only way to attain faith is through truth. Faith is only applicable in the case of something which cannot be understood rationally. Where one can understand something rationally there is no question of faith being involved at all. But there are certain things which can never be understood rationally. How can one come to have faith in the things one must believe in? Faith depends upon truth. If you will only search for the truth with complete honesty you will eventually realise that you must have faith in God, in the true Tzaddikim and in the holy Torah. You will realize this in spite of the fact that such faith is not something that is susceptible to our rational understanding, bound as our rational faculties are by the material nature of our existence. If you think about things with uncompromising honesty you will get a glimmer of understanding that this really is the truth. Reason will not help here. You need faith that is strong and total. Understand this well (*Ibid.* 2).
5) The only way to find truth is to draw closer to the Tzaddikim and follow their guidance. Do not turn aside from their words either to the left or the right. Then the truth will be engraved

within you and you will achieve genuine faith. By the same token, keep well away from bad influences. Pay no attention to the suggestions of those who are the enemies of the truth, who raise every kind of question about the truth. You can succeed in this through observing the mitzvah of *tzitzit*, the fringes. (See *Tzitzit* #1). *Tzitzit* are a hedge against immorality which is directly contrary to the Holy Covenant between God and the Jewish people and is one of the strongest forces which can undermine truth. The guidance and advice of worthless people actually breeds immorality. Through observing the mitzvah of *tzitzit* you will be able to purify yourself and observe the Covenant, which is the foundation of faith. All the teachings of the Tzaddikim are bound up with this (*Ibid.* 3).

6) Pray with strength and put all your force into the letters of the prayers. Through this you attain faith (9:1).

7) The people who deny that miracles are possible and claim that everything that takes place has a natural explanation can actually witness a miracle themselves and still try and glaze over it and explain it away. Naturally, this attitude of mind is very damaging to religious faith. It is harmful to prayer, and people's understanding of the true significance of the Land of Israel becomes obscured. All this contributes to the lengthening of the exile (*Ibid.* 2).

8) The less faith there is, the more the face of God is concealed and the more fiercely His anger burns. At such times the Tzaddikim shy away from accepting positions of authority and honor and the world is left without true leadership. But if people learn to hold their anger in check and to break the force of anger by showing love instead, then God's own anger will be sweetened. The true Tzaddikim will again be willing to accept roles of leadership and honor and the world will be ready for the true leader who has the power to bring each person to his own complete fulfillment (18:2).

9) Nobody should accept a position of leadership and authority unless he has attained the ultimate level of faith. There are people who believe in God but still have a trace of superstition

within them. People like this should never bcome leaders. Then there are those who pride themselves on their devotion to the good of the world. They claim that this is their motive for seeking power. But really they are interested in the prestige. The devotion they claim to have is simply a rationalization. When people like this gain power it can result in a terrible godlessness, the negation of faith. But Heaven takes pity on the world and these people are deprived of the reins of power (*Ibid.*, 3).

10) Make sure that you never let your faith become weakened. A person whose faith is weak is unable to accept honest criticism. This is very damaging to the cause of peace because it results in all kinds of aggressiveness, exile and conflict. The end result is godlessness and idolatry, false ideologies and false religions. True faith is the foundation of everything. It is the seal of holiness. You must guard it well because through doing so you are protecting holiness itself (22:1,2).

11) To attain complete faith you must come to the true Tzaddikim of our era. They alone have the power to explain and communicate the authentic faith of the Jewish people to our generation, and therefore they are the ones who bring faith to the people of this age. They can do this because they have achieved the summit of holiness (*Ibid.*3).

12) Faith and truth are a *shining face*. They are *joy* and *life*. They are the gateway to the *length of days*. But falsehood shortens the days of man's life. Falsehood is *death* and *idolatry*, a *dark-face* (23:1).

13) All the noble qualities of the soul depend upon faith. Faith is the foundation and source of all holiness.

14) Even a person who attains a certain level of religious insight and understanding must take good care to ensure that the perception he has is suffused with faith. Intellect alone is not something to rely upon (24:6).

15) There are people who have an extensive knowledge of Torah yet they lack personal worth. The teachings of people like this stem from "fallen Torah". Their influence can have devastating effects. It can cause people to reject even the most basic tenets of

faith. Those who remain firm to their belief in God find themselves under attack and exposed to ridicule and contempt. When such a situation develops, the remedy is to open your doors to genuine Torah scholars and offer them hospitality. This is one of the ways of coming to genuine faith, and the hold of those who oppose the faith and look down upon believers will be broken (28:1-3).

16) Charity is only perfect when it is combined with faith. The same is true of all the blessings which flow into the world through acts of charity. They are only perfect when there is faith. Faith is the source of blessings. Keeping the holy Shabbat — which is called the "source of blessings"— is the foundation of faith (31:2).

17) All things depend upon faith for their perfection. Without faith, nothing is complete. Even the Torah itself, which is the source of true wisdom, has perfection only through faith. Faith is the foundation of the whole Torah. It is the basis of everything (*Ibid.*).

18) When a person is asleep he enters the category of "faith". and this refreshes his intellect, which is the manifestation of his soul. The refreshment a person gains from sleeping can help him to attain new levels of religious awareness and perception of God. He can actually receive a new soul from the light of God's countenance (35:3-5).

19) Any flaw in people's faith is tantamount to idolatry. Because of this the rains are withheld (*Taanith* 8) and the world has no contentment or peace. No one helps his neighbor. Everyone is for himself, and because of the lack of cooperation people have to travel from place to place in order to find a livelihood (40).

20) Truth is the source of genuine wealth. Anyone who spurns the truth will come to poverty in the end and people will despise him. But one who endeavors to live truthfully will receive abundant blessings (47).

21) Falsehood damages the eyes — physically and spiritually. When a person tells lies it stirs up all the impurities in the blood and he falls into depression. The resulting tears are very harmful

to the eyes. The blood of dishonest people is loaded with impurity. To speak the truth you must first purify the blood (*Ibid.*).

22) Falsehood is evil and corrupt. A person who is false casts God's protective care from himself. But a person who is truthful will enjoy God's care and protection in all ways (*Ibid.*).

23) There is only one truth but a whole multitude of lies. You can only say one truth about any given object — just what it is and nothing else. Silver is silver and only silver. Gold is gold and only gold. But lies can be multiplied without end. Silver can be called copper...or tin...or lead...or any other name you can think of. That is why the truth will come out in the end and all the current opposition to the true Tzaddikim will disappear. The basic cause of this opposition is the terrible spread of falsehood everywhere. Where the truth is acknowledged to be only one there is no place for opposition. So the truth will remain and endure forever because the truth *is* one: that God is one. In the end all the lies and falsehood will pass from the world and this one truth will remain. For "the truth of the Lord is for ever" (Psalm 117:2) (*Ibid.*).

24) Your goal should be to become merged with the One and to connect "after the Creation" with "before the Creation" to make a unity which is all good and all holy. To join "after the Creation" with "before the Creation" means constantly to connect the created world in which we live with the transcendent realm which is *beyond* Creation and its source, and which alone gives this world its meaning. If you want to achieve this, guard yourself from falsehood and speak only the truth. Be perfectly truthful then you will become merged with the One, because the truth is one (*Ibid.*).

25) The gates of holiness are opened through faith (57:8).

26) We only speak of faith when the one who believes does not know why he believes. But even so, for the believer himself the thing he believes in is perfectly clear and obvious to him — as if

he saw it with his own eyes. This is because his faith is so strong (62:5).

27) One of the ways to develop faith is through working to draw those who are far from God closer (*Ibid.* 3-5).

28) When people lack absolute faith they can fall into the trap of confusing the means with the ultimate cause. They may think they believe in God as the ultimate cause of everything. But in practice they put their trust in the means. For example they believe that their livelihood is totally dependent on their business activities and the energy they put into them — as if without them God would not have any other means of providing them with their sustenance. In effect they believe that their business activities are the source of their livelihood and not just the intermediate factor. Or they may believe that it is the medicine which *causes* the cure, as if without it God would not have any other means of sending healing. Once people believe this they inevitably become preoccupied with the means — chasing after the right medicaments, throwing themselves into their work, and so on — and they forget to turn to God, the root of all things and the ultimate cause. It is true that we *do* have to concern ourselves with the means. But we must not make the mistake of confusing the means with the ultimate cause and put our faith in the intermediary. We must have faith in God alone (*Ibid* 6).

29) Everything we do — praying, learning Torah, carrying out the mitzvoth — has one fundamental aim: to reveal the kingship of God (77).

30) If you are very strong in your faith you will eventually reach understanding of what you believe in. The stronger your faith the greater your understanding will be. At the outset you have no option but to have faith because you cannot understand the matter rationally. Through faith you will come to understand it. Except that then there will be new, more exalted levels which are still hidden from you and beyond your ability to understand rationally. Here again you will have to make the effort to believe. You must always have faith in the levels that are hidden from you. In the end you will understand them also. And so the

process goes on. The main thing is that your faith must be so strong that it spreads to all your limbs. This faith will bring you to true wisdom (91).

31) One who always wants to be victorious is very intolerant of truth. The truth may be staring him in the face. But because he is determined to win at all costs he ignores it completely. If you want to find the real truth you must rid yourself of the urge to win. Then you will be able to see the truth if you wish (122).

32) Faith contains the power of growth. A person with perfect faith will grow and develop in his devotion to God no matter what he may have to go through. Regardless of the obstacles or difficulties he may encounter, nothing will throw him off course. He will accept whatever he experiences with patience. People who are put off by the obstacles and difficulties which confront them when they try to serve God have a certain lack of faith. They are left with a feeling of heaviness and depression, a lack of enthusiasm. Why is it that people don't make real efforts to draw closer to those who lead lives of piety and justice? If they really had faith they would run to them as fast as they could. Why do people not pray properly? If they had genuine faith, they would really believe that God stands over them while they are praying and hears every word that emerges from their lips. Then they would pray with tremendous fire and yearning. But instead they are listless and depressed. It is because they lack this real faith. That is why they are far from the Tzaddikim, from the pious and just, and from true devotion to God. When a person has genuine faith nothing can stand in his way. No matter what happens he will grow in the service of God (155).

33) Controversy and divisiveness can cause even God-fearing people to start having doubts about their beliefs. The answer is to be silent. And to leave the battle to the Lord (251).

34) A person should be so honest that when he carries out the mitzvot and all their fine details it is for the sake of God alone. Even if he were completely alone with no one to watch him, he would still carry them all out scrupulously. Being free of the slightest hint of dishonesty, he would never do anything merely

to impress others (*Ibid.*).

35) When troubles strike, God forbid, it is because the truth has become flawed. A person with troubles must be very careful not to become ensnared in error and falsehood because of them (II 2:4).

36) At all times one should give thanks to God for everything one experiences, and especially when one is released from danger. This, combined with the study of the law, will cause truth to radiate in his speech. He will be able to perfect all aspects of his speech. Perfection in speech comes only through truth. He will pray in truth — and this is perfect prayer. He will be worthy of learning Torah from a true teacher who will give true guidance in the path of truth. He will find his true partner in life and true partners for his children. The way to attain all this is through thanks and acknowledgement of God and the study of the law. In this way one can draw the blessing, and holiness and joy of Shabbat into the other six days of the week. Then the simple unity which underlies all the diverse phenomena of this world will be revealed, and one will believe and know how all the different things in the world stem from the blessed unity of God. To know this is very precious. Even in God's eyes it is something wondrous and precious (*Ibid.*).

37) When people's faith in God is weak all kinds of false doctrines and beliefs gain influence. But when their faith in the truth is strengthened, these ideologies lose their grip and become discredited. Even the nations who were far from God abandon their fallacies and come to believe in the truth. They may not actually convert. But although they remain in their place, they acknowledge God and believe and know that there is One who was the First, blessed-be-He. At times, however, they do actually convert and become proselytes (*Ibid.*).

38) Faith is attained through attachment to the Tzaddik who has attained the level of *ruach hakodesh*, the holy spirit. Through this *ruach hakodesh* man's faculty for symbolic thought is refined and cleansed, bound up as it is with the power of imagination and fantasy. Only then can he attain perfect faith in God and in the

constant renewal of the world. This is the foundation of everything. The whole world depends on it (8:7,8).

39) Faith depends on a person's mouth. We must *say* we believe — say it out loud! As it is written in the Psalms (89:1) "I will make known Your faithfulness *with my mouth*." When a person has a crisis of faith, or even passing doubts, it is very good if he says out loud: "I believe." Just expressing your faith in words is itself one kind of faith. Through doing this you can come to genuine faith (44).

40) In the same way one should also be very careful never to say anything which implies even a slight lack of faith, let alone complete disbelief. Even if you believe in your heart, you should never express disbelief even as a joke, or even if you are only quoting someone else in order to ridicule them. It is very wrong to do this and it is very damaging to your faith. Even as a joke it is forbidden to say anything which implies disrespect of God (*Ibid.*).

41) It is far better to have even simple-minded faith than to believe in nothing at all. When your faith is simple-minded you may even believe certain things which are not true. But at least you will also believe in the truth. If you reject all simple-mindedness you may end up rejecting everything and you will become totally cynical. Then you won't even believe in the truth (Rabbi Nachman's Wisdom, 103).

42) Perfect faith is when you believe in God without any sophistication at all — without signs or miracles, speculation or philosophy. Your faith should be simple and pure — like that of women and simple folk (*Ibid.* 33).

43) There are people who are well versed in Torah and still have no belief in God. They are diseased. The name for their disease is *Raasan* (a type of leprosy. See *Ketuboth* 77b). Make sure that you keep well away from these people. The rabbis warned us that the very breath of their mouths can be harmful to honest people and it can arouse their sexual desire. Such scholars are themselves usually sexually immoral (*Ibid.* 106).

44) When you take such joy in Torah and mitzvoth that you

literally dance for joy, it will strengthen your faith (*Likutey Moharan* II, 81).

45) When a person is in a state of "constricted consciousness" and weak in his faith, this is the time for difficult devotions such as fasting etc. But someone with total faith can serve God with all things. Because "God does not act like a despot over His creatures" (*Avodah Zarah* 3a) (86).

46) Faith is accounted as charity (Rabbi Nachman's Wisdom, 44).

47) The power of faith is very great. Through faith and simplicity alone, with no sophistication whatsoever, you can reach the level of Desire, which is beyond even that of Wisdom. Your desire for God will be so strong that you simply do not know what to do because of the great longing. You cry out with yearning (*Ibid.* 32).

48) There are certain cases where people are riddled with doubts about their faith because they were not conceived in holiness. Added to this is the effect of their own misdeeds, because there are certain sins which cause people to lose their faith. A person who finds these thoughts entering his mind should be ashamed and broken-hearted, and he should cast them out of his mind completely (*Ibid.*).

49) A person with faith has a very good life. Without faith there is no life at all. No one in the world can be free of troubles and hardships of one kind or another, because "Man was born to struggle" (Job 5:7). But a person who has faith can find comfort even when he has to endure pain and suffering. He knows that God loves him and intends everything for his own ultimate good, to purify and cleanse him. For everything that God does is for the best. But the sophisticated disbeliever has no one to turn to when trouble strikes. He can find comfort nowhere. There is nothing to encourage him. This is why he has no life at all. He walks without God and he does not come under His protective care. But through faith your life can be good always (Rabbi Nachman's Wisdom, 102).

50) True faith in the unity of God comes through the

Tzaddikim. They are the tip of the letter *dalet* (ד) of the word *echad*, which means One (*Tikkuney Zohar*, 21, 55b; *Likutey Moharan* 10:5).

SIGHING אנחה

1) The sighs and groans of a Jew are very precious. When a person is lacking something, sighing and groaning can bring wholeness and completeness. But only if he is close to the Tzaddik who is the guide and leader of the age. The breath of the sigh is drawn from the breath of life with which God created the world. When a thing is incomplete, it is really lacking in life-force - the breath of life which keeps it in existence. When a person breathes long and deep, he draws new life. But the breath of life is in the Torah. The Tzaddik is totally bound to the Torah. Therefore the breath of life is with the Tzaddik. From him we can draw the breath of life for our groans and sighs, and bring wholeness and completeness where before they were missing (8:1,2).

2) A person may be praying with great devotion or at the height of meditation and then suddenly in the middle he falls from his level. It is a sign that there is some flaw in his faith. He should feel broken and ashamed. How could he fall from heaven to earth? He should arouse tender pity for himself to the point where he literally sighs. This sigh will bring him back to his level (108).

3) How precious when you sigh out of longing for something holy. The sigh you let out because you are far from holiness breaks the bond of impurity which was trapping you. Now you can bind yourself with the cord of holiness. But the opposite is true when you sigh with desire for something wrongful, God forbid (109).

4) One sigh of regret for your sins and the distance which separates you from God is worth more than many fasts and

other forms of self-mortification. The sighs you let out when you want something holy can actually break the force of your bodily instincts. Then the soul can draw nearer to the body and communicate to it something of her own perception of God (*Ibid.*).

EATING אכילה

1) If the food a person eats is pure in accordance with the dietary laws and he eats it with dignity, without swallowing it hurriedly, the powers of his mind will be restored and grow and his foolishness will be subdued. But if he eats like a glutton, then he will be overwhelmed by foolishness. He will lose his intelligence and the light of the Tzaddik will be concealed from him. He will no longer be able to learn the love and fear of God from the Tzaddik (17:2,3).

2) If you are conscious that your eating habits are bad, the remedy is to give charity to the Tzaddik and to poor people who are genuinely deserving. The Tzaddik has the power to draw people who are far from God closer, even if they were sunk in idolatry. Eating greedily causes the light of God to be darkened in the world. But through this charity, God's light is spread through the world. The powers of your mind and soul will be restored and you will see the light of the Tzaddik and learn the love and fear of God (*Ibid.* 5).

3) When a person attains perfect mastery of the Holy Tongue and guards the Holy Covenant in purity he has the power to stir up the sparks of the letters which exist throughout the Creation. All the pleasure he has from eating and drinking and other enjoyments comes only from the sparks of the letters. His heart is illumined and his face becomes so radiant that people are moved to return to God simply by seeing it. Everyone who looks at his face sees his own reflected there as if in a mirror — and sees, in contrast, how far sunk in darkness he is. Without a single word of preaching he will want to be released from his darkness — all through seeing this person's face (19:7-9).

4) Whenever you feel a sudden strong impulse to eat it is a sign that there are forces which hate you. This sudden appetite for food is caused by the animal part of your nature. You must break the animal impulse. Then you will be free from the clutches of those who hate you (39).

5) Gluttony leads to divisiveness and strife. The glutton is an object of contempt. Other people look down upon him: they have no wish to help him, on the contrary they put all kinds of opposition in his way. But a person who succeeds in breaking his greedy impulses will find peace. And peace will also reign in the realms above. A profound and wonderful contentment will reveal itself in the world (*Ibid.*).

6) When a person is sunk in the desire to eat greedily it is certain that he is far from truth. A person like this is under the force of the Divine aspect of severe justice. Greed is a sign of impoverishment to come, and will subject him to contempt and embarassment (47).

7) When a person manages to break his desire for food, God works miracles through him (*Ibid.*).

8) There are people who sleep away all their days. Some of them have fallen into their sleep because of their desires and wrongdoing. There are other cases of people who possess genuine goodness and beauty of character. But their fall came through food. Sometimes a person may eat food which was not sufficiently purified to be fit for human consumption. Then his mind falls into a "sleep". When a person eats in holiness and purity, his face, and the inner "face" — that is his soul — becomes radiant through his eating. But when he eats without holiness the food damages his heart, and the result is that he loses that inner face and he falls into a "sleep". He may still *think* that he is serving God, occupied as he is with Torah and prayer. But he is "asleep", and all his devotions remain below in the lower worlds. God has no pleasure from them. It is vital to arouse him from his sleep. But the only way it can be done is if he stirs himself a little first. The tales and stories told by the Tzaddikim have the power to rouse those who are asleep so that

their days will not be wasted. It is a great thing to be privileged to find a Tzaddik like this who can stir you from your sleep. Otherwise you could sleep away all your days, God forbid (60:6).

9) The food — physical and spiritual — of the Jew must first undergo purification until not a trace of the forces of the *Sitra Achra*, the Other Side, remains. Food which still contains a trace of them can cause one to sin. All the impulses and desires which people experience are aspects of the *kelipot,* the "husks" which surround the spiritual fruit. The husks are characterized by excess and superfluousness. The body can survive without these gratifications. When desires and impulses press in on a person, this is the battle of the *kelipot* against holiness. The principal desires are for food and drink. All the other desires are derived from them. When a person is in their grip, they send his faculty of speech into exile. As it says in the Psalms: "My throat is dry" (69:4). He finds himself unable to say a single word before God. But by fasting he can overcome the power of these desires. Then he will be able to speak. Through this he will be able to draw those who are far from God closer. As more people come to acknowledge God, His glory is revealed over the whole Creation, and our faith in God becomes complete. When a person who is master of his desires eats, it is precious indeed because of the unification brought about between the Holy One, blessed-be-He and the Shechinah face to face (62:1,2,5).

10) When a person eats greedily it is a stain, as it were, on the honor which is due to God's holiness. The more disrespect that is shown to God, the more the arrogant start to assert themselves. The nations of the world abrogate to themselves all the glory that is due to God. They flaunt themselves and boast — and receive the world's respect and deference for it. God hides His face from the world and the Divine aspect of severe justice prevails. But when we break the desire for food, God shows favor to the world. The aspect of severity is withdrawn. The honor due to God's holiness is restored. The arrogant are humbled and lose their power and influence (67:2,3).

11) Never eat more than you need. If you eat unnecessarily it can be very harmful. Even the food which the body needs is then joined with the extra food and causes great damage (257).
12) A person who eats excessively is like an animal. To be human is to eat only what is necessary. Excessive eating brings on fever. Another cause of fever can be if a person eats food which is insufficiently pure for human consumption (263).
13) Greed for food is one of the three lusts which destroy the heart's capacity for awe and reverence for God. The other two are the desire for wealth and the sexual appetite. Each of the three festivals of the year has its own spiritual influence which counters one of these desires. Pesach counters the desire for wealth; Shavuot the sexual impulse. The greedy desire for food is broken through the influence of Succot. Celebrating Succot fittingly will bring an illumination which can help one to control one's appetite for food (II, 1:4,5).
14) The food one eats can affect one's dreams and even cause one to have a "dream sent by a demon" (*Berakhot* 55b). This can bring about a wasteful emission. The *tikkun* for this is to be always happy (5:10).
15) One of the highest of all spiritual experiences is the revelation of Desire which comes at the time of eating. But before one can attain this level one must first find a wise sage for a teacher, one who possesses the wisdom and understanding of how to awaken the radiant light of the Jewish people. If a person finds such a sage and is firm and disciplined in his own spiritual path, then he will be able to experience this revelation of holy Desire when he eats. He will feel an overpowering yearning and longing for the Holy One, blessed-be-He. This Desire is boundless, beyond all understanding. He scarcely knows what it is he desires. It is pure Desire — the yearning of the soul for God (7:10).
16) The bodily sustenance we take in can harm the spiritual sustenance of the soul. Eating and drinking can harm our capacity to experience the awe of God. Awe is the "sweet savor" which sustains the soul. The Tzaddik understands how to guide

Israel. By learning from him and following his guidance, we give strength to the spiritual and counter the effects of our physical sustenance (*Ibid.*).

17) The act of eating plays a vital part in refining and purifying the Creation. The food we eat is refined and elevated when it is transformed into the beautiful words that we speak: the blessings we make over the food itself, the prayers we offer, our words of Torah, and all the other devotions we are enabled to perform by the nourishment we derive from the food. One should keep this in mind as one eats. Then one's food becomes "incense" as it were. One will find true joy and make a crown of lovingkindness and mercy for the King of Peace, as it is written: "Go forth, O ye daughters of Zion and gaze upon King Solomon" — Shlomo, he to whom peace, Shalom, belongs — "even upon the crown wherewith his mother hath crowned him in the day of his espousals, and in the day of the gladness of his heart" (Song of Songs 3:11) (16).

18) Every Jew, even the greatest Tzaddik, necessarily undergoes a certain measure of pain and suffering every day. The deeper his understanding and attachment to God, the greater the pain he must endure. But eating in holiness and with the fear of Heaven can help to sweeten this pain somewhat and prevent it from becoming overpowering (77).

19) One who eats in holiness and with the fear of Heaven is worthy of the status of *Adam*, Man, the pinnacle of Creation. His mouth is the mouth of *Adam*. The Shechinah herself speaks from his lips. But when a person eats without holiness, God forbid, his mouth is the mouth of a mere animal (*Ibid*).

20) The time when we are eating is especially suited to working on ourselves to develop the fear of Heaven. We should be careful to take advantage of the moment and cultivate this fear in our hearts (*Ibid.*).

21) Never eat a fruit before it has become fully ripe on the tree. Unripe fruit can be very harmful. It can damage the very soul. So long as the fruit still needs to grow it has the power to draw to itself the life-force it requires. If somebody eats it before it is

ripe it will suck the vitality it requires from *him*. By making the blessing over fruit with intense concentration and with a sense of true fear of Heaven you can avoid the dangers of unripe fruit. In fact, you should be careful with all the blessings over food, drink, spices and so on, but especially with the blessings over fruit. Many lost objects are actually present in the fruit of the tree. Deep mysteries (such as the transmigration of souls) are involved here. These lost objects need to be refined and elevated. Cooking unripe fruit in order to make it fit for eating will not help if the fruit did not ripen on the tree. However if unripe fruit is left for a time after it is picked until it ripens by itself, it does help and the fruit may be eaten (88).

22) Be careful not to gulp your food down hurriedly like a glutton. It was Esau who said, "Let me swallow some of this red pottage" (Genesis 25:30). Get into the habit of eating at a moderate pace, calmly and with the same table manners you would show if an important guest were present. You should always eat like this, even when you are eating alone. Happy is the one who achieves this! (*Chayey Moharan, Avodat Hashem*, 69).

HOSPITALITY הכנסת אורחים

1) It is a very good thing to open the doors of your home to genuine Torah scholars who possess integrity as well as learning. Offering them hospitality will help you to deepen your own faith. This in itself helps to counter the prevalent lack of belief. Offering hospitality to genuine Torah scholars helps to make a *tikkun* for the "fallen Torah" which has passed into the hands of those who are learned but unscrupulous. The Holy Zohar refers to these scholars as "Jewish demons" (Zohar 3, 253a). They are the source of all the hostility to those who are truly God-fearing. The way to overcome this hostility is by offering hospitality to genuine Torah scholars (*Likutey Moharan* 28).

2) Everyone offers up bad prayers from time to time, and these prayers come back and confuse him when he stands up and tries to pray with devotion. Offering hospitality to Torah scholars is the *tikkun* for this (209).

LAND OF ISRAEL ארץ ישראל

1) With true faith, prayer comes into its own. Prayer is bound up with the concept of bringing about miracles. To attain this level of faith is only possible in the Land of Israel, for it is there that prayer ascends to the worlds above. With faith such as this one can accomplish with one's prayer whatever is necessary: one can work real miracles and wonders in the world (*Likutey Moharan* 7:1).

2) The very essence of Eretz Yisrael as a spiritual concept is bound up with faith and prayer. If we abuse Eretz Yisrael we go down into exile. Prayer goes into its own exile, and then it is impossible to pray and bring about miracles in the world (*Ibid.*).

3) To be a true member of the people of Israel is to move always to higher and higher levels. To do this is impossible except through the sanctity of the Land of Israel. Every upward movement which we have to make towards holiness can only be accomplished through the Land of Israel. The same is true of prayer. The ascent of prayer comes about only in the Land of Israel (20).

4) It is through the power of the Torah that we draw into ourselves that we can attain to the level of the Land of Israel. Likewise when we are present at the time that the Tzaddik draws Torah into the world and teaches in public, we ourselves have a share in the Torah that is revealed then by the Tzaddik. This also gives us the strength to come to the Land of Israel (*Ibid.* 6).

5) It is impossible to come to the Land of Israel without difficulties and suffering. The root of all the difficulties and suffering lies in the slanderous image of the Land which is put about by the wicked. They are the source of all the obstacles.

But the power of the Torah which we draw into ourselves enables us to overcome all the obstacles, the difficulties and suffering. The more profound a person's grasp of the Torah and the greater the *tikkun* he brings about through his attainment, the greater his victory over the obstacles, and he will succeed in reaching the Land of Israel (*Ibid.*).

6) When a person attains to the level of the Land of Israel, he is worthy of being called a "man of strength and valor". Before he attains this level, "Let not him that girdeth on his armor boast himself as he that putteth it off" (I Kings, 20:11). But when he has gone through the battle successfully he is worthy of the name "man of war" (*Ibid.* 10).

7) When people give charity to causes in the Land of Israel, they become merged in the air of the Land of Israel, which is holy breath that has no taint of sin (*Shabbath* 119b). Through this breath the forces of severity and darkness are banished from the world. This is also how it is possible to escape from the distracting, alien thoughts which come during prayer. The mind and the thoughts become clear and refined. This is a *tikkun habrit* — a remedy for abuse of the Holy Covenant (37:4).

8) The Land of Israel possesses a mystical power to stimulate procreation and also to bring relief from the divisiveness and hostility which exist between people. Through the sanctity of the Land of Israel, the true guide and leader of our age will be revealed. Truth will spread throughout the world and even the heathen nations will return to the Holy One, blessed-be-He, and serve him "with one consent" (Zephania 3:9) (48).

8) The mitzvah of the Succah is a *segulah* for coming to the Land of Israel (*Ibid.*).

9) Praying with intense devotion reveals sparks of the radiance of our fathers, Abraham, Isaac and Jacob (see *Tefilah* 51-56). The Patriarchs laid the foundations of our faith. This faith is embodied in the prayers we recite. The lives of the patriarchs were completely bound up with the Land of Israel, as is our faith. Through genuine prayer, therefore, it is possible for us to feel the sanctity of the Land of Israel even today, when we are in

exile and the Land itself is under the dominion of the *Sitra Achra*, the forces of the Other Side. Thus it is written in the Torah that even when the Jews are "in the land of their enemies, if then...their uncircumcised heart be humbled... then will I remember My covenant with Jacob and also My covenant with Isaac and also My covenant with Abraham will I remember; and I will remember the Land" (Leviticus 26:41-42). Through the revelation of the sanctity of the Land of Israel we will witness the destruction of the wicked. Not only will we be delivered from their hand; we will see them suffer the very evil they sought to inflict upon us (55:2,3).

10) The mitzvah of *challah* — separating the priestly portion of the dough — is also bound up with the Land of Israel, and the effect of the mitzva is likewise to reveal the radiance of the fathers and the holiness of the Land (*Ibid.* 8).

11) The motive for making the journey to the Land of Israel should be purely spiritual: to draw closer to God. A person who goes there with this as his aim will certainly benefit. Merely by stepping foot on the Land he will become merged with it and transformed by its sacred character. That is why even "one who walks four cubits in the Land of Israel will assuredly inherit the World to Come" (*Ketuboth* 111). On the other hand, if a person's motive has nothing to do with devotion to God and cleansing himself of his evil, then what help will the Land be to him? The Land will vomit him out "as it vomited out the nation that was before you" (Leviticus 18:28) (29).

12) Through the holiness of the Land of Israel one can attain pure faith. This is the gateway to that long, deep, patient breath which is the remedy for anger and depression (155).

13) Pray to God to give you desire and yearning for the Land of Israel. Then you will succeed in reaching there. And pray also that He should plant yearning for the Land in the hearts of all the Tzaddikim (*Ibid.*).

14) God repays man "measure for measure". Nowhere is the repayment more exacting than in the Land of Israel. But this is really a great kindness. If we know that God repays us according

to our deeds, then by thinking about the situations God sends us we can gain an insight into our own behavior and learn how to improve (187).

15) The holiness of the Land of Israel is the epitome of holiness, encompassing all other levels of holiness. It is there that we can free ourselves completely of the materialistic viewpoint which claims that events take place naturally. We can come to know and believe that everything comes about only through the Hand of God. When man knows this he becomes like God in his power to divide the light from the darkness. The Midrash (*Bereshith Rabbah* 2) comments that *light* refers to the deeds of the righteous while *darkness* refers to those of the wicked. It is very good to recount the deeds of the righteous. Such stories help to cleanse and purify the mind. But for every episode in the life of a Tzaddik we find that a corresponding story is told about one of the wicked — because the realm of evil is a mirror-image of the domain of holiness. For example we are told that Pinchas flew in the air. It is also related that the wicked Bilaam flew in the air — except that he used the forces of witchcraft to do so. The power to divide the light from the darkness gives us the skill to distinguish stories about the Tzaddikim from those which are not. To be able to divide the light from the darkness requires that ultimate level of faith which can only be achieved in the Land of Israel (234).

16) Genuine enlightenment and wisdom come only in the Land of Israel. But even the People of Israel outside the Land have the power to draw enlightenment and wisdom from there. Every single Jew has his share in the Land. According to his share, so is the wisdom he draws from the Land. But those who insult the honor of the Almighty, God forbid, are cut off from the radiance of the Land of Israel and they fall into the mentality of "outside the Land", which is one of conflict and divisiveness. This is the source of all the conflicts and divisions which have become so rampant (II, 71).

17) The enlightenment which can be achieved in the Land of Israel possesses the quality of "pleasantness" — the pleasantness

of Torah, all of whose ways are peace. Giving charity, and especially charity for the Land, forges a vessel with which to receive this pleasantness. Then one can rise above the mentality of "outside the Land." But the more deeply people sink into this mentality because of irreverence, the more difficult it becomes to extricate them from it, and this alien mentality can even begin to infect the Land of Israel itself. Instead of peace there is conflict even in the Land of Israel. This is the reason why today the divisions in the Land of Israel are as deep as they are outside it (*Ibid.*).

18) The graves of the Tzaddikim literally have the holiness of the Land of Israel, as it is written: "The righteous shall inherit the land" (Psalms 37:29). The Land of Israel is a *tikkun* for abuse of the Holy Covenant. That is why one should make every effort to visit the graves of the Tzaddikim. The sanctity of their burial place is a *tikkun* for the Covenant (109)

THE COVENANT ברית

The *Brit* is the foundation of the Jewish people and the Jewish religion. There is no single word in English which conveys the richness of meaning in the word *Brit*, which is usually translated as "Covenant". The *Brit* which God struck with Abraham (Genesis 17) was the source of the special relationship between God and those of Avraham's descendants who observe the obligations which the *Brit* carries with it.

1) If you guard the sacred Covenant in purity you will be worthy of true prayer (2:2).
2) The sexual appetite is the root of the evil inclination. It is the source of all impurity. Confronting the sexual desire is the main trial one has to face in this world. Happy indeed is the one who wins the battle (*Ibid.* 6).
3) Someone who knows that he is guilty of having wasted the drops of his very mind and soul should be careful not to get involved in any of the conflicts and disputes between the Tzaddikim. He should believe in all of them. The various doubts and questions which arise in his mind when he sees the Tzaddikim in conflict with one another stem from the mental weaknesses he himself brought upon himself when he wasted those drops of his very soul. If his mind had not been flawed he would not find anything to trouble him at all. He should understand that all their conflicts are really for his benefit, to prompt him to examine and purify himself (5:4).
4) The guidance given by the Tzaddik and his followers are the foundation of the Covenant. But the smooth talk of those who oppose them, who have their own ideas about the right way to live, is a denial of the Covenant and can only undermine it. The

ideas that a person receives from another are like seeds planted in his mind. Advice and counsel are "drops of wisdom" which impregnate the soul. A person who has given way to immorality in the past must be extremely careful to protect himself from the influence of these enemies of the truth. Otherwise he is in danger of losing his share in the world to come, God forbid (7:3).

5) Sexual desire is subject to the eyes: when the eyes wander, desire is aroused. The mitzvah of *tzitzit*, the fringes on the garment, is a protection against this. It also gives protection against the influence of those who are enemies of the truth. Be very careful to fulfill this mitzvah properly. If you do this you will begin to understand the meaning of the teachings of the Tzaddikim and to follow their ways. When you wrap yourself in the *tzitzit* and recite the blessing, concentrate on the thought that you desire a life of purity governed by the Holy Covenant and by the advice and counsel of the Tzaddikim. This is the foundation of true faith. You will be worthy of coming to the Land of Israel, and bringing the era of Mashiach closer. You will attain true prayer, and with it the power to bring about miracles. Your livelihood will be sent without difficulties — because a person's livelihood is governed by the purity with which he leads his life. In the end you will learn to find wisdom wherever you are: you will see the teachings which are contained in all the things around you. All the wisdom of the world will be revealed to you like a table spread with delights (*Ibid.* 4).

6) Pride and sexual immorality are bound up with one another. By guarding the Covenant in purity a person can rid himself of pride and find the light that will guide him on the path back to God (11:3).

7) The basic reason why people have to struggle bitterly to make a living is because they are guilty of sexual impurity. People who keep themselves pure also have to work. But in their case the work they do is the labor of building the Sanctuary. Our Sages teach us that there were thirty-nine separate kinds of labor connected with the construction of the Sanctuary. Each labor is a light, making thirty-nine lights. But when a person undermines

the Holy Covenant, poverty pursues him. He takes the yoke of bitter struggle and puts it around his own neck. For him, work is the scourge of the thirty-nine lashes with which offenders are punished (Deut. 25:2,3) (*Ibid.* 4).

8) There are two different levels of observance of the Covenant. The first is that of the man who has relations with his wife during the six working days of the week. He too can be said to be observing the Covenant since he only approaches his wife at the times when she is permitted to him in accordance with the rules of family purity. He must of course take care not to come to sin. This is the level of the lower unification. Purity here leads to understanding the *Law* of the Torah — the "secrets." The second level is that of one who has relations only on the night of Shabbat. This is the level of the upper unification, where it is possible to penetrate to the mystical depths of the Torah, the "secrets of secrets." Those whose relations are only on Shabbat must guard themselves scrupulously to ensure that they conduct themselves in perfect holiness. This applies all the more so to those on the lower level, who have relations during the six working days. When the Covenant is observed on both these levels the glory of God is complete (*Ibid.* 5).

9) A remedy for a nocturnal emission is to talk to one's friends about their spiritual difficulties and give them encouragement in their search for God (14:12).

10) Sexual desire is the comprehensive evil. It is the root of all the different kings of evil found in the seventy nations of the world. Each of the seventy nations and languages is associated with its own special form of evil — an evil character trait, a particular desire for which that people is especially known, or whatever. This special evil is what binds this people to the forces of evil. The sexual desire is the sum of all evil. All the different desires found in the seventy nations are, as it were, gathered together and included in this. They all burn together, and the effect is a flaming furnace which urges men on with sexual lust. But God has separated us from the nations and exalted us above all languages. We are therefore obliged to keep apart from all

the different kinds of evil which are found among them. Their desires are totally worthless to us. More than anything we must guard ourselves against sexual desire which is the sum of all evil. The fact that we keep ourselves apart from this is the essential difference between ourselves and the other nations. It is the foundation of the holiness of the Jewish people. Man has the power to uproot this impulse from himself completely. In this lies our sanctity (19:3).

11) The key to subduing and breaking your desires, and especially sexual desire, which is the main challenge, is to strive to gain mastery of the Holy Tongue. This means that you should sanctify your tongue with words of Torah and prayer — the formal prayers and your own spontaneous private prayer. Even if the words you speak are in your own native language they are still considered as the Holy Tongue. (In fact, when you converse with God in your own words, it *must* be in your own language.) The point is to sanctify your tongue by always speaking in a way that is holy. This is what is meant by gaining mastery of the Holy Tongue. Through sanctifying your speech you will have the power to subdue the sexual desire, which is the comprehensive evil (*Ibid.*).

12) Sexual purity and mastery of the Holy Tongue are both connected with each other. The more words of holiness which you speak, the more you will succeed in purifying yourself, and in this way you will make amends for any immorality in the past. By the same token, the purer you become the more your mastery of the Holy Tongue will grow. But, you should understand that a similar relationship exists between sexual immorality, God forbid, and the abuse of language. Each one feeds the other (*Ibid.*).

13) The serpent which beguiled Eve and corrupted her is the embodiment of sexual lust. (Other expressions used for this in our holy literature are the "whirling stormwind," the "spirit of madness," and the "foolish woman.") It is the way of the serpent to try to beguile the "spirit of holiness," which is the Holy Tongue, and to insinuate its way into our speech. The

holiness of language is bound up with sexual purity. Therefore the serpent constantly strives to corrupt our speech. It is written: "sin coucheth at the door" (Genesis 4:7). This refers to the serpent lurking in wait for man, trying to suck his strength by tripping him into sexual impurity. The evil inclination constantly tries to push one to sin. Its main force is directed to the area of sexual desire (*Ibid.* 4).

14) Use words of holiness — Torah and prayer — to cool the heat of your passion. As King David said: "My heart waxed hot within me; while I was musing, the fire was kindled. Then I *spoke with my tongue*" (Psalms 39:4). When you cool your passion with words of holiness, you will be protected from nighttime emissions (*Ibid.* 4).

15) Most people go through life subjected to a constant barrage of discourtesy, rudeness and outright insults and humiliation. All this is sent only because of their immorality. Those who guard the Covenant in purity will be treated with honor (*Ibid.* 3).

16) One who is pure and masters the Holy Tongue can interpret dreams, like Joseph did (*Ibid.* 4).

17) The Tzaddik is one who has attained perfect purity and perfect mastery of the Holy Tongue. Only through the words of *his* lips can you yourself achieve that mastery and thereby free yourself of all your desires. But you must actually go to the Tzaddik and hear the words from his lips yourself. It is not enough to read books of his teachings or even to hear them second-hand from someone else. You must go to him yourself. His holy lips are a fountain flowing with the fear of Heaven. His words are the foundation of the Holy Covenant. They are the comprehensive *tikkun** (*Ibid.* 9).

18) Because of the desecration of the Holy Covenant a sword is let loose in the world. This is the sword that "executes the vengeance of the Covenant" (Leviticus 26:25) (20:10).

19) Crying out loud is a remedy for sexual impurity and can bring an illumination of *da'at*, perception and understanding of

see **Rabbi Nachman's Tikun**, published by Yeshivat Chasidei Breslov 1982.

Godliness. That is why guarding against impurity elevates the mind to higher levels (*Ibid.*).

20) The underlying reason why we should recite the Passover *Haggadah* in a loud voice is that the *Haggadah* is a *tikkun* for the Holy Covenant. The original exile in Egypt was the result of the abuse of the Covenant, as we find explained in the sacred literature. The redemption from Egypt was a *tikkun* for this. The wine of the four cups which we drink on the first nights of Passover symbolizes *da'at*, perception and understanding of Godliness. Drinking the wine is a *tikkun* for the distortion in our consciousness which stems from sexual impurity (*Ibid.*).

21) The Holy Covenant is a protection against the "face" of the *Sitra Achra*, the Other Side. This "face" of the Other Side is the craze for money and materialism which is a form of idolatry and the source of the darkness, depression and heaviness in the world. They are really a form of death. But through the Covenant we become bound to Godliness. In the joy of God's radiance we can attain true contentment, because the light of the Countenance of the King of Life shines upon us (23:2).

22) One who guards the Covenant in purity will come to perceive the source of all the blessings which flow into the world, spiritual and material. This root is pure radiant light. When one attains this perception, all desire for materialism simply disappears (*Ibid.* 5).

23) The Holy Covenant is the foundation of true enlightenment, which is called the "glory of the face", *hadrat panim*. The mind is refined by the wisdom of the Torah, which one learns to interpret with grace and beauty through the thirteen rules of interpretation. These rules are the "glory of the face" (In the Kabbalah they are known as the "thirteen perfections of the beard". The beard, a symbol for wisdom is *zakan*, which also means "old man"; and it is written in the Torah: "Honor (*ve-hadarta*) the **face** of the old man"; (Leviticus 19:32).) The voice also becomes purified. One has only to lift up his voice and utter the sounds of song, even without words, and God will save him in his time of distress. Then he will attain peace, and the power

to draw the entire world closer to the service of God (27:6).
24) Any transgression of the laws of the Torah stains the Shechinah with the blood of impurity and sunders the Shechinah from the Only One, blessed-be-He. To rectify every single sin one by one would be impossible, because each transgression has many implications and ramifications: every prohibition has its fine points and subtleties. The only solution is the *Tikkun Klaki*, the general remedy. This is the *tikkun habrit*, the "restoration of the Covenant." Through this, all of a person's transgressions are rectified. The healing influence of the *Tikkun Klaki* has the power to reach the narrowest, most inaccessible channels of the soul which no other remedy could reach (29:3).
25) One who has not yet achieved the *Tikkun Klaki* has no right to speak. He does not know how to use speech as it should be used. Nor is he able to speak words which radiate Torah. For him to speak would be a transgression of the prohibition against tale-bearing (Leviticus 19:16), because anything he says amounts to slander. He is unable to keep secrets. But the *Tikkun Klaki* confers on the one who achieves it the right to open his lips and speak. His words will be filled with the light of Torah (*Ibid.* 6).
26) Sexual impurity can result in epilepsy, God forbid. The Covenant is a protection against this (*Ibid.* 7).
27) A person who has not yet achieved the *Tikkun Klaki* should avoid wine, because it stirs up the blood and this is the source of all sin. Drinking can have an adverse effect on one's livelihood. The wine becomes like a poison. But someone who has achieved absolute purity can reach profound enlightenment when he drinks wine (*Ibid.* 8).
28) All the suffering which a person goes through when he is travelling is sent to him only because of abuse of the Covenant. One who is pure will be free of pain and torment when he travels (*Ibid.* 4).
30) The Covenant is the source of true freedom (*Ibid.* 5).
31) There are two aspects to the Covenant. The first is embodied in the figure of Abraham. This is the Upper Covenant, which is a firmament separating the upper and the lower waters. The

second is the Lower Covenant, embodied in the figure of Abraham's servant. This is the firmament dividing the pure and the impure waters, that which is permitted from that which is forbidden, the ritually clean from the ritually unclean. The Upper Covenant entails the endeavour for absolute purity, the purity of the perfect Tzaddik. The Lower Covenant involves the observance of the laws of what is permitted and what is prohibited, and this entails learning. Every person must try to fulfill the Covenant on both these levels: to be a Tzaddik and a scholar. "For an ignoramus cannot be a saint" (*Avoth* 2:6). One who fulfils the Covenant on both these levels is likened to an angel of the Lord of Hosts. He will attain true faith and he will be blessed with an abundance of Divine favor and grace. He will be filled with love and yearning for God.

The letters of Torah have two opposite powers: they can be turned to good or to evil. Through the longing and yearning we have for God we invest the letters of Torah with goodness. The very letters themselves push forward and ask to be mouthed on the lips of those who long for God. The letters themselves yearn to be invested with goodness. When one attains this sanctity it is accounted to him as if his very eating had the holiness of the show-bread of the sanctuary. His table brings atonement like the altar. The entire universe - the stars, the planets and all the nations of the world - all labor to provide him with livelihood and blessing (*Ibid.* 5).

32) Sexual temptation is the main test in life. It is sent as a challenge to refine us. When you are subjected to this test it puts you in a type of "exile". You should cry out to God: scream and cry out to Him over and over again, like a woman in labor who cries out from the pain of her contractions. Seventy times she cries out (*Zohar* III, 249b). You must do likewise and cry out to God again and again until He takes pity and helps you to strengthen yourself and break your desire. New ideas and new perceptions will be born within you. The secrets of Torah, which before were guarded, will now be unveiled for you. The greater the determination with which you stand up to the trial, the

greater the revelation you will receive in Torah and devotion to God. You will be able to see the seventy faces of the Torah (36:1,2).

33) The *tikkun* for sexual fantasies is to say the words of the *Shema*: "Hear O Israel, the Lord our God, the Lord is One", and the phrase which follows it: "Blessed be the name of His glorious kingdom for ever and ever". The six Hebrew words of each of these two lines adds up to twelve, corresponding to the twelve Tribes of God. By saying these words one attaches his soul to the Twelve Tribes and separates it from the "Mixed Multitude" who went up with the Children of Israel from Egypt (*Tikkuney Zohar*, Introduction) The "Mixed Multitude" stems from the "harlot woman," the "wicked maid". This is the source of sexual lust, which is the root of all evil character traits (*Ibid.* 3).

34) When one merely has a stray thought or fantasy it is sufficient to say these two verses as we have mentioned. But certain people are plagued with sexual fantasies all the time. They find they cannot rid themselves of it. In this case, they must bring themselves to tears when they take on the yoke of heaven. They must literally weep as they say the words "Hear O Israel" and "Blessed be the Name of His glorious Kingdom" (*Ibid.* 6).

35) The level of religious perception that a person can attain depends on the degree of purity he achieves. It is a fundamental principle that one can only comprehend the words of the Tzaddik if he first purifies himself. Immorality leaves a blemish on the mind. Not only will one fail to understand what the Tzaddik is saying; he is also in danger of putting the wrong interpretation on the words. He can easily stumble if he follows the crookedness of his heart and accepts the distorted logic of the doubts with which his head is filled (*Ibid.*).

36) Sexual temptation can literally make a person go out of his mind. This is why the medical authorities have written that castration is a cure for madness (*Ibid.* 6).

37) Once one breaks his sexual desire, he can easily break all his

desires. This is why the *tikkun* for sexual impurity is called the *Tikkun Klaki*, the comprehensive *tikkun*. The further a person is from sexual desire, the closer he comes to the radiance of Torah. The opposite is also true. This explains why, before a person can receive a new revelation of Torah, he is first tested in the crucible of this passion. If he stands up to the test and breaks his desire, it is like breaking the shell which proceeds the fruit, and he will be worthy to receive the revelation (*Ibid.*).

38) Be careful not to listen to the words of a person who is wicked and also intelligent. The mere words themselves can arouse sexual desire. They are laden with poison and enter the very body of the one who hears them (43).

39) One who abuses the Covenant will have the taste of bitter waters - the "waters of impurity" and the "seed of uncleanness". He will be unable to pray with the fervor of total devotion. He will never taste the sweetness of the words of the prayers. The offering he brings - his prayer - will be eaten by a dog . His prayer will be bitter - a "double-edged sword"... "hell". But when one guards the Covenant in purity his prayers are sweet waters - the "waters of purity", the "seed of holiness". As the words emerge from his lips and enter his ears, their sweetness passes into his very bones and his prayer flows out with fervent passion - as it is written: "All my bones declare, Lord who is like unto Thee?" (Psalms 35:10) Then a lion comes and consumes his offering (50).

40) The "dogs" who snatch at the prayers of one who has not achieved sexual purity are the brash and arrogant peole who disturb him and spoil his prayers (*Ibid.*).

41) One who succumbed to sexual immorality in the past should be wary of dogs and the sword (*Ibid.*).

42) The vanity of beauty leads men to the charm of deceit (cf. Proverbs 31:30). One who is captured by the beauty of women falls victim to its vain futility. There are many ways he can fall into deceit, be it in the way he stands, the way he eats, the way he speaks to people and so on. No matter what he does he must always think how will he *appear*: will he seem charming and

attractive? Each separate act demands a different kind of charm. One who fails to guard himself against the attractions of female beauty will become a slave to the charm that he feels he must project (60:3).

43) The vanity of beauty brings men to poverty (*Ibid.*).

44) Life depends upon breathing. Sexual desire affects the breathing, causing gaps between breaths. This allows the body fluids to dry, which results in damage to the brain and the mind, because mental life depends on the fats and fluids in the body. This is why all forms of madness are caused fundamentally by sexual desire, as is known. Even in the case of those who are not actually insane but who lack stability and strength of character, the root cause is also sexual (*Ibid.*).

45) Anyone who marries a woman for money is a fool and an idiot (*Kiddushin* 72). He will be spiritually crippled and his children will turn out to be immoral (69).

46) Charity given in secret is a *tikkun* for a nocturnal emission (83).

47) Depression and anxiety are the main cause of sexual immorality. The foundation of the Covenant lies in joy (169).

48) The milk that a baby suckles when being breast-fed can have a decisive effect on his sexual behavior later on. If a baby is given to a wet-nurse to be suckled it is essential that she should be a good and pious woman. A child who sucks milk from a woman who is morally lax can be overwhelmed by sexual temptation in later life. But a child who is suckled by an honest, pious woman will only have as much desire as is necessary to fulfill the commandment of God (II, 1:4; see *Tosafoth, Avodah Zarah* 11b).

49) Today publicity and fame go to false figures. The arrogance of these false leaders causes sexual immorality to become rife, with the wanton destruction of seed. The "flesh is stopped" (Leviticus 15:3). This "sealing" of the flesh is the seal of the forces of the Other Side. The only way to escape this is through the strength of the Guardians of the age, the Tzaddikim and those who are truly pious. They are called the "Guardians of the

earth.'. The battle they have to fight is very fierce. But these Guardians have the power to transform the "stopped up flesh" to a "seal of holiness". This seal is the *tefilin*. The greater the victory over sexual immorality the greater the spiritual enlightenment which follows. This enlightenment is the "seal of holiness" which the *tefilin* embody. Every one can draw strength from the "Guardians of the Earth" to break his desires and put all his fantasies out of his mind, filling it instead with holy thoughts. Something you should understand is that the more strongly you are assailed by temptation and desire, the greater the *tikkun* when you fight and break them. Holiness is released from the power of the husks. You will be suffused with the holiness of the *tefilin*: to know and make known God's power and glory in the world. The sole reason why these fantasies and evil thoughts are sent to a person is precisely that he should transform them and sublimate them to the realm of holiness (5:6).

50) One who breaks his sexual desire, and cleanses and purifies his mind, is worthy of dreams sent by an angel. Then he is worthy of the status of Man. But a person whose mind is impure receives dreams from a demon and resembles a beast (*Ibid.* 9).

51) Rabbis and judges who are dishonest and pervert the law cause the filth of nocturnal pollutions. The perversion of the "thrones of judgement" (Psalms 122:5) causes the *love* that is in the Chariot (the Throne) to fall, and stirs up the heat of impure passion. The remedy for this is "binding the chariot" - a reference to the institution of the Sages that before we go to sleep we should say: "In the name of the Lord God of Israel: at my right, *Michael*; at my left, *Gavriel*; before me, *Uriel* and behind me, *Rafael*, and upon my head, *Shechinat-El*" (*Ibid.* 11).

52) The spiritual powers of the mind and the soul are the shield against sexual desire. Each of the three main facets of the mind is a separate barrier against this impulse. The power of the sexual impulse derives from the "spirit of folly" which overwhelms one with lustful thoughts and fantasies. As soon as a person feels himself threatened by them he should remind

himself of the intrinsic superiority of the spiritual realm. He should immediately turn aside from the "spirit of folly" and take refuge in the powers of his soul, setting up the barriers of wisdom and intelligence to protect him against this desire. They are the best shield of all. Understand this well. It is something which cannot really be explained. Each individual will see for himself how to escape the "spirit of folly" and draw closer to his spiritual powers, which are the shield against it (8:2).

53) Every Jew has within him a spark of Mashiach. How much it shows through depends on the purity and holiness he attains. He must be very careful not to weaken this spark in any way. The main thing is to guard against the sexual desire, because even the slightest trace of it can seriously affect this spark. The spirit of Mashiach is a jealous one. The full force of its zeal is turned against every place where there is even the slightest trace of sexual immorality. The holiness and purity of everything associated with Mashiach is so great that even a mere hint of sexual immorality cannot be tolerated. The full force of its jealousy is directed against it (32).

54) When man and wife have relations in purity and holiness untouched by the slightest flaw, their relations brings unification in the uppermost spheres. This is truly precious (*Ibid.*).

55) One who attains absolute purity knows how to send forth the words of prayer like arrows from a bow. His whole being becomes suffused with the spirit of the holy Shabbat. He is totally free. He reaches the ultimate enlightenment. He strips himself of his leprous body, the "skin of the serpent", and is clothed instead in Shabbat garments - a holy body from the Garden of Eden. His guardian angel is raised high. He is blessed with wealth and joy. All the passion in his heart is for good. Depression and cynicism have no place. He has the power to go out into the world and bring life to those caught in the net of degraded passions and irrational fears: in their place, he inculcates them with the love of God and the fear of Heaven. The darkness is lifted from their eyes, and their eyes are opened to wonders around them. So great is his power, it is as if he had

created the world. Those whom he teaches learn the ways of prayer: their pleas and entreaties become infused with deeper meaning and higher purpose. The hearts of men are purified, and the age of Mashiach begins to dawn. The leaven of the evil inclination is destroyed, and in the radiance of Torah the heart takes fire with flames of love. "Many waters cannot quench love" (Song of Songs, 8:7). The "many waters" are the degraded loves and irrational fears. Now they are powerless to quench the passion of this love of God. The Shechinah spreads her wings over Israel in the light of this love, and protects the Jewish people from the power of the wicked and the "waters of the flood." (Cf. *Niddah* 13b) All this is founded on the holy Covenant and sexual purity (83).

56) Today it is easy to resist temptation. When peole withstand a temptation, its evil husks are broken. It then becomes easier for others to resist it. Many Tzaddikim and righteous men have already withstood very severe sexual temptations. Now even an ordinary person can easily withstand this test, if he wants to take pity on himself in This World, and the World to Come (Rabbi Nachman's Wisdom 114).

57) A person who experiences a night-time emission should recite the following ten psalms on the same day: Psalms 16, 32, 41, 42, 59, 77, 90, 105, 137, 150. One who recites these psalms on the same day need have no further fears about the harm such an emission can cause. Any damage will certainly be repaired through doing this. It is a very great *tikkun* (II, 92).

CHILDREN בנים

1) Intense prayer is a *segulah* for having children. The same is true of the mitzvah of *Succah* and the Land of Israel. These three concepts are all connected with one another (48).
2) Those who work hard to draw people closer to God and to the Tzaddik are worthy of having children (53).
3) If you are married, be careful that you sanctify the marriage relationship. You must break the force of your desires, which are rooted in the animal soul. You should imagine that a demon is forcing you (cf. *Nedarim* 20b). Then you will be blessed with children, and they will be protected from premature death (39).
4) The best time for relations between husband and wife is on the night of Shabbat (cf. *Ketuboth* 61b). Then they will be blessed with children (*Ibid.*).
5) One with an evil eye will not leave male offspring behind. The same goes for one who talks *lashon hara*, slander, and bad language (*Ibid.*).
5) A *segulah* for having children is that prior to having relations, the husband and wife should recite the account of the additional offerings which were brought on the New Moon. This also helps for a child who is sick (151).
6) A woman who usually has a difficult labour should recite the Psalm of Thanksgiving (Psalm 100). It is also a *segulah* for her to give generously to charity and to help others as much as possible with favors and acts of kindness (II, 2:3,4).
7) A person who has no children should make it a practice whenever he attends a religious celebration to be especially joyful. When he studies Torah it should be with joy. The same goes for all the mitzvot. The joy should be so great that he

literally starts dancing for joy. Then he will be worthy of having children (81).

8) Faith brings children (cf. Genesis 15:5,6) The Hebrew word for faith is *emunah* (אמונה). The numerical value of the word *emunah* is one hundred and two. The word for children is *banim* (בנים). The numerical value of *banim* is also one hundred and two (Rabbi Nachman's Wisdom 34).

9) It is best for children if you leave them alone for the most part rather than sticking to them and playing with them constantly. Don't pay overmuch attention to them. Do what you have to in order to give them their religious education, and training them in mitzvot when they reach the appropriate age. But don't play with them too much (*Ibid.* 59).

10) If you are joyous, it can protect your children from death (*Ibid.* 65).

TRUST בטחון

1) Those with deep trust in God are the "organs of conception and birth," as it were. Everything that is born in this world, all the blessings that flow into it, everything comes about through trust. The way to develop trust is through listening to the stories of the Tzaddikim. There are many people who sleep away their days. They need to be aroused, and the way to arouse them is by showing them the radiance of Torah. But because they are asleep, it could be damaging to expose them to the full light of Torah too suddenly. The Tzaddikim veil the wisdom of the Torah in stories which have the power to arouse those who are asleep. These people are literally like the dumb. They are totally incapable of uttering a single holy word. But when they are roused from their sleep, the power of speech is liberated. Then they begin to speak with tremendous force. Holy speech strengthens our trust in God. Those who were barren are able to give birth and attain true awe of Heaven (60:6-8).

2) When you trust in God and you look to Him alone for all your needs, a vessel is formed with which you can receive His blessing. What you need will be sent to you as and when you require it (76).

3) There are higher and higher levels of trust reaching to Infinity. The greater a person's wisdom and understanding the deeper his trust. The more trusting he is, the more generous he will be in giving charity. Charity is the gateway to the perfection of the faculty of speech, which is the essence of man's superiority over the animals (225).

4) Besides trust in God there is the trust of the Other Side, which is "trust in a trickster" (Proverbs 25:19). The making of

marriage bonds in holiness and purity causes this false trust to be broken like a piece of earthenware. This is the meaning of the custom of breaking a piece of earthenware at the marriage ceremony (60:8).

To explain the concept of trust a little more fully: the essence of genuine trust is summed up in the words of the Psalm: "Trust in God and do good" (Psalms 37:3). One should never let oneself be diverted from Torah study, prayer or devotion because of worries about not having enough to live on. A man should continue to serve God in the confidence that God will always send him whatever he needs. Not everyone has such absolute trust that they are prepared to separate themselves completely from the concerns of this world. But even those engaged in business or work of some kind must make sure to fix regular times for Torah study, to pray at the appropriate times, and to carry out all their other religious obligations. They should not allow themselves to be pushed off course by worries about earning a living. They should trust in God to give them their livelihood. When it comes to giving charity and helping others or paying whatever is needed for the various mitzvoth, they should trust that God will provide them with whatever they need and bless them in the merit of their deeds. Sometimes people are aware that their behavior is not what it should be and they feel that their ways do not find favor in God's eyes. Still, they should not let this feeling become a barrier to trusting in God. No one should say, "Who am I to trust in God and rely on His help seeing that I have done so much that was wrong." God is good to all: "His love never fails, nor does His kindness cease" (from the *Amidah*). A person may be small in his own eyes, but he should not let this worry him. He should remain firm in his trust no matter who he may be. The main thing is that he should always have in mind that his intention is for the sake of Heaven. This is the meaning of genuine trust in God. It is the complete opposite of the false confidence that leads people into wrong-doing — be it stealing, cheating, forging documents, lying, smuggling contraband or whatever - in the hope that God will protect them and help them succeed and not get caught. This kind of confidence is the trust of the Other Side, "trust in a trickster" (Proverbs 25:19). It is no better than a broken potsherd which cannot be repaired. Even if a person simply takes big business risks and borrows heavily to do so, trusting that God will bring off the business venture, this is also the trust of the Other Side. Even if a person's business is not on a large scale he should still trust that God can give him whatever income he needs. Anyone with intelligence will understand from what we have said that the way to avoid the trust of the Other Side — which is contrary to the teachings of the Torah — is to remain firm in genuine trust in God, regardless of his own opinion of his merits.

MODESTY בושה

1) One should have a strong sense of humility before God. One should feel ashamed to do anything which would not be in accordance with the will of God, and certainly ashamed of actually sinning, God forbid. Having a sense of humility is the foundation for developing genuine fear of Heaven. A person who has no shame in this world will be put to shame in the World to Come. This is the worst of all punishments. The pain of the feeling of shame in the World to Come is even worse than the bitterest suffering in Gehinnom. Even the Tzaddikim will feel embarrassed before other Tzaddikim who reached higher levels than they themselves. Our Sages said, "Alas for that embarrassment, alas for that shame!" (*Bava Bathra* 75). They were talking about the shame the Tzaddikim will feel. How much more will sinners be ashamed and confounded. In this world it is impossible to form any conception of the bitterness and suffering which the shame and embarrassment of the World to Come will cause. But someone who develops a true sense of shame in this world acquires the instrument with which to keep himself from sin. He will discover true prayer and joy and inner strength. He will draw close to the Tzaddikim and learn from them how to develop perfect faith (22).

2) You should be totally honest when you talk to God. Get into the habit of expressing yourself with such honesty that your heart is stirred and the words begin to pour forth with fire and passion. As you draw yourself closer to God you will see how small and insignificant you are compared with His greatness. You will be filled with feelings of humility before Him. For up till now you simply cast your sins behind your back and ignored

them. But as you start to acknowledge them frankly you will be overwhelmed with a feeling of shame at having rebelled against the Master and Ruler of the Universe, the Source of all the worlds. At first this humility will not actually show on your face. This is because sin sullies the intellect and stops it from radiating on the face. Before a person repents his mind is so weakened that he can have no conception of the true gravity of sin and the greatness of the One before whom he sinned. But as he returns to God and strips himself of his folly, gaining wisdom and understanding, so his shame will become more and more visible on his face. The sense of humility is symbolized in the *tefilin*, which are the sign of our attachment to the Creator. The light of the *tefilin* is a ray of the light of God's inner countenance. When a person achieves this sense of humilty all his sins are forgiven and he becomes attached to the Tree of Life (38).

3) There are certain people who are so brash and arrogant that they feel no shame or embarrassment at all before the Tzaddik or those who are truly pious. This brashness is a sign of impure ancestry: it is very doubtful if their ancestors stood at Mount Sinai (*Nedarim* 20). They have impugned the holiness of the *tefilin*, which is rooted in the Tree of Life. Instead they have attached themselves to the Tree of Death. They will be cast out of the Garden of Eden and thrown into Hell. But a person who repents and feels ashamed of his sins will immediately be forgiven, and the wisdom and understanding of his soul will be restored. He will be able to expel the spirit of folly from within him and become worthy of the radiance of the *tefilin* (*Ibid.* 5:6).

4) Shame and embarrassment are the basic qualities which help us to return to God. The merest sin one may have committed should give one a deep sense of shame, because in reality every Jew ought to be far removed from sin. The soul of the Jew is rooted in a source so exalted that in essence he is completely detached from sin. For a Jew to sin in any way at all is totally unbecoming. Even when he wants to perform a mitzvah, a positive action, he should also feel a sense of shame and embarrassment. What right does he have to perform this

mitzvah? How does he dare to enter the court of the King and perform the mitzvah when he considers the greatness of the One before whom he does it? The true significance and preciousness of each mitzvah is totally beyond our comprehension. A person has only to look at himself to see how far he is from God and how unworthy he is of performing the mitzvah. How can he stretch out his hand to take the *tefilin*, the very crown of the King... and simply put them on his head all of a sudden? A person who felt genuine shame would be embarrassed even to take food and put it in his mouth before God. What right does he have to this food? To acquire a sense of shame one should examine oneself in comparison with the Tzaddik. This will move him to repent and attain true humility, the humility of Moses. This humility is the root of life — the eternal life of the World to Come (II, 72).

CLOTHES בגדים

1) You should be very particular about your clothes. Never treat them carelessly, and make sure they are not stained or dirty. A person's clothes become his judges if he does not show them the respect they deserve. The greater the man the more care he must take over his garments, because the higher one's level the more scrupulously one is judged (29:3).

2) A person who fails to protect his garments from stains causes a division between the Holy One, blessed-be-He, and the Shechinah. This gives strength to the "wicked maid," which is an expression for the forces of evil. Such a person is like a rebel against God's kingship, and therefore his whole livelihood will only come to him with great exertion and difficulty (*Ibid.*).

3) By making a beautiful garment for a Tzaddik the Shechinah is clothed in radiant garments, and the severe face which God shows to the world becomes sweetened (42).

4) See to it that your clothes are always in good condition. Never wear clothes that are torn. Torn clothes are an indication of weakness in the fight against evil, because the concept of clothing alludes to the mystery of the *chashmal* (Ezekiel 1:27) which is bound up with the idea of watchfulness (127).

5) The Evil One and the forces of the Other Side grab people by their clothes. They burden people with all kinds of worries about clothing. The trouble people have to go to for various items of clothing they need can easily become a serious distraction from religious devotion. Someone who is firm in his faith will not be concerned about this. Even if he has nothing to wear he will still do what he can to serve God to the full extent of his capability. In the end God will look down from the Heavens and see what he needs (Rabbi Nachman's Wisdom, 100).

PRIDE & HUMILITY גאוה וענוה

1) The humility of the Tzaddik brings him to the level of Nothing. This is what gives him the power to atone for sins (4:7).
2) A person who is truly humble becomes stripped of all his material aspects and merged with the Infinite. He then attains the awareness of how everything that happens to him is only for his benefit. To know this is to taste the life of the World to Come (*Ibid.* 9).
3) Pride brings poverty (*Ibid.* 8).
4) Humility is the foundation of true repentance. The essence of repentance is to feel your own lowliness and insignificance, to be aware of the wrong you have done, and to understand that even the suffering and murderous opposition you may have to encounter in your quest for the truth are perfectly just (6:2).
5) A person may have fasted a great deal and undergone harsh personal discipline and self-mortification. Even so, he should not arrogantly assume that he has attained the level of a Tzaddik, with the power to bring about redemptions or to accomplish great feats through prayer. If he examines himself carefully he will see that in spite of all his fasting and asceticism, his physical desires are still firmly lodged in his body — not only his own desires, but even the lust his father had at the time he was conceived. As soon as he recognizes this he will be overcome with trepidation and he will no longer delude himself with the thought that he is a Tzaddik. Instead he will turn to the true Tzaddik to ask him to intercede on his behalf; he will bind his own prayers to the Tzaddik, and in this way he will restore prayer to its rightful place, which is with the true Tzaddikim. They alone understand the secret of prayer and the way to

elevate prayer. God yearns for the prayers of the Tzaddikim and sends an eloquent flow of words to their lips (10:4).

6) There are certain arrogant people who not only refuse personally to go to the Tzaddikim to ask them to pray on their behalf, but who also try to prevent others from going as well. Such people deprive God of the prayers of the Tzaddikim for which he yearns so strongly (*Ibid.*).

7) Pride is a form of idol-worship. The way to crush it is by drawing closer to the Tzaddikim (*Ibid.* 5).

8) To break one's pride is the foundation for attaining wisdom, long life and vitality. The severe face which God shows is sweetened, and one attains faith, joy, the understanding of Torah in its revealed and hidden aspects, and *ruach hakodesh*, the spirit of holiness (*Ibid.* 11).

9) A person who is arrogant cannot even open his mouth. He lacks the faculty of speech and is unable to speak words which radiate with light. When words of Torah pass across his lips, not only do the words themselves fail to radiate within him and draw him to improve, worse still, the Torah itself becomes coarsened and dimmed on his lips (11:2).

10) Arrogance and sexual immorality are connected. A person who succeeds in resisting temptation and extricating himself from pride will attain the light that will illumine his path to repentance. In the end he will reach an understanding of the depths of Torah (*Ibid.* 3).

11) There is a form of humility which is the ultimate in arrogance. This is when a person acts humbly because he knows that people look down upon those who flaunt themselves. All he wants is to gain their respect and approval. His humility is for show: he really wants honor. It takes a good deal of intelligence and self-examination to rid yourself of pride: you must cleanse yourself of it completely. As our Sages said: "Be *very, very* lowly in spirit" (*Avoth* 4:4). The exile of the Jews from our land was caused by "seven idolatrous temples" (*Gittin* 88). This is a reference to pride. Even today people are still chasing after

honor and prestige, and this is why the exile has still not ended (*Ibid.* 7).

12) Torah can only be acquired with meekness. There are four distinct areas where you must break your pride: you must be humble before those who are greater than you, before those who are on your own level, and before those who are less than you. And at times — if you are the smallest of the small — you must make yourself humble even in front of yourself: you must look upon yourself as if you were on a lower level than you actually are (14:5).

13) There are many different things which make people arrogant. You should be very careful about all of them. Intelligence, power and material possessions are the three main things which give people a sense of superiority. You must rid yourself of any trace of arrogance you may have in these three areas. Whatever intelligence, power or wealth you have been blessed with should give you a sense of meekness and humility (*Ibid.*).

14) The more you succeed in breaking your pride the greater your attainments in Torah will be. You will have the power to draw those who are far from God closer, and then the glory of God will be exalted and magnified. When glory is taken from the hands of those who have abrogated it to themselves and restored to God alone, the awe of God spreads. Through awe you can attain harmony within yourself, and this is the way to discover true prayer and to achieve universal peace, peace in all the worlds (*Ibid.*).

15) Arrogance can actually cause a person to be imprisoned (*Ibid.* 22).

16) There are times when people generally fail to guard their tongues. The danger then is that even those who are righteous and God-fearing will succumb to feelings of pride. It is essential for every individual to keep a careful watch on himself and ask if the honor and prestige he enjoys are really justified. Otherwise he runs the risk of falling into arrogance. Pride is the cause of the "Exile of the Shechinah" (58:10).

17) The less importance a person attaches to himself, the more drawing power he has: he is able to draw down the Shechinah to the lowest worlds to dwell with us. This was God's desire from the day He created His universe. Such a person has the power to draw men closer to the service of God, and he can channel blessing and goodness to the Jewish people. And he himself is able to draw closer to the Tzaddik (70).
18) Experiencing the sanctity of Shabbat is one of the ways of attaining true humility, which means to seeing one's own lowliness and understanding the greatness of the Jewish people and being willing to sacrifice oneself for them, like Moses did (79).
19) A person should look upon himself as if he were less than he really is. That is true humility. And at the very least he should not look upon himself as if he is more than he really is (*Ibid.*).
20) When a person is meek and lowly, no one will ever be able to shake him or push him from his place. No one can take away his livelihood, God forbid (*Ibid.*).
21) Humility protects against sexual temptation. Pride arouses it (130).
22) One of the ways of ridding yourself of pride is to celebrate the festivals with open-heartedness and joy, and to honor them in the most lavish manner you can afford (135).
23) If someone is humble, it is a sign that he is bound to the Tzaddik, because being close to the Tzaddik breaks one's pride (*Ibid.*) (See #5, #29).
24) When a person is so humble that he is literally *nothing*, he can attain Torah and greatness at the same time. Otherwise it is hard for the two of them to dwell together (162).
25) When a person is arrogant, it is a sign that he will end up in trouble. The opposite is also true: a person who is humble and lowly will come to great honor (168).
26) Whatever glory and greatness any kingdom or leader or ruler may possess, their true basis lies in humility. The greater the humility of the ruler or leader, the more his power and dominion will spread (*Likutey Moharan* II, 16).

27) Most people have very mistaken ideas about what it is to be humble. You must be very careful not to fall into the trap of false modesty. Pray to God about this and ask to be worthy of true humility in accordance with His desire (38).

28) In the resurrection which is destined for the future, the part of each person that will be restored to life is the modest, humble part and that alone. The indescribable bliss of the eternal life of the World to Come cannot be experienced by anyone except inasmuch as true humility and meekness are found within him (72).

29) At the root of every single Jew there exists an aspect of the humility and lowliness of Moses. Every limb of the body is suffused with them. However they are hidden and concealed to the point that they are "dead" as it were, and for this reason the average person does not consciously experience them at all, and he is far from being humble and lowly in the way Moses was. But as a person draws closer to the Tzaddik — when he sees the Tzaddik, and especially when he hears Torah from his lips — he is able to develop a sense of genuine shame and to achieve repentance. The humility and lowliness concealed in him will then come to life, and he will attain the true humility which is the gateway to enduring life in the World to Come.

30) We must pray and plead with God to make us worthy of true humility and lowliness. We really have no conception of what humility is. The aim is certainly not to be slovenly and act as if we consider ourselves worthless. Humility is the source of the life which is in every single limb. Humility *is* the life of the world to come and the essence of its joy (*Ibid.*).

31) If things are not going well for a person, he should understand it as a sign that there is still some residue of pride within him. He must repent and lower himself and bring himself to the level of *Mah*? — "What?" Then things will begin to go well for him (82).

UNDERSTANDING דעת

1) True understanding is in the heart. Even the heathen nations possess understanding but not in their heart. The heart must be filled with awe. It is not enough to acknowledge God in the mind alone. It is necessary for one to draw his understanding down into the heart and to be so aware of the Creator that one's heart is filled with awe and fear of the greatness of God and one is aroused to serve Him with true devotion in the knowledge of His utter exaltedness. The way to achieve this is through meditation, through examining oneself and weighing all one's actions. This is the path to the "light that is treasured up for the just" (15).

2) If people feel they have problems and difficulties in life or that they are lacking certain things they need, be it sufficient income, children, physical health or whatever, the reason for their feeling is that they lack true understanding. When understanding is perfect, nothing is lacking. The essence of the eternal life of the future is bound up with the degree of understanding that will exist then. All will have knowledge of the Creator, and through this they will all be merged in His unity and live eternally just as God does. It is through knowing Him that we become merged with Him, and this is the main joy of the World to Come. For this reason a person should be very careful to guard his thoughts in purity and holiness and to avoid any bad thoughts. He should think only about Torah and devotion, and should constantly aim to attain higher levels of perception of God. Everything depends on this (21:11).

3) In order to attain *Da'at*, understanding (see #5), you must sanctify your lips, your nostrils, your eyes and your ears. Guard

your lips from all falsehood. Sanctify your nostrils with the fear of Heaven, as it is written: "...he will *scent* the fear of God" (Isaiah 11:3). Use your ears to listen to the words of the Sages and have faith in what they say. Lower your eyes and avert them from evil. Then you will attain perfect understanding and through this your heart will burn with passion for God. Because it is through the activity of the mind that passion is born in the heart. The more one thinks about Torah and devotion, the more one's heart becomes fired for God. The deeper one's understanding, the more one's passion burns. This passion purifies the heart and prevents it from being inflamed with evil desires, which merely pollute it. When a person's heart is pure, he will never be at a loss for words when he speaks to God. He will always find new words and new approaches (*Ibid.* 2; see also 156).

4) The way to sanctify the nostrils is through meekness and humility. You must be patient and not allow anger to burn within you* even if people treat you badly. The way to sanctify the ears is with loyalty and discretion. If people tell you a secret, be sure to keep it and not reveal it to anyone (21:6).

5) One who sanctifies these seven "lights of the head" can attain awesome levels of perception of God. These heights of understanding are a blessing from God which is bestowed from above without any preliminaries and introductions. This is the gift of *ruach hakodesh*, the holy spirit (*Ibid.* 2).

6) There are certain questions which trouble many people, such as the problem of how free will can exist if God knows the future. It is necessary to realize that it is beyond the capacity of the human mind to understand these matters. The answers to such questions lie in a sphere of wisdom that is so transcendent that the human mind is unable to attain it. This wisdom can never enter the human mind. It encompasses the mind from outside. One who apprehended this wisdom would not be human at all, he would be an angel. It is precisely the fact that

*The biblical expression for anger is a burning in the nostrils.

we do *not* understand these questions about free will that actually gives us the freedom we have. In time to come, when men's minds will expand and the secrets of free will and providence will be revealed, free will as such will disappear. Man's mind will emerge from its limits and he will become like an angel — with free will (*Ibid.* 4).

7) When a person lacks respect for the Tzaddik, the light of wisdom and understanding is hidden from him. He will never have original Torah ideas or reach new perceptions. He is no better than a dead person (*Ibid.* 6).

8) There are times when understanding can be very elusive. It is very good then to cry out as one prays or studies. In this way fresh understanding and insight are born (*Ibid.* 7).

9) The mind is man's very essence. Wherever a person's thoughts are, that is where he himself is — all of him. This explains why it is so important to avoid all bad thoughts. Otherwise that is where your place will be. You must force yourself to think good thoughts so that you will be worthy of knowing and understanding God. Then your place will be with Him: you will be merged with Him. The greater your perception of God the more you will become merged with him, and then you will achieve eternal life (*Ibid.* 11).

10) Lack of understanding strengthens the hold of the Divine face of severity and harsh judgement, giving rise to anger and unkindness. This is why sick people — who are under the sway of harsh judgements and constricted consciousness — are so often filled with anger. Expanding one's understanding helps to sweeten the harsh judgements: then anger and unkindness are dissipated and in their place comes lovingkindness. A person who has understanding realizes that God is wholly good and therefore all the experiences that are sent to him are for his own good (*Ibid.*).

11) The very prosperity and greatness of the nations of the world will in the end turn out to be for our own ultimate good. It may be impossible to understand this at the present time: we cannot deny the realities of our situation and our experiences. But in the

future, *Da'at*, understanding will grow to the point where even the nations of the world themselves will know and understand that all the greatness and advantages they enjoy today are really for our own benefit (*Ibid.*).

12) Understanding and perception of Godliness give hope and consolation in times of trouble. They constitute the very essence of the life of the World to Come, and they are the source of all its bliss. In time to come the whole world will be purified and all will become worthy of knowing God, even the nations of the world. As it is written: "For the earth will be filled with the knowledge of God like the waters cover the sea" (Isaiah 11:9). But there will be a great difference between the understanding they will attain and ours. Even within the Jewish people itself there will be great differences between the various Tzaddikim, and even more so between the just and the wicked. The perceptions granted to each one will depend on the struggles and bitterness he endured in this world for the sake of God. These Tzaddikim will become "burned" by these perceptions in the sense of being stirred and aroused by them, even though they seem very simple in the eyes of the Tzaddik who attained them in this world. In the World to Come his own perceptions will be unimaginably greater. Similar distinctions will exist on all the different levels. Understand this well and be warned. Make sure that you prepare yourself for the eternal life of the World to Come. "If you become wise, the wisdom is yours..." (Proverbs 9:12) (*Ibid.*).

13) A person who fills his mind with thoughts of Torah and devotion will always attain higher and higher levels of understanding. He will have nothing to fear from lurking evil and accusers. The forces of evil will flee from him. He will not be afraid of them at all (*Ibid.*).

14) The month of Elul is especially propitious for attaining new levels of understanding which are still beyond you. When you succeed in bringing these levels within the range of your comprehension you will then see further horizons beyond you. In this way you form new garments for your soul and you will

be saved from all evil (*Ibid.*).

15) When a person performs a mitzvah, this mitzvah has the power to arouse all the worlds and draw them closer to God, and blessing spreads over all the worlds. The essence of the blessing which flows from the upper worlds is wisdom and the vision of Godliness. As the blessing descends to the lower worlds, the effect it has on each individual depends on the strength of his desire for God. One who wishes to develop spiritually should always aim to draw this blessing down upon himself. But he must also be sure that his intellectual vision is infused with faith. It is no good to rely upon wisdom alone. The spiritual blessing of wisdom and understanding which descends through the fulfillment of the mitzvot expands the boundaries of man's intellect until he is worthy of perceiving the light that is beyond the *nefesh, ruach* and *neshama* which make up the soul. This is the light of the Infinite which cannot be perceived through the understanding itself but only through the performance of the mitzvot in joy. It can only be "attained, yet not attained" (*Zohar* I, 65a) (24).

16) Each individual must strive to free himself from the power of fantasy and imagination and acquire true wisdom. It is no good to follow one's animal instincts or the attractive images they evoke in the mind. He should pursue wisdom alone, which is completely opposed to impulse. The power of impulse derives from the faculty of fantasy and imagination. Animals also have this faculty, and therefore they also have these desires. Such desires are nothing more than the stubbornness of the heart, and one who follows them is literally like an animal. A man must free himself from stubbornness and break his heart of stone. He must follow intellect alone (25:1).

17) A person may succeed in breaking the hold of his desires and fantasies and thereby establish his commitment to a life founded on wisdom. But his intellect is still only *potential*. He must bring it into *actuality* by using it to think deeply about how to serve God. When he succeeds in attaining the ultimate level of wisdom that man can achieve, he will have won eternal life for himself

after his death. Because the only thing that is left to a person after his death is the holy wisdom he acquired through his Torah and devotion (*Ibid.*).

18) When a person's words lack understanding, they lack goodness — and then they will neither be heard nor accepted. They do not come into the category of "speech" at all. For speech that is not heard or accepted is not worthy of the name "speech" (29:1).

19) The way to develop the faculty of speech is by recounting the greatness of the Tzaddikim, their achievements, their levels and so on. Praising the Tzaddikim enhances our power of understanding, and the faculty of speech then receives from this understanding. Now our words contain goodness, and they will therefore be heard and accepted. This is the comprehensive *tikkun* for the faculty of speech (*Ibid.* 2).

20) Each individual must strive to reach the understanding of how the whole earth is full of God's glory. There is no place devoid of God. He fills all the worlds and transcends all the worlds. Even a person whose business activities involve him in contacts with non-Jews should not try to excuse himself. He cannot claim that it is impossible for him to serve God on account of his being constantly surrounded by gross materialism due to his business involvements. Godliness can be found everywhere — in all material things, and even in the languages of the non-Jews. Without Godliness they would not be able to exist or endure at all. It is only that as the levels become lower Godliness is more "contracted" and veiled in many garments (32:2).

21) This means that even if you are sunk in the very lair of the "husks" on the lowest of all levels, even if you believe you are so far from God that it is impossible for you to draw closer, you can still find Godliness even in the place you have sunk to. Even there you can attach yourself to Him and return to Him in perfect repentance. God is not far away even there. It is only that in the place where you are, the veils are thicker (*Ibid.*).

22) A person who masters his evil inclination and subdues it is

really like an angel of the Lord of Hosts, and he can find letters of Torah even where materialism is rampant. Even when he is in contact with non-Jews and sees their behavior, he is aware of the Godly vitality — the letters of Torah — which are clothed in it. The secrets of Torah — the hidden Torah of the Ancient of Days — will be revealed to him. He will taste the light of the love which is beyond time and beyond finitude, and he will attain a perception of the light and goodness which are hidden away — the hidden Torah and the hidden Tzaddikim (*Ibid.* 3).

23) As one goes from level to level and draws closer and closer to God, his knowledge and understanding of God will become greater and greater, and his ability to love God will grow more and more (*Ibid.* 4).

24) Each individual must bind his heart to his understanding. Every Jew knows in general terms that God exists. By rights the mere fact that he knows this should be enough to make him subdue all his animal impulses and bad character traits. But "the evil are under the sway of their hearts" (*Bereshith Rabbah*, 34) and the heart is the seat of all the passions and character traits of the individual. This is why it is so important to bind one's heart to one's understanding. When a person is in control of his heart, all his passions and impulses and character traits will be under the sway of his understanding, the part within him that knows God and is aware of how the whole earth is full of His glory. As he develops this awareness he should be able to break and eliminate all his impulses and then he will be worthy of the light of love which is within *Da'at*, understanding. This is the hidden light, which is the hidden Torah and the hidden Tzaddikim (*Ibid.* 7).

25) Wisdom is the root of all things. This is why one must guard his mind from all extraneous ideologies. True wisdom has as its goal the pursuit of perfection. The wisdom that is necessary for this is the holy wisdom of the Torah, which is concerned with Godliness. All other idea-systems are futile — they cannot really be called wisdom at all (35:1).

26) From the time a person is born his understanding is in a

state of contraction. It only starts to grow when he begins to use it to think about how to serve God. But when a person admits alien thoughts and ideologies into his mind, the holiness of his mind and soul is diminished in direct proportion to the space occupied by the alien ideas. All kinds of negative character traits develop from this alien mentality and cluster around it (*Ibid.*).

27) This is why one must be so careful to protect one's mind and not allow alien thoughts and ideologies to enter. The way to achieve true repentance and make amends for all one's sins is to make a determined effort to expel all alien thoughts from one's mind. The mind is the manifestation of the soul. When a person sanctifies his mind — and therefore his soul — everything becomes elevated and restored to its source. This is the essence of repentance (*Ibid.*).

28) It is not sufficient merely to guard yourself from alien ideas. You must always try to bring new vitality into your mind, and in this way your soul will be revived and refreshed. For the mind is the manifestation of the soul (*Ibid.* 2).

29) None are more prone to the attacks of the evil inclination, the "primordial serpent," than those who study the Torah. Because of their deeper understanding and the higher level of their souls, the evil inclination makes redoubled efforts to insinuate itself within them and make them sin. It is therefore essential for them to guard their minds from evil thoughts, because these are the basis on which the evil inclination builds (*Ibid.* 1).

30) The mind — and therefore the soul — is renewed through sleep. When the mind is tired from exertion, sleep refreshes it. While one is asleep, the mind — that is, the soul — enters into the category of faith. This is expressed in the words of Lamentations (3:22,23): "His compassions fail not. They are new every morning; Great is Your *faithfulness*" (*Ibid.* 3).

31) There are different kinds of sleep. There is physical sleep, which gives rest to the mind. Learning Torah may also be considered as "sleeping" in relation to intense devotion to God through prayer, meditation and contemplation. "Learning" here

refers to the study of the simple meaning of Torah. There are people who involve themselves in very intense devotions. When their minds become tired from the high level of their devotions, they should turn to the study of Torah on the level of the literal interpretation, and for them this is a kind of "sleep." Another kind of "sleep" is business activity when conducted in faithfulness and with integrity. When a man conducts his business affairs with the requisite faithfulness and integrity, his mind and soul are thereby refreshed, acquiring fresh illumination from the Inner Light of God. In all these different kinds of "sleep" the essential thing is always faith, and it is necessary to guard one's faith very carefully. Then, when his mind becomes tired, he can infuse it with fresh life through his faith by turning to one of these kinds of "sleep." In the case of material sleep in the literal sense one can actually feel how the mind has been renewed. And because, as we have said, the main thing is faith, before going to sleep we have to bind ourselves with our faith. This is the reason we recite the Shema before retiring to sleep at night. When we do so, we should say the words with intense concentration in order to bind the soul with faith during the hours of sleep. The soul will then be refreshed, as it is written, "New every morning; Great is Your *faithfulness*" (Lamentations 3:23). Our sleep will bring us a new mind and a new soul from the Inner Light of God. This binding of the soul with faith also applies to those who turn to the study of Torah in its simple interpretation as a form of relaxation from the intensity of their devotions. When their minds begin to become distracted and they can no longer remain attached to God through intense devotion, they should lay aside their efforts and bind themselves to faith in simplicity. They should study the simple sense of the Torah without any sophistication at all, simply with faith. Regardless of the devotions a person uses to bind himself to God, the basis of his attachment must always be through faith. One should never rely on intellect alone (see 15 above). So, too, where business activity serves as a kind of "sleep" refreshing the mind, the essential thing is also faith. The business activity must be carried out with integrity in accordance with the Torah laws governing business and commerce. Then the soul — which is the mind — enters the category of faith and is there renewed (*Ibid.* 4-6).

32) In all your business activities you must seek to fulfill the verse in the Psalms (15:2) "And he speaks the truth in his heart." This is how to preserve your faith intact (*Ibid.* 7).

33) Every Jew, before making some advance in Torah or devotion, must first be tested and refined through "exile" amidst the seventy nations of the world. Each of the seventy nations is particularly associated with its own unique bad character trait. It is these bad traits that keep the nations far from the seventy faces of the Torah. The new advance which this Jew has to make will draw him closer to the seventy faces of the Torah. But the shell comes before the fruit, and whoever wants to eat the fruit must first break the shell. Therefore before the soul can come to any fresh revelation of Torah, it is obliged to go into "exile" amidst the seventy nations — that is, to be tempted and tested by their impulses and desires — in order that it may break through and attain the new revelation. The main test is sexual desire, which epitomizes all the evil of the seventy nations and all their desires. When the soul is brought to the test and a person feels overwhelmed by lust and desire, he must raise his voice and cry out again and again. He must cry at least seventy times, like a woman giving birth, who utters seventy cries. Then he will be able to break the temptation, and he will be worthy of a great revelation in his understanding of Torah and his devotion to God. The more purified he becomes, the more the seventy faces of the Torah will be revealed to him (36:1).

34) One should aim to achieve perfect understanding. One should strive to reach an understanding of everything that is within the grasp of the human mind in the realm of holiness. The only way this can be achieved is through working with other people to draw them closer to God. Through this his own understanding will develop and eventually become complete. He will be worthy of having children, and he will have the power to

cause the barren to give birth (53).

35) It is because of this that the Tzaddikim make such great efforts to chase after people and draw them closer to the service of God. It is not that they want prestige, God forbid. Their goal is to attain perfect understanding (*Ibid.*).

36) A person should think about the various different situations God sends him day by day. Each day has its own thoughts, words and actions. All of them are completely unique to that day. God has as it were "contracted" His Godliness, which is infinite and without end, in such a way that Godliness is present even in the innermost point of the finite, material world in which man finds himself. Thus God sends each individual thoughts, words and deeds appropriate to the day, the person and the place. Within them are clothed hints whose purpose is to draw this individual closer to God's service. A person should therefore pay attention to the various things which happen to him and reflect on their significance. He should think about every thought, word and deed which God sends him each day in order to discover the hints God is giving him to draw him closer every moment. This holds true of every single person, no matter who he may be and what situation he is in (54:2).

37) But caution is necessary when thinking about these matters. It is necessary to keep within certain limits, and one should not delve too deeply. Otherwise there is a danger of passing beyond the bounds of holiness. It is dangerous to fly off into speculation. A person should keep within the bounds of human understanding and expand his horizons steadily. He should not try to go beyond his own level, because "that which is too wonderful for you, you must not search out" (*Chagiga* 13a) (*Ibid.*).

38) Very tall people are usually foolish (55:6).

39) Don't be over-sophisticated. Being clever, or even wise, is no good unless you act correctly in your practical life. In order to draw closer to God the most important thing is a steadfast heart. The main source of the heart's strength lies in good deeds. A person whose mental attainments outweigh his practical actions

lacks the strength of heart needed to keep his intellect within the bounds of holiness. His intellect can easily lead him astray and cause him to sin. Worldly wisdom — as opposed to the wisdom of the Torah — is futile. The worst thing of all is philosophy. One should simply abandon all one's pretensions to wisdom and defer to the men of truth who follow the path of truth as we know it by tradition from our Rabbis of blessed memory (*Ibid.*).

40) There is nothing in the world that does not contain Godliness, however hidden it may be. There are two degrees of concealment. The first is simple concealment; the second is "the concealment within the concealment." When God is hidden with one concealment it is hard indeed to find Him, but still, with great effort and searching it is possible, because at least one *knows* that God is hidden from one. But at the time of the "concealment within the concealment," even the fact that God is hidden is itself concealed. The individual has no idea that God is concealed from him, and then it is hard indeed to find Him. The concealment of Godliness comes about through sin. When a person sins once and then repeats his sin a second time, the sin becomes permissible in his eyes. This is what causes the first concealment. But if one sins more and more, God forbid, one falls to the level of "the concealment within the concealment." Nevertheless, even within "the concealment within the concealment" Godliness is present, because without His life-force nothing in the world could exist at all. Through devotion to Torah it is possible to strip away all the veils and reveal that God is present even when "the concealment within the concealment" is most intense. Then the unremitting cry of the Torah is heard at last: "How long, ye thoughtless, will ye love thoughtlessness?" (Proverbs 1:22). In the end one will be able to return to God no matter where one may have fallen to (56:3).

41) The greater one's *Da'at*, understanding, the easier it is for one to make a living. The more one lacks understanding, the more one must struggle and labour for one's income (*Ibid.* 6).

42) The more understanding, the more peace. For strife, anger and unkindness are rooted in lack of understanding. The more

understanding the more love, kindness and peace. Through this comes healing (*Ibid.*).

43) When a person is angry his understanding is withdrawn and the image of God disappears from his face. He no longer has the face of a *man* (57:6).

44) In order for a man's understanding to develop, he must pay attention to three things; he should teach what he knows to others and draw them under the wings of the Shechinah. He must cultivate the fear of sin over and above his learning. And he must be careful about the way he communicates what he knows to others in order that his words will be words of grace. For "The words of a wise man's mouth are gracious" (Ecclesiastes 10:12). Then his words will not be despised. His understanding will bring him the three blessings of food, drink and clothing (58:5).

45) One whose understanding is developed to perfection has the power to draw even the weakest among Israel to the service of God and to crush the enemies who chase after them and oppress them. He has the power to expound original Torah ideas on Shabbat — "two for every one" (*Ibid.*).

46) The bliss of the World to Come lies in the praise and thanks we will give to the great and blessed name of God. It is through knowing and acknowledging God that we come as close to Him as it is possible to come. The more we know and acknowledge God, the closer to Him we become. In the future everything else will be of no account whatsoever. The only thing left will be to give thanks and praise to God and to know Him (*Ibid.* II, 2).

47) The essential part of man is his *Da'at*, understanding. A person without understanding is not a person at all. He is not worthy of the name "man." He is nothing more than a wild animal which resembles a man. The most important aspect of understanding itself is the understanding one has of the Holy Torah: to know that God exists and has power and control over all the world, and to carry out His will and fulfill His commandments. A person who is worthy of attaining this understanding will be saved from all sin and transgression. For

"one only transgresses if the spirit of folly enters one" (*Sotah* 3a). A person who is aware of God at all times will certainly be saved from sin (7:2,3).

48) The main reason why people are far from God is that they are not clear-headed. It is essential to think about the *purpose* of this world, with all its desires, distractions, etc. There are the desires which are bound up with the body, and then there are the other desires — for prestige and honor etc. — which are not directly concerned with the satisfaction of bodily functions. Think what is the purpose of everything, what is the ultimate goal. Then you will surely return to God (10).

49) If you are always happy you will be able to achieve a clear, settled mind. Joy settles the mind and then you can control it as you wish. You can reflect on the ultimate purpose of life. But when a person is depressed, his intellect and understanding go into "exile" and it is very hard for him to concentrate. Depression is a terrible obstacle to serving God (*Ibid.*).

50) A person with complete understanding knows that time in this world is really nothing. The sensation of time stems from deficient understanding. The greater one's understanding, the more one sees and understands that in reality time does not exist. We can actually feel how time flies like a passing shadow and a cloud that will soon disappear. If you take this to heart you will be free of worries about mundane matters and you will have the strength and determination to snatch what you can — a good deed here, a lesson there — in order to gain something that is truly enduring out of this life. You will gain the life of the eternal world, which is completely beyond time (61).

51) True humility is when a person uses his intelligence to keep well away from any kind of sophistication. It takes both wisdom and great effort to make oneself like an animal [without sophistication] (83; Rabbi Nachman's Wisdom 15).

52) You must be very worthy to be able to meditate for a given time each day and regret what you must. Not everybody has such clarity of mind. You must make sure you set aside a time each day when you can reflect calmly on everything you are

doing and the way you are behaving and ask if this is the right way to spend your days (Rabbi Nachman's Wisdom 47).

SPEECH דיבור

Its power for good or evil.

1) Idle pursuits and abusive, slanderous language bring one to poverty. The remedy is to give charity to Torah scholars: this brings wealth (4:8).
2) The way to study Torah is by speaking the words out loud. The words will then become a light which will illuminate for you all the places where you must repent and make amends. Eventually you will achieve perfect repentance, and then you will come to understand the very depths of Torah (11:1).
3) You must strive to sanctify the way you speak until your words are the words of the "Holy Tongue." Speak many words of Torah. Say many prayers and make many entreaties before God. Talk to Him; plead with Him. And at the same time be careful to avoid any falsehood and derogatory comments about other people. If you are careful about the way you speak it will help you to achieve personal sanctity and to guard the Holy Covenant. And the more you purify and sanctify yourself the more you will be able to perfect the way you speak (19:3).
4) Words which are neither listened to nor accepted cannot be called "speech" at all. The way to discover the true meaning of the gift of speech is through speaking the praises of the Tzaddikim. This is the complete *tikkun* for speech (29:1,2).
5) Speech is the vessel with which we receive the flow of blessings. According to the words, so is the blessing. One who attains perfection in the way he speaks, can receive abundant blessings by means of the vessels formed by his words. This is the reason why when we pray, we must actually pronounce the words with our lips (34:3).
6) Speech is the breath of the lips of the Holy One, blessed-be-

He. To abuse it is to make it into a wild blast, the "raging storm-wind" (Psalms 148:8). This "raging stormwind" is the "great accuser" — the source of all the trials and challenges which confront man. This wild spirit wastes away man's very flesh. It is the root of all the slander and falsehood and evil which people speak about each other. It is called the "end of all flesh" (Genesis 6:13) because it works for the destruction of man's flesh and life. All this comes from abusing the faculty of speech (38:2).

7) It is a great thing if you persevere in learning Torah in spite of poverty or other trials and pressures and difficulties. This is the way to achieve perfection in your speech. A thread of lovingkindness will be drawn down over you (*Chagigah* 12b) and the forces of stern justice and impurity ranged against you will be thrust aside. Your speech will become cleansed and elevated. The words will flow out in song and praise to God, you will pray with strength and fire, and your heart will be aroused to serve God with true devotion. In the end you will be worthy of speaking the pure truth before God, the truth in your heart will flow forth, and you will be filled with a fiery passion to return to God (*Ibid.* 4-5).

8) Empty words devoid of holiness give strength to the temples of idolatry. The hand of falsehood is strengthened and the exile deepens. All contact with the spirituality of the Land of Israel becomes lost. Truth is concealed, divisiveness and strife multiply. The Shechinah is locked in strife with her children, exiled as they are from their land and the table of their Father. But words of holiness put strength into the hand of Truth (45).

9) Talking in a derogatory way about other people reinforces the power of fantasy and illusion within us. When people use bad language and speak derogatorily about others, their *Da'at*, understanding, is taken from them and they fall from the love of God into animalistic passions and desires. The source of these passions and desires is in the faculty of fantasy and imagination, which is part of man's animal nature. It feeds upon falsehood and slander. It is directly opposed to the faculty of memory,

through which we keep the true facts of our situation and our eternal destiny in the forefront of our minds. Those who abuse language fall instead into "forgetfulness," which is "death to the heart" because their heart dies within them and they never remember that the true goal of our life in this world is the eternal life of the World to Come. People like this are dead even in their lifetime, because they have no conception of their true goal and purpose (54:5).

10) Excessive greed for food and drink causes speech to go into "exile." The words become trapped in the constriction of the throat. One who is a glutton is unable to say a single word before God. The remedy for this is fasting (62:5).

11) There are many different kinds of degenerate speech: talking unfairly and untruthfully about other people; telling people what their friends and acquaintances said about them or did to their disadvantage; telling lies; cynicism and sarcasm; flattery; embarrassing people publicly; obscene talk; unnecessary remarks and so on. Worst of all is when people cast aspersions on the Tzaddikim and on those who are honest and God-fearing. Talk like this gives wings to the primordial serpent. It flies through the world wreaking havoc. This "serpent" is the sophistry of the philosophers and other apostles of atheism. Today this has spread throughout the world and is gaining ever-increasing prestige and power. But words of holiness form wings for the domain of the holy (63).

12) You must struggle until you are serving God with every drop of blood you possess. You must speak many words of Torah and prayer until all the blood within you is transformed into these holy words. Then you will find peace, and the spirit of strife and contention will be broken. For contention and rivalry have their source in the drops of blood with which a person has not yet served God (75).

13) Words of Torah and prayer have the power to raise up the fallen sparks and restore and renew all the fallen worlds. The one who speaks them is accounted as if he had created Heaven and Earth and all the worlds afresh. We must speak only words

of holiness and nothing else. Then the sparks will be raised up, the worlds will be restored, and Mashiach will come (*Ibid.*).

14) You must speak words of Torah and prayer to the point where your body becomes totally nullified, as if it literally did not exist. To achieve this you must develop true awe of Heaven. This will bring you peace and harmony, and the world will be filled with blessing (*Ibid.*).

15) Words of holiness — Torah and prayer — are a very high concept. Holy words are the Shechinah, the Divine Indwelling, because the kingship of God and the truth of His existence is revealed through them. Holy speech is the "breath of Mashiach." It is *ruach hakodesh*, the Holy Spirit, and it includes the concepts of the revival of the dead and of the unification of the Holy One, blessed-be-He, and the Shechinah (78).

16) Speech is a "mother of children" (Psalms 113:9). Just as a mother always stays with her child and never forgets him even if he goes to the filthiest of places, so the power of speech never leaves a person even if he finds himself in the filthiest of places. Even one who is sunk in the lowest of levels can always remind himself of God's presence if he speaks words of holiness — Torah and prayer. Regardless of his situation, he should make an effort to speak words of Torah and prayer, to meditate and speak to God, and to discuss religious matters with his teacher and his friends. Then he will always be able to remind himself of God's presence regardless of how far he may be from God, even if he falls to the "filthy places." The faculty of speech will never desert him, and he will never be able to forget God. Understand the tremendous power of speech. This idea can save you from destruction (*Ibid.*).

17) Speech derives from the Divine aspect of *Gevurah*, which denotes strength and severity. Therefore all speech must be sweetened through studying Torah and speaking words of goodness and holiness. This is the reason why we must be so careful to avoid any form of degenerate speech, especially derogatory comments about other people. More than anything else this applies to the way we talk about the Tzaddik. To cast

aspersions upon the Tzaddik arouses the force of severity in the world, and can cause the Tzaddik to fall from his level if he lacks sufficient force to sweeten it. He may even die because of this, and then the harsh forces are sweetened by the departure of his soul from the world.

18) When a person sits down and starts discussing somebody else it is a "day of judgement," for he is in effect sitting in judgement on his neighbor. You must be very careful about this. Take a good look at yourself and ask if you are worthy to pass judgement on your friend. Judgement belongs to God, as our Rabbis said: "Do not judge your neighbor until you come into his place" (*Avoth* 2:5). Who really knows the *place* of his neighbor and who can come there aside from God alone? (*Likutey Moharan* II, 1:14).

19) Trust is the foundation of perfect speech: when we acknowledge God, praise Him and learn His law, all the lines of truth spread their radiance throughout the different aspects of speech and bring it to perfection (2).

20) Speech has tremendous power. Speak many words of Torah, say many prayers, and make all kinds of appeals and entreaties to God. More than anything else, talk to God in your own words. If you are determined and make a practice of this every day of your life, you will certainly attain the ultimate good both in this world and in the World to Come.

SECLUSION & MEDITATION התבודדות

1) To taste the hidden light of Torah — the secrets which will be revealed in time to come — you should seclude yourself as much as you can to pray and speak to God. Take a good look at yourself and make a reckoning. What are you doing with your life? How is your time spent? Is this the right way to spend your life — to behave as you do before the Holy One, blessed-be-He, who bestows goodness upon you every moment of the day? Weigh all the different aspects of your life very carefully. If you make yourself the judge over everything you are doing, you will be able to rid yourself of all fears and worries. You will never be afraid of earthly powers — princes or rulers, wild beasts, robbers or the like. Nothing in the world will frighten you. Only before God will you stand in fear and reverence. This is the way to elevate the fear that is within you to its true root, which is in *Da'at*, understanding. You will attain perfect knowledge, because you will know before Whom to stand in awe: God alone, in His greatness and glory. Then you will be able to understand the revealed Torah and you will attain genuine humility. You will learn how to put your whole soul into your prayers. All sense of self and physical being will be totally nullified as you pray, and you will be able to pray without any thought of personal gain. When you reach the point where your sense of self and physicality totally disappear — as if you were simply not in the world at all — then you will discover the hidden secrets of the Torah. This is the concealed light which is destined to be revealed in time to come. All this you can achieve through *hitbodidut,* secluded prayer (15).

2) When a person meditates and speaks to God, the very words

he speaks are *ruach hakodesh*, the holy spirit. As soon as a person makes this meditation a regular practice and prepares himself, indeed *forces* himself to speak to God, then God Himself sends the words to his mouth. Make sure that the words you say are always new and fresh. Search out new ways to appeal to God. Always choose words that will find favor. Purify your heart by devoting your mind to thoughts of Torah and holiness, and then you will find the right way to meditate and speak to God (see *Da'at* 3) (21, 156).

3) When you speak to God, make it a habit to express the longing and yearning you feel to extricate yourself from evil and attain true good. It is by praying and pleading like this that you draw your spiritual power and strength from the realm of the potential and possible to the realm of the real and actual. The longing and yearning by themselves create only the *possibility* of spiritual strength. But the *words* of your prayers and conversations with God draw this spiritual strength into the realm of the *actual*: it becomes realized in actual fact. This is the way to accomplish what you yearn for. Letters of Torah are present throughout the Creation. By expressing your yearning and desire in words, you invest these letters with strength for good. You give new life and strength to everything, drawing goodness and blessing into all the worlds. Numberless souls are stirred to make their own return to God — all through the words of the prayer you utter before your Maker. How precious are the longing and yearning which you express before God. The main thing is actually to pronounce the words. Make a regular practice of this and spend a lot of time each day working on it. It will help the whole world (31:8,9).

4) Within every Jew there is a good "point" — and it is precious indeed — whose only desire at all times is to do the will of her Master. But lust and desire break the heart. This is why people's hearts are remote from this good point. Make it a habit to speak to God. Then your good point will send its radiance into your heart, and you will be able to destroy the "foreskin of the heart" (Deut. 10:16) — the impulses and desires which break and

destroy the heart (See Tzaddik 42) (34:7,8).
5) In all your prayers and conversations with God, be sure to be absolutely honest and truthful (see *Busha* 2 and *Dibbur* 7) (38:5).
6) Everyone must strive to be totally merged with the Source of his being. To achieve this requires *bittul* — self-nullification. The only way to attain *bittul* is through secluded prayer with God. When a person goes aside to converse with God he nullifies everything else and attaches himself only to God. In this way he becomes merged with his Source (52).
7) The best time to seclude yourself to pray is at night, when everyone is asleep. Ideally you should go to a place outside the city and follow a solitary path somewhere that people don't go even in the day-time. Empty your heart and your whole consciousness of all your involvements in the everyday world. Then work to nullify all of your character traits, one after the other, until in the end you nullify all sense of self completely. First work on one character trait, then another and another, until you reach the point where you are free of any self-centeredness and any sense of independent existence. You must be as nothing in your own eyes. Then you will be worthy of attaining true self-nullification and your soul will be merged with its root. The whole universe will be merged with you in your Source. You and everything with you will be merged in the Unity of God (*Ibid.*).
8) The ideal time for *hithbodeduth* is at night: seclude yourself and express yourself before God. Speak with all your heart and search out the goodness of your soul. Find the good points which are within you and cleanse them of all the evil in the soul until you pour out your heart like water before God. This is the way to attain true joy and to subdue the power of fantasy which is the source of all lust and desire. Through this you can acquire a good memory — which means always to remember the World to Come and never to lose sight of the end purpose of this life and its ultimate destiny. This is how you can return to God (54).
9) A person may be praying with great intensity or at the height of meditation, when suddenly he falls from his level. This is

because somewhere there is a flaw in his faith. He should feel heartbroken and ashamed. How could he fall from heaven to earth? He should arouse tender pity for himself because of his plight. He should literally sigh! This sigh will bring him back to his level (108).

10) When a person speaks to God and uses every kind of argument and appeal to "conquer" God, then God Himself has great joy and pleasure. He Himself sends words to this person's mouth so that he will be able to "conquer" Him. How else could flesh and blood win a victory against God? It is only because God Himself helps him (124).

11) When a person speaks to God and pours out his pain and anguish, confessing his sins and grieving at the enormity of what he has done, the Shechinah herself rises before God and pours out her pain and sorrow. Because every flaw in the soul of man is also a "flaw" in the Shechinah. And the Shechinah will seek to bring him comfort and devise ways and means of repairing the damage (259).

12) How good it is to pray to God and meditate in the meadows amidst the grass and the trees. When a man goes out to the meadows to pray, every blade of grass, every plant and flower enter his prayers and help him, putting strength and force into his words (*Ibid.* II, 11).

13) It has already been explained how important it is to seclude yourself and pray, and how powerful a method this is. It is *the* path by which we can come close to God. Everybody should set aside fixed periods every day and express himself before God in his own native language. It is much easier to say what you need to say when you are using your own language. You should set forth whatever is in your heart. Use every kind of appeal and argument. Use words that will endear you to God and win His favor. Plead with Him to draw you closer. Every individual knows his own personal pain and sorrow and the distance that separates him from God. It is impossible to convey the true greatness of this method. It is superior to all others. It is *the* way of serving God, and through following it everyone can attain the

ultimate good in this world and in the World to Come. There is nothing that cannot be accomplished by prayer and entreaty. The greatest of the Tzaddikim achieved what they did only through this practice. Think about it carefully and you will see the greatness of this path. Set aside one hour every day for this, the rest of the day be happy — and then you will be truly blessed (25).

14) It is a good thing to turn the Torah which you learn into prayers (*Ibid.*). (See there for fuller explanation).

15) It is true that weeping and crying are good when you plead and entreat before God. But don't fall into the trap of saying psalms and prayers with the constant thought and expectation that you are going to burst into tears and cry. It will only confuse you and prevent you from concentrating. The most important thing is to say what you are saying honestly and with all your heart. Let your ears hear and your heart attend to the words which your lips are uttering. If you are moved to cry, good. If not, don't be distracted because of this (95).

16) All the Tzaddikim and all of the truly righteous attained what they did only through secluded prayer and meditation. This practice has never been more necessary than in our age, situated as we are at the end of the period of the exile, subject to the full force of the evil inclination and the forces of the *Sitra Achra*, the Other Side. People are weak, spiritually and physically. The only way to escape from the power of the evil inclination and all the other obstacles holding us back from God is to follow this practice determinedly and make a fixed time every day to talk to God in our own native language. Be totally honest and open your heart before God, whether to beg for forgiveness for what happened in the past or to appeal to God to help you in the future by releasing you from the traps you are caught in and drawing you closer to Him. Even if you find you are unable to express yourself before God, even if you can say no more than a single word, this is still good. Even if you can say nothing except "Master of the Universe" it is also good. The mere fact that you make an effort, that you prepare yourself to

speak, that you feel a longing to speak —even if you find you can say nothing — all this is very precious in God's eyes. If you are determined and persistent and you *make* yourself speak before God, in time God will help you and then you will be able to express yourself with words filled with vitality, freshness and grace. Your words will bring blessings down from the Heavens and you will attain true and enduring good. This is *the* path to serving God, because all the different ways of serving God require prayers and appeals to God if we are to accomplish them well. If you remain firm in following this path you will be blessed indeed. Small or great, no one can serve God honestly and truthfully except through *hithbodeduth*, secluded prayer (25, 100).

17) Whenever you say psalms and other prayers or rise to say *Tikun Chatzot*, the Midnight Lament for the destruction of the Temple, you should endeavor to find *yourself* in the words of the prayers. The Rebbe had truly extraordinary things to say about this (101).

18) Even when you feel your heart is not in what you are saying, don't let this discourage you. Persevere, and you will usually find that in the end your heart will be aroused and the words will flow from you with genuine fervor. Speech has tremendous power to arouse a person's heart. And even if the days and years pass by and you think that all your words and meditation have accomplished nothing, don't let yourself be thrown off course. The words *have* left their mark. There is no doubt about it. It is the same as when water is dripping onto a stone. It may seem as though mere water is incapable of having any effect at all on the hard stone. Certainly the effects of the water are not visible. But if the water continues dripping for a long time without interruption you can see for yourself that it will wear a hollow in the stone. The same is true of the heart, even when the heart is as hard as stone. The words and the prayers may all appear to have no effect. But with the passing of many days and years the heart will be worn away by the words.

When a person is meditating, it is a good thing to say:

"Today I am just *beginning* to attach myself to You." You should always make a fresh start, because every activity is greatly influenced by the way you start it. In the words of the popular saying: "Starting is half the battle" and this way you can never lose. If things were going well before, now they will go even better. And if God forbid they were not going well before, then in any case you would have had to make a new start! (Rabbi Nachman's Wisdom 234).

19) When you speak to God you should arouse your heart to the point where your soul all but flies out of you. This is true prayer (*Likutey Moharan* II, 99).

20) When God helps you to pray you will be able to express yourself before Him in the same way that a person speaks to a friend. You should get into the habit of talking to God like this. As if you were speaking to your teacher or your friend. For God is close by. He can be found everywhere. The whole earth is full of His glory (*Ibid.*).

21) How good it is if you can pour out your prayer before God like a child complaining and pestering his father. And it is good if you can stir your heart so much with your words that the tears literally pour down your cheeks like a child crying to his father (Rabbi Nachman's Wisdom 7).

22) It is possible for you to scream in a "still small voice" (Kings I, 19:12) without anyone in the world hearing you. Not a sound emerges from your lips. You just imagine in detail exactly how you would scream (*Ibid.* 16).

23) A broken heart is precious indeed. You should understand that a broken heart has nothing to do with depression. When a person is depressed it is a form of anger and irritation. But someone with a broken heart is like a child nagging his father or a baby crying and screaming because his father is far away. A broken heart is precious in God's eyes. It would be good if one could go through the whole day with a broken heart. But this would easily lead the majority of people to fall into depression, and depression is very destructive. Therefore, the best thing is to set aside a certain period each day to pray with a broken heart

and then to spend the rest of the day in joy. (See *Simcha* for guidance on how to be happy at all times.)

ENCOURAGEMENT התחזקות

1) To return to God one must be expert in the law, the *halachah*, which literally means "going." A person must be skilled in travelling the necessary path so that nothing in the world will discourage him or make him feel rebuffed. Whether he makes progress or not, even if he feels himself sliding back, regardless of what he may go through, he should always be firm and follow the teaching of King David in the book of Psalms (139:8): "If I ascend to heaven You are there, and if I make hell my bed, behold there You are." For even in the lowest pit of hell it is possible to draw oneself closer to God, because He is to be found there too. "If I make hell my bed, behold there You are." (6:4).

2) The greatest revelation of God's greatness comes when those who were very far from Him draw closer. His blessed name is then glorified and exalted in the worlds above and the worlds below. What this implies is that no one should ever despair of coming closer to God even if he feels very far from Him, because of his sins. It may be that he has committed great wrongs. But if so, then it is precisely through *his* returning to God that God's glory will be exalted and magnified (*Ibid.* 10:1).

3) It is a good thing for friends who are attached to the Tzaddikim to give encouragement to each other. The main source of strength they have to draw on is the Tzaddik himself: his power is so great that he can draw up even the most damaged soul, even a soul that has not yet begun to emerge from the profane to the holy by a single hair's breadth. The thought that the Tzaddik can renew such a soul should give everyone a feeling of encouragement. However low a person's

level may be and no matter what he may have been through, there is genuine hope for him so long as he attaches himself to the Tzaddik. A person should remind his friend about this in order to give him encouragement. He should also find other ways of encouraging him and strengthening his devotion to God. It is a good thing to pass on to his friends as much of the teachings of his teacher as he himself can understand (13 end).

4) God takes pride even in the most insignificant Jew, even in the sinners of Israel, so long as they go by the name Jew. There is a special pride which God takes in each individual Jew. One should therefore never despair of God's help regardless of any wrong one may have done. God's love for him will never cease, and he can still return to God. The main thing is to be attached to the Tzaddik and his followers, because they possess the ability to uncover the goodness and glory which is present even in the worst people and return everything to God (17).

5) When it is time for a person to advance from one level to the next, he must first experience a fall before he can rise up. The whole purpose of the fall is to prepare for the advance. Try to understand this and you will realize the determination which is necessary in order to serve God. No matter how you may fall, you should never allow yourself to be discouraged. Remain firm and resolute and pay no attention to the fall at all. In the end the fall will be transformed into a great advance. This is its whole purpose. This applies to all the different ways one can fall. There is much that could be said on this subject because everyone always thinks that his own situation is so bad that this idea does not apply in his case. People think it only applies to those on very high levels who are continually advancing from level to level. But you should realize that it holds true even for people on the lowest of levels. For God is good to all (22:11).

6) One may be on such a low level that one is literally "inside the earth." But in order to serve God one must start advancing from level to level. This applies to everyone in the world. Each time a person emerges from one level in order to rise up to the next, the "husks" attack him again in the form of temptations, fantasies,

strange thoughts, confusions and all kinds of other obstacles. They range themselves against him and refuse to allow him to enter the gates of holiness. There are many sincere people who get very discouraged when they find themselves suddenly confronted by all these temptations and obstacles. They start thinking they must have fallen from their previous level because for some time now they had not experienced all these temptations to the same degree. They were dormant. But they should understand that what they are experiencing is not a fall. The time has come for them to advance from one level to the next. This is the reason why these temptations and obstacles have reared their heads again. Whenever this happens it takes a lot of strength and courage not to lose hope and to master all the temptations and obstacles again (25).

7) In this situation it helps to give charity to those who are worthy. When the recipient of the charity is himself worthy, the act of charity reveals the greatness of the Creator. This revelation helps the individual to break the husks confronting him on every level (*Ibid.* 4).

8) Another way to face this situation is to make yourself happy with the thought of the good point which is within you. You are of the seed of Israel, and you have succeeded in drawing closer to the men of truth who are leading you and guiding you along the path of truth. Regardless of your situation you still have hope of attaining the ultimate good. The joy these thoughts will arouse will help you break the husks which confront you at each level (*Ibid.* 5).

9) When a person succeeds in breaking through the barriers and rises from level to level, this also benefits his fellow Jew who was previously standing on the level he himself has now attained. For it means that the other Jew was obliged to rise to the next level, since it is impossible for two people to be on the same level at the same time. This is how one Jew can help to raise up another (*Ibid.*).

10) The places which seem lowest of all and furthest from God actually contain the most exalted life force of all, albeit

concealed: namely the "secrets of Torah." One who has fallen very far should therefore understand that in the very place where he has fallen he can draw very close to God, because of the exalted life force which is concealed there. When he succeeds in returning to God, exalted levels of Torah will be revealed through him. These are the "secrets of Torah" (56:3).

11) When a person wants to return to God and change his life accordingly and make the journey to the Tzaddik, a new evil inclination rises up against him far stronger than the one he had before. The more strongly a person is devoted to God, the stronger the onslaughts of the evil inclination. It is a constant battle to control it. This explains something which is often found when a person wants to journey to the Tzaddik. At first he feels a great enthusiasm, but when he actually starts on the journey his desire becomes weakened. At times it happens that when he finally comes to the Tzaddik himself he loses his desire completely. The reason is that as soon as he felt the desire to journey to the Tzaddik, he killed the evil inclination which he had before and a new and stronger evil inclination came into being. Because "whoever is greater than others has a stronger evil inclination" (*Succah* 52). If you genuinely wish to draw close to God, you must be very firm in the battle against the evil inclination, because it keeps on rising up with ever renewed strength (72).

12) There are many different aspects to the evil inclination. Most people have a very crude and materialistic evil inclination — literally the "spirit of madness." But one whose understanding is somewhat developed and who can begin to form some slight conception in his heart of the greatness of the Creator will realize that an evil inclination like this is mere foolishness. For him even sexual temptation is mere folly requiring no special exertion to fight it. His own evil inclination is on a far higher level (*Ibid.*).

13) On a higher level still are those whose evil inclination is a "fine shell". This is sent only against one who has outstanding spiritual strength. But this is still not the evil inclination of the

Tzaddikim. Theirs is truly a holy angel (*Ibid.*).

14) Even the desire one experiences to return to God may have its source in the evil inclination. This is the case when one has too much enthusiasm without the proper limits. Thus before the giving of the Torah on Mt. Sinai, God told Moses to warn the people, "Let them not *break through* to come up to the Lord." (Exodus 19:24). You must beg God to take pity and save you from this kind of excess (*Ibid.*).

15) When a person is in some kind of trouble and experiences the severe face of God, he needs to make a special effort to escape from the evil inclination. This is because the evil inclination then attacks him with even greater force since its source is in the Divine aspect of severity and harsh justice (*Ibid.*).

16) Depression is very harmful and gives strength to the evil inclination. A person should use the various methods explained elsewhere to make himself happy. Joy and gladness are the main source of strength, as it is written, "for the joy of the Lord is your strength" (Nehemiah 8:10).

17) When God appears to reject us, His purpose is really to draw us closer. A person who wants to draw closer to God often finds that all kinds of hardship and suffering and other obstacles descend upon him, at times with great force. He may start thinking that he is deliberately being rejected. But really these experiences are very beneficial and they serve to draw him closer. The most important thing is to be very firm and resolute, to stand up to the test and not let oneself be deterred by the suffering and obstacles and the sense of rejection. It is a mistake to think that one is being rejected. He should have simple faith that whatever he has to go through is for his own good — to bring him to strengthen himself and draw even closer to God. The whole purpose of this apparent rejection is to draw him closer to God (74).

18) The way to remain firm is by using the power of speech. Even if you fall, be resolute and speak words of truth — words of Torah and prayer and the fear of Heaven. Talk to God. Talk to your friends also, and especially your teacher. Speech has a

great power to remind a person of God's presence and give him strength even in situations which are very far removed from holiness (78).

19) You should always be happy and serve God with joy. At times you may fall from your level. If you do, you can give yourself encouragement by thinking about occasions in the past when you experienced a certain illumination. Use that experience as a source of inspiration now (222).

20) A person who has to have contact with non-Jews for business purposes must be very careful to see that his sanctity as a Jew is not affected. It is dangerously easy to get caught in their net, God forbid. He should always be steadfast and remind himself constantly of the holiness which is his heritage as a Jew. He should pray to God not to be influenced by their behavior (244).

21) The main source of strength is the heart. A person whose heart is steadfast will never be afraid of anyone or anything. He can achieve remarkable feats and win fierce battles simply through the strength of a heart which fears nothing and does not run from the battle lines. This applies literally to serving God. Understand this well (249).

22) When a person falls from his level he should understand that this is something sent to him from Heaven, with the sole purpose of drawing him closer. The intention is to encourage him to make new efforts to come closer. The thing to do is to make a completely fresh start. Start serving God as if you had never started in your whole life. This is one of the basic principles of serving God. We must literally begin all over again every day (261).

23) As soon as a person starts thinking about himself and sees how far he is from true good and how full of sins he is, he can become so discouraged that he may not be able to pray at all. He must try and search until he finds one good point within himself. How is it possible that throughout his life he never did a single good deed or mitzvah? There must be at least one good point. If he starts to examine it, he may see that really it is

thoroughly blemished and there is "nothing sound in it." Perhaps his motives were not the right ones or other things were not as they should have been. Even so, it isn't possible that within this little bit of good there is not at least one very tiny point of good. After this he should continue searching until he finds another good point. This may also have been mixed with much that was improper. Even so, it must contain at least some good point. He should carry on searching until he succeeds in finding a number of good points. The merit and goodness he discovers will take him out of the scale of guilt and place him on the scale of merit. Then he will be able to return to God. If you follow this method you will give yourself fresh vitality and joy no matter what condition you may have reached. You will be able to pray and sing and give thanks to God (282).

24) A person should be very careful to follow this method. It is a great principle for anyone who wishes to draw closer to God and not to lose his eternal reward completely. The main thing is to keep as far removed from depression as possible. Depression is the reason why most people are distant from God: when they see the seriousness of the damage they did they become discouraged. Everyone is aware of his own personal pain. Most people give up hope for themselves completely, they pray without any devotion whatsoever and they do not even try to serve God in the ways they used to be able to. Think very carefully about this, because many souls have sunk completely because of it. Despair is the worst thing of all. Follow this method of searching out the good points. It will give you a constant source of strength, and you will always be able to pray with desire, vitality and joy, and return to God in truth (*Ibid.*).

25) Certain fallen souls can only be revived with special kinds of "tasty delights" which restore the soul. One who breaks the force of his sexual desire becomes worthy of an exalted spiritual illumination. From it are made words of nobility and truth which have the power to revive and restore these fallen souls (*Ibid.* II, 5:8,9).

26) Despair is forbidden no matter how you may have fallen.

You may be lying in the lowest pit of hell, but you should still not despair of God's help in any way at all. Even there it is possible to draw close to Him, because "the whole earth is filled with His glory." The true Tzaddik is only worthy of the name because he has the power to revive and raise up even those who have fallen very far: he can strengthen them, arouse and awaken them and reveal to them that God is close by. He is at their very side, for "the whole earth is filled with His glory." This is the message of the Tzaddik to those on the lowest levels. But to those who are on higher levels he must show that they still know nothing of the Creator: for "what knowest thou? what have all thy searchings achieved?" (*Zohar* I, 1b) (7:7).

27) At times people undergo the most terrible decline, and then the fall can be very, very low. There are some who fall so low that the only term for where they are is the "filthy places." Such people can become wracked with doubts, morbid thoughts and mental turbulence. Their hearts race, because the "husks" torment and circle the heart with every kind of confusion. It may seem impossible to find God in such places, but the very act of searching for God from there, asking and seeking "Where is the place of His glory?" — in itself can bring healing and reconstruction. The more one sees how far one is from God's glory the more grief-stricken one should become. He should search even more intently and ask: "Where is the place of His glory?" Through the very act of searching and seeking and longing for God's glory with anguish, cries, questions... through this alone he will attain the ultimate ascent: he will be worthy of ascending to the level of "Where?" which is the most exalted holiness. The essence of repentance is to search at all times, "*Where* is the place of His glory?" Then the fall will be transformed into a great advance. Understand this well, for it is very deep (12).

28) Serving God requires great obstinacy. Understand this well, because everyone who wants to enter God's service must inevitably undergo an endless series of rises and falls and endure all kinds of rejections. There are times when a person is

deliberately thrown down from serving God. It takes unremitting firmness to stand up to it. At times you may find that the only way you can strengthen yourself is through sheer obstinacy. Remember this, because you will need it many times (48).

29) All this climbing and falling and turbulence are a necessary preliminary to entering the gates of holiness. All the Tzaddikim have endured all this (*Ibid.*).

30) If you are so far from God that you feel that your every movement is a blemish in His eyes, understand that if a person has reached such a pitch of crass materialism, then every single gesture which he makes in the effort to extricate himself — even the merest motion he makes to move a fraction closer to God — is great and precious in God's eyes and causes a movement of thousands upon thousands of miles in the highest worlds (*Ibid.*).

31) In this world man has to pass over a very narrow bridge. The main thing is not to be afraid at all (*Ibid.*).

32) When you consider the utter greatness of God and His unfathomable exaltedness, the merest movement, the merest glance of ours which is slightly out of place in relation to the glory of God, should make us liable to whatever we should be liable to, God forbid. But He is filled with love and the whole world is filled with His kindness. God desires this world very greatly. So my beloved friend and brother, my very soul and heart, take courage and trust in God. He will not abandon you. Whatever you experience is all for your good. Rely upon God's abundant love, which is absolutely without end. There is no limit to the greatness of God. Somehow everything will be transformed to good. Even the intentional sins will be transformed into merits. Only remain firm (49).

33) That man has the evil inclination is really a great thing. Thus man can serve God with the very evil inclination itself. Even when he is exposed to the burning of the evil inclination, he can *still* strengthen himself even then and try to draw some of its passion into the service of God. If man had no evil inclination his service would be worth nothing. This is why God gives the

evil inclination such power against men, especially those who genuinely seek to draw closer to Him. The onslaught of the evil inclination brings men to all manner of sin and devastation. But even so, in God's eyes all this is acceptable because of the preciousness of the gestures which people make when confronted by the full force of the evil inclination — those gestures of fighting and escaping. In God's eyes this is more precious than if a person served him for a thousand years without the evil inclination. All the worlds were created only for the sake of man. The whole preciousness and greatness of man lies in the fact that he is confronted by this strong evil inclination. The more it arrays itself to attack, the more precious in God's eyes is every single gesture one makes to strengthen oneself against it. God Himself will send help, as it is written: "The Lord will not abandon him into his hand" (Psalm 37:33) (*Ibid.*).

34) The evil inclination bites a person again and again. Repeatedly it tempts him and tries to lead him on. One may refuse to listen and turn away. Even so it comes back and bites him a second time, a third, a fourth and more. But if one is absolutely determined, obstinately refusing to bow to it in any way, then eventually the evil inclination will just leave. The same thing is true when it comes to the confusing thoughts which rise up in the mind when we are praying. The same thought comes again and again and tries to disturb the person. He must be firm and pay no attention whatsoever (51).

35) When a person reaches a very exalted level of holiness, for example when he draws closer to the true Tzaddik, at times it can happen that precisely at this moment he experiences an impure emission, God forbid. He should not lose heart because of this: it may well be a sign that he has indeed entered such a level, and it can be very beneficial to him (117).

36) There is no reason for despair at all. The very fact that a person sees how very far he is from God should itself give him a way to find encouragement. At least he *knows* that he is far from God. It is possible that he could have been so far that he would not even have known that he was far. Far he may be, but the

fact that he knows it is itself precious in God's eyes. This alone should encourage him (68).

37) Even the most ordinary people, even the wicked, even the nations of the world... all draw vitality from the Torah, each in their own way. A person may be perfectly ordinary, he may be unable to learn or he may be in a place where he cannot learn. Still, he too receives vitality from the Torah. Therefore even in situations like these he should remain as steadfast as he can in his fear of Heaven. Even at times when he is prevented from pursuing his studies, or if he is a person who doesn't know how to learn! All receive their vitality from the hidden Torah through the agency of the great Tzaddik. At times this Tzaddik may act with absolute simplicity (78).

38) A person may have fallen very far, he may be sunk in the lowest pit of hell. But he can still restore and rebuild, with the help of the true Tzaddik. Because through the Tzaddik all can receive vitality from the realm of holiness regardless of their situation. Therefore despair is absolutely ruled out. No matter where you may have fallen, remember that there is still hope for you to return to God. The main thing is to *cry out*: "From the belly of hell I cried out" (Jonah 2:3). Even a cry from the lowest pit of hell is not lost. Cry, cry and cry again. Do not despair and do not stop crying out to God. Cry and plead with Him no matter who or what you are, until He looks down from the Heavens and sees (*Ibid.*).

39) Even in the lowest pit of hell it is possible to be close to God (*Ibid*).

40) If you believe it is possible to destroy, believe it is possible to repair.

PERCEPTION & REVELATION OF GODLINESS

השגות והתנוצצות אלקות

1) Sometimes we see a person experience a sudden burst of enthusiasm during his prayers. A stream of words suddenly pours from his lips with tremendous fire. In His love, God opens the light of the Infinite and it radiates to him. When the person sees the radiance — and if he himself doesn't see it, his *mazal*, his guardian angel, sees it (*Megillah* 3a) — his soul takes fire with a passion to bind himself to the light of the Infinite. As long as the revelation lasts, the words pour forth with intense devotion. He surrenders himself, throwing his entire energy into them. For these moments he becomes nullified before the Infinite, and he is in a state of unknowing, as it is written: "and no man knows" (Deut. 34:6). He himself has no knowledge even of himself. But it is impossible to remain in such a state. If he did, he would die before his time, God forbid. But during his lifetime the only way to attain this state is in a mode of "running and returning" (Ezekiel 1:14). God does not want us to die! He wants us to live in order that we should serve Him. Only when the time comes for God Himself to take one's soul is it possible to remain in this state of self-nullification, and then he will be merged with the Infinite completely in accordance with his merits (*Likutey Moharan* 4:9).

2) When a person "returns" from the state of self-nullification to his normal state of awareness and sense of self, a trace of the awesome light which he perceived still remains with him, giving him an apprehension of the unity of the Infinite and His goodness. Now he can understand how all is good and all is one. This awareness is a foretaste of the World to Come. The way to attain these levels of awareness is through expressing oneself

before a Torah scholar, confessing one's sins and pouring out one's heart (*Ibid.*).

3) For the Tzaddik, repentance is a continuous movement. He works on it every day of his life. Even if he knows that he has already achieved a state of perfect repentance, he must still "repent" for the perceptions of God he attained in earlier periods of his life, because they were gross and materialistic compared to his present perception of God's utter exaltedness. Every day the Tzaddik moves from perception to perception and from level to level, repenting for his earlier levels. The world to come, which is called "wholly Shabbat, wholly teshuva (repentance)," has precisely this quality of movement towards an ever-enhanced perception of God. With every climb a person makes in the level of his perception, it is necessary to repent for his previous levels. Anyone with a brain in his head will be able to realize from this something of the true greatness of the Creator and the greatness of the Tzaddikim. Happy are they and happy are those who are attached to them (6:3).

4) Know that there is a light which is above the *nefesh, ruach* and *neshama* of human souls. This is the light of the Infinite. It cannot be attained through intellect. And yet thought endeavors to chase after it. It is through fulfilling the mitzvot in joy that we can become worthy of attaining this light. We chase after it, only to encounter "that which holds back." We can "reach, yet not reach." In this way nine palaces are formed which are neither "lights" nor *ruach* nor *neshama*. It is impossible to remain attached to them. They cannot be known. Happy is the one whose thought chases after this awareness, even though the mind has not the power to attain it (see *Zohar* I, 65a; *Likutey Moharan* 24).

5) The whole purpose of life is to come to know God. But it is impossible to attain any apprehension of Godliness except through innumerable "contractions" from level to level, from cause to effect, from the Supreme Mind to the Lower Mind. Therefore one must search for a teacher who is on such a level that he has the power to guide one and communicate all that one

needs to understand. To be able to do this, the teacher must possess true greatness. The lower one's level, the greater the teacher one needs, because only the greatest will have the skill to elucidate the subject in the right way, with the appropriate preparatory explanations and introductions. These are the "contractions" through which even one on a very low level can come to a perception of Godliness (30:1,2).

6) Torah and mitzvot are the path to the apprehension of God. Because every letter of the Torah and every detail of every mitzvah is a "contraction" (*Ibid.* 3).

7) Wisdom and understanding are the foundation of any perception of God. But the only way to acquire them is if one "hates covetousness" (Exodus 18:21). One must hate materialism absolutely. Someone who is attracted by it will inevitably fall from the necessary level of wisdom and understanding into folly, stupidity, anxiety and depression. He will be captured in the net of the "husks" and the forces of the Other Side, which are the opposite of wisdom and understanding (*Ibid.* 4).

8) The joy we experience on the three annual festivals can arouse new perceptions of Godliness (*Ibid.* 5).

9) Every single Jew is a part of God above. The essence of Godliness is to be found in the heart. The Godliness in the heart of the Jew is infinite. There is no end to the light of the flame which burns there. The holy desire which is there is infinite. But this same burning passion would make it impossible for him to accomplish anything at all in his service of God, nor would he be able to reveal any good trait, if he did not hold his passion within certain limits. He must "contract" it, so to speak, in order to be able to serve God in a measured, orderly way. For God desires our service. There are specific actions and devotions which He asks of us. He wants us to develop our character traits and behavior in an orderly, systematic way. This is how His kingship will be revealed (49:1).

10) The more one draws close to God the more one must understand how far one is from Him. When a person believes he

has already succeeded in achieving closeness to God and attaining an understanding of Him, it is a sign that he does not know anything. If he did, he would know that he is very far from God and that he knows absolutely nothing. It is impossible to explain this satisfactorily in words. The greatness of God has no limits (63).

11) A person should learn to live in a state of self-nullification. He should always fix his eyes upon the ultimate goal, which is truly good and enduring. The only way to do this is by closing his eyes to this world and concentrating on the true goal to the point that he becomes united with it. You must keep your eyes firmly shut as far as this world is concerned — even if you have to hold them closed with your finger! Pay no attention whatsoever to this world. Then nothing in the world will cause you any pain or suffering. But you should understand that it is impossible to remain in this state of self-nullification all the time and still be a human being. Inevitably self-nullification can only be achieved at certain moments in the mode of "running and returning" (Ezekiel 1:14). In the period of "returning" a trace of the state of self-nullification remains and shines with the sweet and pleasant light of Godliness. It is impossible to describe this experience to anybody else. It brings a tremendous joy, which can lead us to new horizons in understanding Torah. These new perceptions can be a source of strength and fortitude in the face of all the sufferings and harsh experiences a person may have to undergo. Even in this world he will be worthy of experiencing a taste of the World to Come (65:3,4).

12) When a person attains a certain perception of Godliness, he must be careful to observe certain limits: he must "contract" the experience, as it were, in the sense of putting certain limits on the way he explores and follows through his perception. Even in the realms of holiness, there are places where it is forbidden to travel. One must never go beyond one's limits. Every created being has its boundary. Only thus far is it permitted to go to receive the radiance of God. To go further is forbidden, lest one "break through" (cf. Exodus 19:24). (*Likutey Moharan* II, 5:7).

13) King David, peace be upon him, said: "For I know that the Lord is great" (Psalm 135:5). "*I* know," said King David — because the perception which a person attains in his own heart can never be communicated to anybody else (Rabbi Nachman's Wisdom 1).

14) Even to yourself you cannot communicate such a vision. Today you might be inspired and see a certain vision. But tomorrow you will not be able to communicate the inspiration and the vision even to yourself! (*Ibid.*).

15) God is so great — "His greatness is unfathomable" (Psalm 145:3) — and yet nobody knows it. Remarkable things are happening in the world. There is no end to the works of God. All the time there are changes, new creations, wonders, miracles...yet nobody knows it. One cannot even speak of it. Each person has only his own perceptions to go by. The more advanced his perceptions, the more he can understand just a bit how ignorant he really is. And even then he is still far from the true goal of knowledge, which is to realize that one is truly ignorant. But so far he hasn't begun to know anything! The Rebbe had remarkable things to say about this subject, and he showed how a person can always fortify himself so as never to lose hope. Regardless of where he may have fallen, he should never despair of crying out to God. In His greatness, God has the power to turn everything to good (*Ibid.* 3).

CONFESSION וידוי דברים

1) It is a good thing to pour out your heart and confess all your sins before a Torah scholar. Sin is in essence a denial of Godliness. Therefore when a person confesses his sins it is an acknowledgement of the sovereignty of God. God's sovereignty is then exalted and restored to its root, and the power of the forces denying Godliness is broken. Through confessing in this way and expressing what is in your heart you will eventually come to understand how everything that happens is for your own good. You will acknowledge that "God is good and does good." This is the formula of the blessing we make on hearing good news. Today, we still have a separate blessing for news that is not good. But our Sages said that in time to come there will only be one blessing — the one for good news (*Pesachim* 50a). This will be when we will realize that everything is for the best. To achieve this realization is to have a taste of the World to Come (*Likutey Moharan* I, 4:3).

2) The sins a person commits are engraved upon his very bones (Ezekiel 32:27) But when he confesses them before a Torah scholar, the entire accumulation of evil engraved on his bones is lifted. All his sins are forgiven and atonement is granted (*Ibid.* 5).

3) A person may come to visit a great scholar and even contribute money to him. But until he comes before him and confesses his sins and pours out his heart, he still does not know the path he should travel. For "there is a way which seems right to a man, but its end is the ways of death" (Proverbs 14:12). Through his confession, the scholar is able to set him straight on the path which accords with the root of his soul (*Ibid.* 8).

4) Each time a person visits the scholar, he should pour out his heart before him. Through this he will come to be merged with the *En Sof.* (*Ibid.* 9).

5) It is necessary to specify exactly what the sin was, and the confession must be put into words. Thought is not enough. Whatever you may have done, you must verbally articulate what you did. There are many obstacles to doing this. Sometimes the sin passes out of your mind and you forget it. In certain cases people find it very difficult to bring out the words and confess. There are many other obstacles. The way to conquer them is with joy — the joy of a mitzvah, such as a wedding celebration and so on. You should work yourself up until you literally dance for joy. Then you will be able to confess what you must and right the wrongs caused by your sins (178).

MEMORY זכרון

1) Prayer is a *segulah* for developing a good memory (7:5).
2) Fasting and giving charity, especially charity for causes in the Land of Israel, help against forgetfulness, and you will be able to develop a good memory (37:3,4).
3) Clapping your hands when you pray sweetens the force of severity in the world. This is one of the ways of ridding yourself of forgetfulness and developing a good memory (46).
4) You must be very careful to cultivate a good memory and not to fall into forgetfulness. What is a good memory? It means constantly keeping the thought of the World to Come in the forefront of your mind and never forgetting about it. It would be a very good thing if every Jew were to make it a daily habit, as soon as he opens his eyes in the morning and before he does anything else, to bring to mind that the World to Come is the only true goal. He should do this as soon as he wakes up. This is the concept of memory in general. And it has to be followed through into every detail of the day. With every thought, word and deed which God sends you every day, you must broaden your understanding and perception of God. You must understand that every one of them is a hint which God sends you in order to draw you closer to Him. God Himself is infinite and without end. But He "contracts" Himself, as it were, to our level, using all the experiences which He sends us each day, in order to signal to us and guide us. It is up to us to recognize this and find the messages in all the thoughts, words and deeds which are sent to us, in order that we may reach a deeper insight and come closer to God. But it is necessary to understand that the only way to broaden and deepen your perception of God is

in a measured, orderly way (54:2).

5) There are people who have the ability to interpret the messages contained in all the things around them, including even secular affairs. But it would be wrong only to pay attention to these signals to the exclusion of other sources of spiritual guidance. The perception of God which comes from the study of Torah is on a higher level. Thinking about the hints contained in material affairs is good up to a certain limit, but that is not sufficient. You should pay attention to them only as much as you need to but no more. And even, as here, when you take from the world just as much as is sufficient for you, you should still give a part of what you take to charity (see *Mammon* 27). If you develop your memory in the right way, as we have explained, great *tikkunim* will be brought about in the upper worlds and the unity of God will be revealed. However, the great mass of people do not have the level of understanding which is necessary to grasp the significance of the hints God sends. For them the same effects are accomplished through sleep, and when they observe the mitzvot of *tzitzit* and *tefilin*, learning Torah and praying and going about their business honestly and in accordance with the law (*Ibid.*).

6) If you want to guard your memory, take care not to fall into the trap of an evil eye. This spells death to the heart and gives strength to the power of forgetfulness (*Ibid.* 4).

7) The evil eye can appear in many different guises. People can become very jealous when their friends are successful, and they look on them with an evil eye. This in itself can manifest itself in different ways. You must be extremely careful never to be jealous of a friend at all. Pray to God and ask Him to save you from the evil eye. And if you find that someone else is directing the evil eye against you, if you feel you lack the strength to stand up against it and humble its power, then you must run from it and flee in order to escape (*Ibid.*).

8) You must also take care not to talk in a bad way. Talking maliciously and derogatorily about other people is very damaging to one's memory. If you work on yourself and even

force yourself to be happy, it is a help in developing a good memory (*Ibid.* 5).

9) When it comes to Torah and serving God, you must guard your memory carefully. But still, forgetfulness does have its advantages. Anything which distracts you from serving God you should forget about completely, especially the distractions which come when you are praying. Usually they consist of worrying about the past and wondering if you did this or that right. But as soon as something is over and done with, you should simply put it out of your mind completely. Make this a habit. Just ignore it completely and don't even start to think about it. The same applies to all your worries about past transgressions and other mistakes. Just put them out of mind completely and forget about them, especially during your prayers and devotions. In fact, there is nothing much to be gained from thinking about them any time of the day except in the special time you set aside for meditation. This is the time to be heartbroken and to express all your thoughts before God. You should think about everything you did wrong. But for the rest of the day you should forget about these things completely. Simply serve God with joy, especially during your prayers (Rabbi Nachman's Wisdom 26).

ALIEN PHILOSOPHIES & IDEOLOGIES

חקירות וחכמות חיצוניות

1) The only true wisdom is the wisdom of the Tzaddikim. It brings them to a lofty perception of God and gives them the power to communicate their perception to those who follow them. Compared with this wisdom, all other ideological systems are utter foolishness. But because of our many sins, it can happen at times that this genuine wisdom falls into the hands of the heathens and the forces of the *Sitra Achra*, the Other Side. Their new-found wisdom gives them power and dominion, and then the heathens gain the upper hand, God forbid. Who can bear the sound of the great and terrible cry when this wisdom falls into their hands and fools affect to be wise? They try to adapt this genuine wisdom to their own purposes, as if it could be made a part of their own ideologies — as if their own foolishness had anything to do with the knowledge of God. They start claiming that they alone are the wise ones and there is no wisdom greater than their own erroneous speculations, parasitic as they are on the fallen, genuine wisdom. God Himself cries out because of this. Every Jew has a part to play in the task of identifying how this wisdom that has fallen into their hands can be separated from them and elevated in order to return it to its source. The way to achieve this is through acts of charity and kindness under the guidance and inspiration of the Tzaddikim (30:6).

2) Wisdom is the root of all things (Psalms 104:24) One should always guard one's mind against false ideologies. The only way to achieve fulfillment in life is through the pursuit of genuine wisdom, namely the wisdom of Torah, which is concerned with Godliness. Compared with this all other systems of ideology are

sheer emptiness, they have nothing to do with wisdom at all (35:1).

3) When a person is born his intelligence is limited. When he begins to use it to think about how to serve God, it starts growing. But if a person fills his mind with alien ideas, the intelligence of his holy soul is diminished in direct proportion to the space taken up by these ideas. This unholy "intelligence" becomes the source of all kinds of negative appetites and character traits (*Ibid.*).

4) This is why a person has to be so careful to guard his mind and his thoughts and make sure that he never admits alien ideas or ways of looking at things. All our problems and defects and sins come from abusing the sanctity of the mind, God forbid, by admitting alien thoughts and ideologies. To achieve true repentance and to make amends for all one's sins, one must cleanse the mind of all these alien ideas. Wisdom and intelligence actually *are* the soul. By clearing the mind of alien ideologies the faculty of thought is elevated to its source. This is the essence of returning to God (*Ibid.*).

5) When the Jewish people adopt the ideas and outlook of the other nations, God forbid, the Tzaddik falls from his level and his perceptions become covered over and obscured (49).

6) Too much intellectual sophistication can be harmful, especially when it takes the form of excessive philosophizing and speculation. The basis of true wisdom is a strong heart and a strong character. The only way to attain them is through good deeds. A person whose intelligence outstrips his practical attainments in the form of good deeds will lack the strength of character to contain his intelligence within the necessary bounds. His intelligence will only make him sin. It can be very dangerous when people with lax moral standards dabble in philosohy. Their intelligence drives them on to even greater transgressions and it harms them, and indeed the entire world, more than all the snakes and scorpions, wild animals and other dangerous things in the world. They use their intelligence to hurl insults and abuse at the heavens and to cast aspersions on the Holy

Torah and especially the Sages of the Talmud and the Tzaddikim of blessed memory who followed them. All this is well known. May God in His mercy take pity on the remnant of Israel and guard them from this band of people and their babblings (55:6).

7) Within the bounds God has set for man's intelligence it is a great mitzvah, a positive duty, to sharpen the mind and understand as clearly as possible whatever the human mind is capable of grasping. However there are certain questions the answers to which are beyond the capacity of the human mind to understand. Only in time to come will the answers be revealed. (An example is the paradox of free will.) On no account should one delve into these questions. Of those who try, relying on their own intelligence and speculation, it is said: "None that go unto her return" (Proverbs 2:19). It is impossible to solve these questions through reason. We must have pure faith. Even when it comes to the questions which do have an answer, there are times when the paths of the intellect become blocked and one is unsure how to answer the unbeliever speaking in one's heart. The remedy then is to study the codes of Torah law. If one still finds oneself confused and unable to understand the way to answer the questions, one should rely on faith alone even here. The main thing is to have faith (62:2).

8) It is forbidden to delve into philosophical works. There are certain questions which stem from the *chalal hapanui*, "the empty void," to which it is impossible to find any answer. In time to come the answers will be revealed. But in this world it is impossible to put these questions to rest merely with thought and ingenuity. Whole philosophical systems have been built up around them. Anyone who delves into them will be sunk in them and lost eternally, as it is written: "None that go unto her return" (Proverbs 2:19). God is not to be found in these philosophies. Through intelligence alone it will never be possible to solve the intellectual tangles they contain. The Jewish people, with its faith in God, is *beyond* all these philosophies and their complications. Israel believes in God and His Holy Torah

without needing philosophical justifications. They have pure faith. The Hebrew word for "beyond" is עבר, *e-ver*, and the Jews are called עברים, *Ivrim* — Hebrews — precisely because they are *beyond* all this speculation. With a faith which transcends philosophy we do not need to speculate about the truth. We know it. We have received it from our fathers, of blessed memory (64:2).

9) Certain of the great Tzaddikim were obliged to go into these philosophies in order to extricate and elevate the souls which have fallen and become sunk in them. You cannot argue that it is permissible for others to enter them on the grounds that many of the great scholars of the past were involved. In their case it was an obligation. And through the great sanctity they possessed, they had the power to release the souls which were trapped. But people who are not on a comparable level of sanctity, and needless to add, the ordinary people of our own age, should never enter these realms and risk being eternally lost (*Ibid.* 3).

10) The song of the true Tzaddik has the power to draw up the souls that have fallen into this form of atheism, from which there is otherwise no return (*Ibid.* 5).

11) The materialist philosophers, who claim that everything operates only by virtue of the laws of nature, are a breed of wild animals who have made terrible inroads into our people and caught many of our sons in their clutches. Many Jewish souls are sunk in this like birds caught in a snare. If you love your soul, keep well away from these wild beasts, who would otherwise snatch your soul and consume it. Keep well away from books of speculative science, even those written by our own great Sages. There is no greater evil (*Likutey Moharan* II, 4:6).

12) Acts of charity and kindness have the power to break the force of the serpent, which is the root of materialistic ideology. And then these wild animals will have no power over you. However at times even after you have crushed them they are soon back again, placing fresh doubts in your mind about whether the world is governed only by the will of God. If this

happens you must make fresh efforts at charity and kindness. Charity has the power to subdue the ideology of materialism and reveal that everything is governed only by the will of God (*Ibid.* 9).

13) Serve God with simplicity and purity, using no sophistication at all. This is the true goal. No one who goes by the name of Jew should ever so much as open a book of philosophy. This is no part of the heritage of Jacob. All speculative philosophy contains the stumbling block of Amalek, which is calculated to make people fall. In one moment they can lose whole worlds. There is no greater evil. Even the books written by Jews discussing speculative philosophy should be left well alone, because they can harm the holy faith which is the root of everything. Thank God we have today many holy books which are filled with sound guidance and the fear of God and which are free of all speculation derived from the so-called "wisdom" of the Greeks. They are firmly founded on the holy words of the Sages of the Talmud and the Midrash. In particular there are the books based upon the teachings of Rabbi Shimon bar Yochai. Explore them, and go through them again and again. You should have nothing to do with books based on the viewpoints of the other nations of the world (19).

14) There are many searching questions about God. But anyone with even a modicum of genuine understanding will see that it is only right and fitting that such questions should exist. For how can we, with our limited human intelligence, understand how God governs the world? Of course there are things which baffle us. The utter greatness and exaltedness of God are only magnified when we find that there are questions we cannot solve. Understand this well (52).

MARRIAGE חיתון

1) Intense prayer can help a person to find his marriage partner (*Likutey Moharan* I, 9).
2) Dancing at a wedding sweetens the force of the harsh judgements in the world (32).
3) There are deep Kabbalistic reasons for the custom that the bride sends the groom a *tallit*, and for crying out "Shabbat" and making humorous remarks at the wedding celebration. There is also a deep significance in the other wedding customs, like covering the bride and pelting the groom with baked goods, interrupting the groom's Torah discourse and giving him a gift for his discourse, the custom of the entertainers' bending themselves over double, etc. There are awesome reasons for all of these things, and they express the will of God (See Rabbi Nachman's Wisdom 86).
4) When we acknowledge God and give Him praise, it has an influence which helps those who need to find their marriage partner to do so. The same is true when we study the legal codes (*Likutey Moharan* II, 2).
5) Immorality and abuse of the Covenant make it hard for a person to find his true marriage partner. The *tikkun* is by following the spiritual path explained in the Kabbalistic writings about the themes of the month of Elul (*Ibid.* 87). See also *Likutey Moharan* I, 6; and *Hitchazkut* and *Brit*).
6) When a person is unable to find his marriage partner, it can help if he goes to hear original Torah teachings from a man of deep wisdom (*Likutey Moharan* II, 89).
7) The reason for breaking a piece of earthenware at the marriage ceremony is to remind the groom of Gehennom in

order to prevbent him getting trapped by his desires. He must sanctify himself in the marriage relationship. It is also a hint to him that if his wife turns out to be a bad woman he should still not maltreat her or divorce her. Because of her, he will never see hell. One should see to it that he never comes to the point of divorce (90. On the subject of breaking a piece of earthenware at a wedding, see also *Likutey Moharan* I, 60:8; II, 90).

MIDNIGHT PRAYER חצות

1) How precious it is to rise at midnight in order to pray and meditate and study Torah. Try to make it a regular practice. Then you will be worthy of succeeding in the task of separating the good from the evil in the world. You will also develop a good memory — which means always to remember your purpose in life and to keep in mind the enduring life you are destined for in the end. You must recognize that everything you do in this world only has meaning in relation to the World to Come. You should reflect on every experience which God sends you: consider all the different situations you find yourself in each day. The only purpose of all of them is to offer you hints as to how you can draw closer to God at every moment. This is the only true and enduring goal in the world. The entire purpose of man's being sent into this world is only to come closer to God. All the days of his vanity, all the experiences he has on each one of them are only for this (*Likutey Moharan* I, 54).

2) Rising at midnight sweetens the harsh judgements. This practice is as valuable as presenting a redemption (149).

3) Throughout the year, the correct time for the midnight prayer is when the first six hours of the night have passed. It lasts for two hours until the end of the second "watch." In the morning, it is a good thing to look up at the sky. This will give you *Da'at*, knowledge of God.

4) The exile has already lasted so long. God is only waiting for the moment to return to us and rebuild the Holy Temple. It could happen at any time. Our task is to see that from our side we do nothing to obstruct the rebuilding of the Temple. On the contrary, we must make every effort to hasten it. This is why we

should be so careful to get up each night at midnight and mourn for the destruction of the Holy Temple. Perhaps in a previous incarnation we ourselves were responsible for something which brought about the destruction of the Temple. Even if not, it could still be that our sins in our present lifetime are holding up the rebuilding of the Temple, and this is as bad as if we had actually destroyed it. This is the reason why we must weep and mourn every night at midnight. When we do so, it is as if we were actually making a tremendous effort to rebuild the Holy Temple. Then we will be able to draw closer to truth — to the true Tzaddikim and those who are genuinely God-fearing. They are in fact the embodiment of truth, in its beauty, splendor and pleasantness. Through drawing closer to them your eyes will be opened and you will be able to see how far your own development has advanced and in which areas you need to work in order to return to God and to know and acknowledge His great and holy Name (*Likutey Moharan* II, 67).

5) The merit of rising for the midnight prayer protects us from destruction by fire (*Ibid.*).

6) The main devotion of the Jew is to get up every night in the winter for the midnight prayer. In the summer, when the nights are short and we do not rise for the midnight prayer except in the Land of Israel, he should be sure to get up with the dawn each morning (Rabbi Nachman's Wisdom 301).

JOURNEYING & TRAVEL

טלטול ונסיעות לדרכים

1) In the periods when the people ignore attempts to criticize them and offer them spiritual guidance, the end result is exile, expulsion from the lands they are living in, and bitter wandering (*Likutey Moharan* I, 22:1).
2) Before going on a journey, one should give money to charity. Then nothing will delay him or trouble him on the way (31:4).
3) All the traveling a person has to do is because of flaws in his faith in God. Such flaws are actually a form of idolatry. At times traveling can be a *tikkun* for these flaws, and this removes the force of anger from the world and draws down the influence of love (40).
4) Neglect of Torah causes exile (*Ibid.*).
5) A person may spend his life as a "fugitive and a wanderer" (Genesis 4:14) and at times he may come to places which are very far from God — the homes of the wicked, or even the homes of heathens. Even so a Jew has the power to elevate all these places to God. He should simply do his part and bring himself as close as he can to God regardless of where he may be (II, 76).
6) When a person has heart there is nowhere that presents an insufferable barrier against his serving God. It is no excuse to say that in a certain place the barriers are so great that it is impossible to serve God. When a person *has* a heart, all the places in the entire world are his (56).
7) Whenever you are on a journey, make sure that you go to the *mikveh*. The *mikveh* has the power to save us from murder (*Chayey Moharan, Avodat Hashem* 30).

AWE & DEVOTION יראה ועבודה

1) You should never fear anything except God. If ever you begin to feel afraid of anything, remember the great fear which is due to God. Throughout the day, fill your entire consciousness with this sense of awe. It will help you to pray with all your strength — to utter the words with such force that they are like thunderbolts! Then you will hear the words which are on your lips. This is the way to achieve true joy, and to perform the mitzvoth with a joy derived from the mitzvot themselves. Then you will attain the understanding of how to nullify all harsh decrees even after the decrees have been made, God forbid (5:5).

2) In order to achieve these levels, you must combine your fear of Heaven with love. A person's main strength lies in the love he has for God. Nevertheless fear must come first (*Ibid.*5).

3) If you wish to savour the taste of the hidden light — the secrets of Torah which are destined to be revealed in time to come — you should meditate and speak to God. Express everything in your heart before Him. Examine yourself and judge yourself. Weigh up all the different things you are involved with. In this way you will be able to banish your extraneous fears of forces other than God — these are called "fallen fear" — and you will be able to elevate your fear and experience the true awe of Heaven. When a person neglects to examine and judge himself, he is examined and brought to judgement from on high. God has many ways of executing His judgements. He has the power to clothe them in anything in the world, because all things are His messengers, and he can use whatever means he chooses to execute His judgements. We can actually see this in practice. When something bad happens to a person, the

particular cause which precipitates the problem is often apparently quite insignificant. One would never have expected a small thing like this to bring on such a train of consequences — illness, suffering and the like. The explanation is that the Divine decree passed against him has been clothed within these mundane circumstances in order to give him his deserts. But when a person examines and judges himself of his own accord the decree above is removed. There is no need for him to be afraid of anything. Worldly objects and events will no longer be used as a veil and a cloak for executing the decree of God. By bringing himself to a reckoning he has removed the judgement above. He is already sufficiently aroused and spiritually awake without needing things of this world to shake him. This is what is meant by elevating fear to its root. He is afraid of nothing except God. Because of this he will be worthy of the hidden light (15).

4) To attain true fear and love of God is only possible with the help of the Tzaddikim of the generation (17:1).

5) Fear of Heaven is the foundation for sanctifying the way one speaks and using the Holy Tongue perfectly (see *dibbur*). But to reach this level of fear it is necessary to journey to the Tzaddik in order to hear words of truth directly from his lips. It is not enough to study *mussar* literature — works giving guidance about spiritual development. When a person hears a Tzaddik, the actual words of the Tzaddik possess a quality of perfection. They are uttered with true fear of Heaven, and this is the foundation for the fulfillment of the Covenant and achieving moral purity. Even if a person hears what the Tzaddik said from the lips of somebody else who himself heard the Tzaddik say them, it still does not help as much, because the words have descended from their original perfection. In order for the words of the Holy Tongue to possess perfection, they must be heard from the lips of the Tzaddik himself. This is where the treasure-house of the true fear of Heaven is to be found, and this is the foundation for attaining perfection in the Holy Tongue (19:3,9).

6) Having a sense of shame is the basis for attaining the fear of

Heaven. One must feel ashamed before God — so ashamed that one could not possibly sin. To have a sense of shame is a very high level (22).

7) Be sure that you make your days very long. With each new day and each fresh moment, make sure that the time is longer, fuller and richer with added holiness. So it must be with every day that comes. You must continually extend the days by filling them with more holiness and more purity. This is the secret of a long life. When you start each day, at first the day is very short. The spiritual accomplishments you need to achieve this day weigh heavily upon you. It takes great determination not to be discouraged as you feel the weight of the devotions you have to undertake this day. But be courageous and don't lose heart. Make a start — even if at first things seem heavy and strained and difficult. If you are determined enough they will become easier and you will find that you can accomplish what you must in God's service. With every hour that passes see to it that you enrich that hour and lengthen it with extra holiness. Do the same with every new day of your life. Let each day be filled with more holiness than the day before. Then you will be blessed with length of days. The root of this skill in living lies in cultivating true fear of Heaven (60:2).

8) Such fear is the foundation of a long life. It can bring you great wealth — the wealth of holiness. And through this wealth it is possible to attain profound understanding. There are certain paths of Torah which possess a degree of profundity which can only be attained with the help of great wealth. This is the reason why so many of the greatest of the Tzaddikim were extraordinarily wealthy, such as Rabbi Yehuda HaNasi, the compiler of the Mishnah, and Rav Ashi, the compiler of the Talmud. The source of this wealth is in "length of days," which is attained through awe (*Ibid.* 3).

9) There are three aspects to fearing God: the fear of Heaven, fear of your teacher, and fear of your father and mother (*Ibid.*).

10) When a person has true fear of Heaven, he is no longer trapped by the beauty of women. He is free from the attractions

of falsehood. He will be saved from poverty and attain wealth (*Ibid.*).

11) The Tzaddik has the power to arouse men from their sleep through the stories he tells about the years of old. Through this he can cause the barren to give birth, which arouses great awe at the might of God throughout the world. This awe is the instrument for attaining all the spiritual levels we have mentioned (*Ibid.* 5,6).

12) The key to everything is the way you start. All beginnings are difficult, because you are trying to turn things from one direction to the opposite direction. But once a start has been made, you begin to get used to the direction you are going in and things are no longer so hard. The level of awe and devotion a person attains each day depends on the way he starts. Every day you should go backwards — in the sense that you should always try and draw inspiration from the start, which was the hardest thing of all. You must always make a frest start. Each time you come to the Tzaddik, you must likewise make a fresh beginning. It must be as if you had never come to him before, as if this time it is an entirely new experience for you. Because perhaps the first beginning was not as it should have been, and if so all the devotion which followed will not have been as it should have been. Because everything depends on the beginning. Therefore you must marshal all your strength and steel yourself to make a vigorous beginning. Start again every time with new fire and passion for God. Start as if you had never begun at all before. The strength of your new beginning will bring power and vigor into all your devotions. You should always ask yourself if the start was as it should have been. Make the effort to start again, and come to the Tzaddik afresh. Do this every time (62).

13) When a new soul enters a person, he must raise it and rear it with love and awe (67:6).

14) If a person does not consider the purpose of everything, what is the point of his life? (268).

15) One of the basic rules in serving God is to think only of today. Pay no attention to yesterday or tomorrow. This applies

to the work you have to do to earn a living and provide your needs. Our sacred literature tells us that we should only be concerned with today. The same applies to serving God. You should only think of today, the present hour. When a person wants to begin serving God it seems like a heavy burden which he will never be able to bear. But if you think that you have only today, it will not be a burden at all. Don't put things off and say, "I'll start tomorrow... tomorrow I will pray with strength and devotion," etc. Man's world consists of nothing except the day and the hour that he stands in now. Tomorrow is a completely different world. "Today, if you would but listen to His voice!" (Psalms 95:7). Exactly! Today! (272).

16) Every mitzvah which a person does in this world, creates a lamp with which he can explore the treasure house of the King after his passing. This is the ultimate bliss of the World to Come (275).

17) There are two kinds of fear of Heaven. There are people who fear God because of His greatness and exaltedness as the Ruler and Master of the Universe. This level of fear adds completeness to God's Name. Secondly there is a lower form of fear which is attained through the fear one has of other, lower things — a wild animal, a person wielding great power, or the like. Such things can evoke the awareness of God within a person, and this second level of fear is the source of the influx of blessing into the world. To receive the blessings one has to make a vessel. The vessel is formed through the longing and desire which he has to travel to the true Tzaddikim. This creates the *shape* of the vessel, and the vessel itself is formed when one comes to the Tzaddik in person. The more obstacles a person encounters in his efforts to draw close and the more energy he devotes to breaking them, the greater the vessel he forms (185).

18) Every Jew is created with the ultimate purpose of wielding power over the angels. This is his destiny. But the angels are very jealous of a man who has power over them. He must protect himself and see that he has the strength to remain in this

position of power without being cast down through the angels' envy (*Ibid.* II, 1:1).

19) Materialism, immorality and gluttony distort and corrupt the fear in a person's heart. The remedy is through honoring the three festivals of the year and celebrating them in the proper way. This causes the fear which is latent in the heart to become manifest, and through it one can attain the experience of prophecy. This is the avenue to true prayer and healing. One becomes bound to the very root of the souls of Israel, and here alone there is protection from the envy of the angels (*Ibid.*).

20) When a person falls into materialism, immorality and greed, God sits and cries out like a lion (*Ibid.*).

21) A person's devotions, his mitzvot and good deeds are his "children." This is especially so of the Tzaddikim. Before a woman gives birth she has to undergo contractions and birth-pangs, and she cries and screams. It is literally the same when you serve God. When you want to carry out a particular devotion or return to God in truth, it inevitably takes a tremendous effort. You have to cry out and groan, bending and jerking in all directions. The hardest thing of all is the start. All beginnings are difficult. This is when you need to cry out and groan the most. Even after the start things do not necessarily come easily, and it takes a lot of effort before you achieve something worthwhile. But don't be discouraged by what you have to endure. According to the effort, so is the reward (4:5).

22) Charity helps to open the gates to holiness. This is why it is good to give charity before doing any mitzvah or good deed. The charity helps to widen the opening to the holiness which is the goal of this particular devotion, and then it will not be so hard to enter (*Ibid.*).

23) Through giving charity you can attain fear of Heaven, and this will lead to lovingkindness. When you attain this you will be able to serve God without being restricted by the difficulties of earning a living (*Ibid.*).

24) In times when the elders of the generation fail to achieve perfection, it gives strength to anti-religious ideologies. The task

of each individual is to ensure that with every day that passes he gains additional holiness and deeper understanding. Each new day must be filled with more of the radiance of devotion to God. Only when a person achieves this is he worthy of the name "elder." When a person wastes his days without adding extra holiness, he may grow old but he cannot be termed an "elder." Instead of enjoying "length of days," his days are actually short. It is because of this that materialistic ideologies are able to become entrenched in the world. The remedy lies in the giving of charity (*Ibid.*).

25) God's main joy and pleasure come only from this low world of ours. God has the whole array of angels, *serafim, chayot, ofanim* and all the higher worlds — all of them serving Him. But when we in this low world of ours magnify and sanctify His Name and carry out His will, this is what gives Him the greatest joy, because He sees the service of this low world rise to the realms above (*Ibid.* 7).

26) When people study and discuss one of the original Torah concepts of the true Tzaddikim they can become filled with the fear of Heaven (*Ibid.*13).

27) Your main aim should be to serve God with simplicity, with no ulterior motive. Follow His ways in order to know Him. This is what He wants. A person who serves God in order to earn the World to Come is just hungry: he wants to fill his stomach with the reward. But even so, it is better to serve God for the sake of the reward of the World to Come than it is to chase after this world. At least someone who serves God for the sake of the reward is wiser than one who struggles for this world all his life. This world is transient, but the World to Come is the world of eternal life. But even so, the main aim should be to serve God with no ulterior motive whatsoever (37).

28) What profit is there when people run after the superficialities of materialism and gratification and neglect the task of achieving self-perfection? There are many people who waste away their days struggling to leave a big inheritance for their children. But this is no better than when a person gets himself dirty and then

takes more dirt to cover up the dirt. Other people try their best to leave a good name behind them for their children's sake. But this is still not the real purpose of life. The aim of the true Tzaddikim is only to satisfy the will of God (*Ibid.*).

29) Man always has free will. This applies to everything he may be involved with. In all situations, the Jew always has the option of exercising free choice. As far as the other nations of the world are concerned, there are certain things which restrict their free will and compel them to act in a particular way. With a Jew, however, no matter what he does — be it to travel to a particular place, or whatever — there is always some devotion involved, something which relates to his service of God. Because of this, the Jew has free will in everything (54).

30) The profit a person can have from this world is indescribable. You don't need to spend your own money to make a profit here. God spreads the opportunities before you and you can simply stretch out your hand and take abundant profit. "No eye hath seen it" (Isaiah 64:3) (55).

31) You should throw yourself upon God and rely upon Him completely. At the start of every day you should entrust all your actions of that day, and all the actions of your children and other dependents, to God, asking that everything should go as *He* wishes it (Rabbi Nachman's Wisdom 2).

32) Fear is the key to achieving spiritual perfection. The basis of fear of Heaven is to be afraid of being punished. Even Tzaddikim need to have this fear. This is what gives us our initial motivation to serve God (*Ibid.* 5).

33) If you want to serve God, you must keep on making new beginnings. Even in the course of a single day you may have to start all over again several times (*Ibid.* 51).

34) Whatever you see in this world exists only to create the possibility of free will. The whole world and all that is in it was created only for the sake of free will (*Ibid.* 300).

35) There are people who serve God for a whole lifetime without being shown what they have achieved. Only in the World to Come will they see what they have achieved (244).

36) The main devotion of the Jew is to get up every night in the winter for the midnight prayer. In the summer, when the nights are short and we do not rise for the midnight prayer except in the Land of Israel, he should be sure to get up with the dawn each morning (*Ibid.* 301; see *Chatzot* 3)

ANGER כעס

1) You must break the force of your anger with love. If you feel yourself becoming angry, make sure you do nothing unkind because of your anger. You must make a special effort to be kind to the very person you are angry with. Sweeten your anger with kindness. When you do this, you will be able to draw benefit from the Tzaddik and then you will be able to understand the true goal of all things. You will taste the delight of the World to Come, and you will see how everything in the world is part of the movement to this ultimate goal. Your perception will be according to the root which you have in the soul of the Tzaddik (18:2).

2) Through breaking the force of anger with love and kindness, the true Tzaddikim receive honor and greatness and the world finds a true leader — one who will have pity for the world and lead it in the right way, bringing each individual to his ultimate goal (*Ibid.*).

3) Anger and unkindness arise when people's understanding is limited. The deeper their understanding the more their anger disappears, and kindness, love and peace spread. This is why the study of Torah, which deepens the understanding, brings love and peace into the world and banishes anger (56:6).

4) Immersing in the *mikveh* is also an antidote to anger, because immersing in the *mikveh* brings understanding (*Ibid.* 7).

5) When a person gives way to anger, it stirs up the great accuser — Esau, or Edom. The accuser in the upper world is the source of a flurry of accusers and enemies who come down and take charge of this angry man. His anger puts his wisdom to flight, and the image of God disappears from his face. He no longer

has the face of a man. This is why he is in the power of his enemies. Because he has the appearance of a beast they are not afraid of him (57:6).

6) The remedy for anger is to fast. In fact, the main value of fasting lies in this. That is why when a person is fasting the Evil One comes against him and creates all kinds of pretexts for making him angry. The Evil One wants to spoil the fast. One has to be very careful to avoid getting angry on a fast day. The whole value of the fast lies in subduing one's anger (*Ibid.*).

7) Through the holy act of eating on Shabbat, anger is crushed (*Ibid.*).

8) Anger can make a person lose his money. When a person gets angry he spoils the blessing of wealth which was due to come to him. He causes a stain upon his good name and, indeed, his very soul. But when a person holds his anger back and behaves patiently even in the most trying of circumstances, he attains wealth, a good name and an unblemished soul. All the other souls yearn to be merged with his soul and he can succeed in drawing many souls closer to God. Through this the glory of God is revealed (*Ibid.*).

9) When a person fights his anger and breaks it, the spirit of Mashiach is drawn into the world. Such a person is accounted as if it was through him that the world and all that is in it was created and brought into being. He will be worthy of rich blessings, and he will attain true prayer, directing himself to God alone without any extraneous motives of gaining people's respect and admiration. He will succeed in carrying out all the mitzvot and other holy acts that he must accomplish (66:3).

10) Through the sanctity of the Land of Israel it is possible to break the force of anger, depression and laziness completely. For this reason one must plead with God to be worthy of coming to the Land of Israel speedily. There a person can attain tranquility in the face of any experiences he may undergo. He will never be angry or upset with anyone, no matter what they may have done (*Ibid.* 155).

HONOR כבוד

1) People should minimize their own dignity and give as much honor as they can to the Creator. One should avoid honor and make no attempt to win people's admiration. Then he will be worthy of receiving honor from God, and no one will raise questions about whether he is really entitled to the respect he enjoys. But someone who chases after the respect and admiration of his fellow men will never be worthy of God's honor. Even if he does attain a position of respect, people will constantly look at him askance and want to know who he is that he should be accorded such respect (*Likutey Moharan* I, 6:1).

2) The test of true repentance is when a person can allow himself to be abused and ridiculed in silence, patiently accepting all the insults which are thrown at him. Through this he reduces the flood in the left ventricle of the heart — this is the seat of the animal soul — and slaughters his evil inclination. Then he is worthy of the honor of God (*Ibid.* 2).

3) A person should guard God's honor in all ways. He should be "vile and despised in his own eyes" (cf. Psalms 15:4), accounting himself and his dignity as of no importance before the honor due to the Creator. Then he will be able to speak words of Torah that will radiate with light, illuminating for him all the aspects of himself that he needs to work on in order to achieve perfect repentance. Through this he will attain profound understanding of the depths of Torah (11:2).

4) The greatest revelation of God's glory comes when those who were farthest of all from Him draw closer: then His Name is exalted and honored above and below, and His glory is magnified. It is a duty for everyone to make efforts to draw

people closer to God. And no one should say, "How can *I* come closer to God seeing that I am so removed from Him because of my wrong-doing." On the contrary, the further away a person, the more God's glory is exalted through him when he makes an effort to return and draw closer (14:2).

5) When people have respect for the righteous, honor is elevated to its source. One should be very sincere in the respect one gives them. This makes up for any flaw in his fear of God, and in the end he will attain peace (*Ibid.* 6).

6) Nobody should accept a position of leadership or power unless he has attained the level of absolute faith. There are people who although they believe in God still retain a residuum of superstition. Such people should not accept positions of leadership. A person may persuade himself that he has great love and pity for the world and this is why he wants to be in a position of leadership. But really he wants the glory for himself, even though he makes out that his motive is one of love and pity. This can lead to atheism and disbelief. But God in Heaven takes pity on the world, and the leadership is not allowed to fall into the hands of such people (8:3).

7) Those leaders and governments which show love and respect for the wise have chosen the firmest possible basis for their power. Love of the wise gives stability to leaders and governments. When a king or a ruler displays signs of hatred for the wise, it is a sign that Heaven has decreed that he should be brought down. For the world cannot endure without wisdom (*Ibid.* 4).

8) An old man who has forgotten his learning through no fault of his own should be accorded every respect. The very honor which is given to him will cause his forgetfulness to disappear and the vital soul — the Torah that he knew — will be revealed again. The darkness and harsh judgements will be put to flight and light, love, life and the wisdom of Torah will spread through the world (37:5).

9) We should also be very careful to give respect to the children of very ignorant, ordinary Jews. In certain cases the children of

very ignorant people have souls that are very precious: this we can see from their Torah learning. If we see that they are learned in Torah it is a sure sign that they must have a very precious soul, and we should be careful to accord them honor and respect. Through this honor, the Torah that is hidden within them will be revealed more fully, and this gives strength to spiritual forces — form, light, wisdom, life, love and memory — as opposed to bodily forces — substance, desire, darkness and folly (*Ibid.* 7).

10) There are leaders who go by the name of rabbi but whose learning has been picked up from the "superficialities" and "waste" of Torah. They are unable to control even themselves, let alone other people. But they still have pretentions to greatness and seek to lead and guide the whole world. You should be very careful to accord them no recognition whatsoever so as not to add in any way to their power or authority. They themselves can be forgiven for what they do: they are no more than the victims of a strong lust for power. It is the people who give them credibility and power and who are prepared to accord them the title of rabbi who will have a heavy penalty to pay (61:2).

11) When rabbis lacking in integrity are ordained and given authority, it weakens the influence of the Holy Writings of the Jews, and the writings of the nations of the world become invested with power. Decrees are passed according honor and authority to these writings alone, and not to our writings, and forcing Jews to learn their literature. In the end, decrees of expulsion are passed against the Jewish people, and they are forced to move from places where they have dwelled by long tradition to places they have never been. This is a form of "exile from the Land of Israel" (because places where Jews have lived for a long time have become sanctified with the holiness of the Land of Israel.) As a result, it becomes impossible for great souls to be born and brought into the world, and because of this the secret of astronomical calculation is taken from us and put into their hands instead, God forbid (*Ibid.*).

12) But when a Sage of true integrity is ordained and accorded the title of rabbi, our Scriptures are again invested with radiance and strength, and even the nations of the world submit to the authority of the writings of the Jews in governing their own affairs. Then the air is sanctified with the holiness of the air of the Land of Israel, and relief comes from the troubles which were brought about through the ordination of unworthy rabbis (*Ibid.*).

13) When some new honor comes to a person, it is something to be quite apprehensive about. At times honor is sent to a person as a prelude to his soul being taken. Therefore a person should always be careful to receive any honor in great holiness and only for the sake of God, not for his own benefit or enjoyment. Otherwise the honor could turn to be very harmful, and his soul could be taken, God forbid. The soul is very precious. One must guard it with the utmost care. One should pray to God that this new honor should not harm him in any way and that his soul should not be taken from him. The root and source of all the souls is in glory, and when a soul is taken, it is taken up into glory, which is its root (67:1).

14) Usually, however, the honor comes for good. For when a new soul comes to a man, it is clothed in honor. Thus when a person receives the honor as he should, he is able to receive the new soul which is clothed in it (*Ibid.*).

15) A greedy appetite is a blot upon the honor of God. God hides His face, and the world comes under the shadow of His harsh severity. Glory falls to the arrogant, who abrogate all the dignity to themselves. Power, kingship, authority and honor fall into the hands of the heathens, the wicked and the insolent, and when a situation arises where the Jewish people needs to take some firm action to ensure the survival of our holy faith, it is necessary to have recourse to their strength. But when we break the lust for food, the honor of God is vindicated and the insolent are left without power, authority or dignity. The countenance of God radiates to the world and the harsh judgements are broken (*Ibid.* 3).

16) Charity cleanses the stains upon God's honor. Glory and power are taken from the Other Side and restored to the wise, who are the world's true leaders (*Ibid.* 5).
17) In the morning prayers, when we reach the words "and You rule over all," it is customary to give charity in order to take glory and power from the hands of the Other Side and restore them to the forces of Holiness (*Ibid.* 7).
18) When honor is restored to the wise, who are the true leaders, at the beginning of their ascendancy there is likely to be factionalism and strife (*Ibid.* 6).
19) When some new honor comes to a person, he should do his utmost to cultivate the fear and love of God within himself in order to give birth to the new soul which comes to him clothed in this honor, to raise it and bring it to maturity (*Ibid.* 7).
20) By giving respect to an old man who has forgotten his learning, cool waters are drawn to revive the fainting soul. Giving such a person respect makes up for all the prayers which people say without sincerity, because it is prayers like these which cause the faintness of the soul (*Ibid.* 8).
21) For a Tzaddik it is very hard to be widely known. A Tzaddik who is revealed and famous has to bear much suffering on behalf of the people. However there are cases where it is the will of Heaven that a certain Tzaddik should be revealed and widely known (71).
22) When the leaders become arrogant, God sends people to make trouble for them and speak out against them in order to break their pride (95).
23) A person who wants honor is a fool (194).
24) The more a person lacks understanding, the more punctilious he is about any affronts to his dignity (202).
25) A person who conducts himself in office with honesty and purity will rise to greatness at the end of his days. Whatever the criteria of greatness in his particular time and place, he will be accorded this greatness (236).
26) One must be very cautious about entering any position of authority. This applies especially to those with fear of Heaven,

who have a particularly strong desire to influence others. If they accept a position of authority they are in danger of losing the blessing of prophecy which they might have been able to attain through their awe of Heaven (*Likutey Moharan* II, 1:7).

27) There are people who impose themselves as leaders and rulers over our poor, bereft nation not because they have been appointed by Heaven but purely through their own arrogance and assertiveness. The sword of pride which they wield draws strength from the proselytes, who bring arrogance into the Jewish people. They can attain so much power that they can even exact penalties from those who do not wish to bow to their rule. But the correct phrase for this is not "exacting penalties" but "causing damage," because ultimately they are a destructive force in the world. The arrogance of these leaders brings rampant immorality to the world. The only escape is by turning to the Guardians of the Earth (5:5).

28) The foundation of true spiritual leadership is love. No one can be a true leader unless he has genuine love for the Jewish people. But he must understand how to show this love. It is forbidden to show love to the wicked, to murderers and robbers. He must know how to guide and direct each individual along the path which will lead to his ultimate good. The essence of the love he must show to the Jewish people is to draw them from their sins. There is no greater love than this (7:1-3).

29) It is very dangerous for a Tzaddik to be revealed and widely known and to occupy a position of leadership. The danger is obvious in the case of one who is not fitted to the task and who wears a *tallit* which is not his own. But it is present even in the case of men of true stature who genuinely serve God. When they accept positions of leadership and teach Torah publicly, they are running the risk of falling into immorality, theft and murder with every step they take (18).

30) The only purpose of the entire creation is the revelation of God's glory. This is why everything was created for the sake of man. Because the revelation of God's glory depends entirely on man. Therefore when some new honor comes to a person, he

must be scrupulous about not taking any of it for himself. He must make sure that he gives all the glory to God. In this way he is building and sustaining the world, because the whole world and all that is in it was created only for His glory (71).

31) A person who insults God's honor falls from the mentality of the "Land of Israel" — which is the source of true understanding and wisdom — to the mentality of "outside the Land." This is the root of strife and factionalism (*Ibid.*).

32) A person who is jealous of a friend who rises to greatness can lose his faith and turn into an atheist. One must be extremely careful about this (80).

33) In our times there is no one whose motive for seeking power is purely for the sake of Heaven. In previous generations there were such people. But today no one should seek out positions of power. All honor and authority should be avoided (*Ibid.*).

34) Anyone with a clear mind can see that all the affairs of this world are utterly futile and foolish. This is especially true of earthly prestige and power and fame. The truth is that they give no pleasure or satisfaction even in this world. They are always attended by suffering and abuse from other people (Rabbi Nachman's Wisdom 47).

MOCKERY לצנות

1) People who make fun of the words of the Sages are punished with boiling excrements (*Gittin* 56a). Stinking vapors rise up to their brains, leaving them twisted and confused. No matter how much they may study Torah, they will never be able to derive true guidance from it about the way to lead their lives. Their hearts are as filthy as a privy. They never have a clear idea how to live at all. This kind of cynicism leads in the end to severe decrees being passed against the Jewish people. They are expelled from the countries they were living in, and the end result of the upheavals is that whole areas of Torah wisdom become lost to us, notably the mystery of *Ibbur,* which underlies the structure of the Jewish calendar with its intercalated leap-years. The loss of this wisdom causes strife and factionalism (61:1-3).

2) An enormous number of religious books are available today, and in the future even more will be written. On no account should one ever make fun of any of them. The world needs every one of them (*Ibid.* 5).

3) When a person makes fun of something holy, it is "the laughter of the fool" (Ecclesiastes 7:6). The remedy for mockery is *tikkun haBrit*, guarding the Covenant (*Likutey Moharan* II, 83).

4) One of the biggest obstacles in the search for truth is other people, especially those who make fun of religion with "sophisticated" jokes. They are under the spell of philosophical speculation and other current ideas. The damage they cause is quite obvious. They have the power to corrupt people completely, God forbid. What is even more insidious is the

sharp wit of people who give the appearance of being respectable and well meaning, but who have a way of turning all kinds of religious matters into a joke. Many people are deterred from true religion because of this. At least where the blatant mockery of the philosophers is concerned most people have the sense to be wary and keep away, knowing as they do that philosophy has the power to deprive you of both worlds, this one and the next, and to throw you down into the lowest pit of hell, God forbid. But the "wit and wisdom" of those who give the impression of being decent and religious can be more dangerous because their words possess a certain aura of truth. Travel the path of purity and you will walk in trust. Keep well away from this crowd and pay no attention to their humor and wise ideas. Walk with simplicity and purity along the ancient path of our forefathers (Rabbi Nachman's Wisdom 81)

MONEY & LIVELIHOOD ממון ופרנסה

1) Worthless pursuits and malicious gossip can only lead to poverty in the end. Pride also causes poverty. The remedy is to give charity, which brings blessing and prosperity (4:8).
2) Immorality can deprive a person of his livelihood (7:5).
3) Intense prayer makes one worthy of one's livelihood (9:2).
4) The less careful a person is about upholding his moral standards, the more unpleasantness and hardship he will experience in his efforts to earn a living (11:4).
5) In order to draw God's providence upon ourselves completely, it is necessary to break the desire for wealth. The way to do this is by giving charity. When a person gives money to charity, it cools his urge to acquire. He will conduct his business affairs truthfully and honestly, he will be satisfied with his portion in life, and he will have pleasure and contentment from what God has blessed him with. Because he is not desperate to get rich, he is free of the constant struggle to make extra profit. The burden of this struggle is the fulfillment of the curse: "by the sweat of your brow you shall eat bread" (Genesis 3:19). Giving charity frees a person from this. It is accounted to him as if he had made an offering of incense before God (13:1).
6) The desire for wealth is literally a form of idol-worship. So long as it continues to exist, the world is under the shadow of God's anger. But the more completely it is uprooted, the more God's anger is lifted and the world radiates with the blessing of His love. The messianic spirit begins to spread; understanding springs forth, and it is as if the Holy Temple had been rebuilt. New horizons of Torah are revealed — the Torah that is destined to be revealed in time to come (*Ibid.* 2-5).

7) People who are obsessed with the idea of getting rich lack faith in God's power to send man his livelihood with little effort on his part. Instead they get involved in all kinds of complicated enterprises in the struggle for extra profit. Only after great toil and anxiety do they eat their daily bread. They are constantly worried and depressed. They have attached themselves to the "countenance of the forces of the Other Side" — the domain of darkness, depression, idolatry and death. It is completely different for those who go about their work in a spirit of faith and trust in God. Having decided to content themselves with what they have, they are happy with their portion regardless of what it may be. They know and believe with perfect faith that God alone is the source of man's wealth and income — except that He desires that man should make some small movement of his own to initiate the chain of events that will bring his income to him. People like this are attached to the light of God's countenance, which is the realm of radiance, life and joy (23:1).

8) A person who is sunk in his craving for wealth is not just enslaved to one kind of idolatry, but to every single idolatrous cult belonging to all of the seventy nations of the world. This is because all forms of idolatry are rooted in materialism. Again and again the Shechinah cries out in pain because of these idolatries. "Woe for the pain in my head! Woe for the pain in my arm!" (*Sanhedrin* 46). There are seventy cries (corresponding to the seventy nations) for the pain in the head, and seventy for the pain in the arm, making one hundred and forty. This corresponds to the *gematria* of *Mamon* (money):

mem	מ	40
mem	מ	40
vav	ו	6
nun	ן	50
plus the four letters		4
		140

9) Another way of breaking the desire for wealth is to contemplate the spiritual source from which material wealth and

blessings flow. By concentrating on this root, the desire for material wealth is dissipated. Because here at the root, radiant with translucent light, the joy is purely spiritual. By comparison the object of the craving is very degraded. Only a fool would throw aside spiritual joy for the sake of some crude pleasure. But the only way to attain this spiritual perception is through self-purification, as it is written: "And from my flesh will I perceive God" (Job 19:26). Only when a person has sanctified himself and his body can he contemplate Godliness. This explains why the basic remedy for the desire for wealth is through fulfillment of the Covenant. When a person achieves this, he will not fall into this desire (*Ibid.* 5).

10) Whenever a person falls from his level, the fundamental reason is always the desire for money. This is basically why people fall into heresy and idolatry. For the same reason when the enemies of the Tzaddik stir up opposition against him and God wants to chase them away, He causes them to fall into lust for money. There is no greater fall than this. As a general rule, in times of controversy and strife, the greater the purity with which a person guards the Covenant and the closer he is to the Tzaddik, — who is the embodiment of the Covenant — the greater his power to resist his opponents and throw them down. And when they fall, it is into lust for money. For this reason a person who finds himself involved in a dispute should be very careful not to succumb to the temptations of wealth (*Ibid.* 3).

11) The mitzvah of *mezuzah* is a remedy against the lust for money. When you observe this mitzvah carefully your livelihood will fly into your hands! (*Ibid.* 4).

12) As long as a person is reluctant to spend money on the mitzvot he performs, his mitzvot are deficient because they have not yet entered the category of true faith, which gives them their perfection. But when a mitzva is so precious in his eyes that he does not mind parting with his money and he spends liberally for the sake of the mitzva, this is called Faith. Because the essence of a person's faith is seen in his relation to money. When he breaks

his desire for wealth he becomes attached to the "countenance of holiness" (*Ibid.* 5).

13) People who are sunk in the desire for wealth are always in debt. We can actually see this. When people are dissatisfied with what they have they start trying to speculate — and saddle themselves with a mighty burden of debt. They borrow from others in the hope of making big profits from the investment. But in the end they die as debtors. And even if they are not literally in debt when they die, they are always effectively in debt to their own lusts, as we can see. There are many people who have more than enough to cover their needs. Yet they spend all their days chasing after profit. They are prepared to struggle and submit to all kinds of risks and inconvenience just for the sake of money. In fact they behave exactly like someone with real debts strung around his neck — except that their only real debt is the debt they owe to their desires, which are so demanding that it is as if they really did owe an enormous sum. In effect they are debtors all their lives, and they die in debt — to their desires. Even a whole lifetime is not long enough for them to pay off the debts they owe to their desires, because there is no limit to them, for "No one in this world achieves even half of what he wants before he dies." (*Koheleth Rabbah*, 1) All their days they are depressed, worried and bitter because of their appetite for money. The more money people have the more depression and worries they have, because they are entangled in idolatry, which is the very source of depression, darkness and death. Their money eats up the days of their life with problems and worries (*Ibid.*).

14) You should realize that it is nothing but a "fool's game" when people make money dishonestly or refuse to give any of their money to charity. (Our Sages laid down that we should give between a tenth and a fifth of our net income to charity in lieu of the priestly tithes.) It is a "fool's game," because the money plays with them as one amuses a little child with coins. And in the end the money itself kills them. The *Tikkuney Zohar* speaks about this game of the fool. "Who is the fool? It is the "other god," the child's croop. It smiles at them with the allure of wealth in this

world, and then it kills them. Why is it called a "child?" Because those who are trapped in it do not have the sense to escape from it" (*Tikkuney Zohar* 140a). The way to escape the allure of wealth is through the purity of the Covenant and by drawing closer to the Tzaddik, who is the embodiment of purity and of whom it is written, "He who is good and walks before God will be saved from it" (Eccl. 7:26). The Tzaddik possesses true wisdom and understanding, and knows how to escape this trap. Even the greatest of men need deep wisdom and understanding if they are to escape the pain and toil which can be involved in trying to earn a living. Most ordinary people suffer terrible bitterness all their lives because of this. They lose both worlds, this world and the World to Come. There is no limit to the bitterness of this world. As the Holy Zohar says: "Were it not for salt* the world could not endure the bitterness" (*Zohar* I, 241b). Were it not for the strength of the Tzaddikim, who observe the Covenant with absolute purity and who are called the "eternal covenant of salt" (Numbers 18:19), the world would not be able to endure at all because of the terrible bitterness caused by the desire for wealth. The closer a person comes to the Tzaddik, the more he can sweeten this bitterness. But those who are far from the Tzaddikim and from personal purity, and especially those who are actually opposed to the Tzaddikim, will be the victims of the full force of this bitterness. How many are sunk in this! Pay heed to these words and perhaps you will escape (*Ibid.*).

15) With every step that a person takes and every word he utters in his efforts to make a living he should have in mind that his purpose in making a profit is to be able to give money to charity. Charity is the *tikkun* for business activity (29:5).

16) Only a person who "hates covetousness" (Exodus 18:21), which means that he absolutely hates materialism, can acquire true wisdom and understanding and thereby reach a perception of Godliness. And so the opposite (30:4).

17) When a person conducts his business honestly and with faith, his soul — his mind and intellect — is renewed through this faith.

* salt has the property of neutralizing bitterness

Through the business activity itself he can develop spiritually and draw fresh wisdom and a new soul from the light of God's countenance. Not everyone is on such a level of Torah scholarship that he can grow intellectually in Torah through his business. But even so, simply by virtue of conducting his business in faith and honesty, a great *tikkun* is brought about, and a second Jew whose soul is drawn from the same root as his own can benefit greatly, because *his* intellect is refreshed and expanded through the honest dealings of the first and he is inspired with new energy to learn and devote himself to God (35:6).

18) The whole body of Torah law dealing with business affairs is relevant to practical business activity. Anyone who wishes to conduct his business with faith and honesty must be expert in all the laws of business in order not to slip up in any of them (*Ibid.*).

19) A person who genuinely wants to conduct his business with faith and honesty must guard his faith very carefully from any possible flaw. He must be as scrupulous as Rav Safra, (see *Makhoth* 24a) and he must "speak the truth in his heart" (Psalms 15:2). Even if he merely decided something in his heart, he must not change it later on. If he guards his faith carefully his soul and intellect will be refreshed and renewed through his faith (*Ibid.* 7).

20) When a person conducts his business with faith and honesty, it is as precious as the daily offerings and incense brought in the Holy Temple, which caused the husks to fall away and all the sparks of holiness trapped within them to ascend. His mind is elevated and refreshed, and it is accounted as if the Holy Temple had been rebuilt in his time (*Ibid.* 8).

21) The main reason for the economic hardships which have hit the Jewish people in recent generations is that many of the *shochetim*, the ritual slaughterers, have not been worthy. The blessing which a worthy *shochet* makes at the time of slaughtering is a powerful influence on the livelihood of the whole Jewish people. The blessing elevates the living soul which was incarnated in the animal. But there are *shochetim* who fail to concentrate properly on the meaning of the blessing and harbor improper thoughts. A *shochet* like this, standing with the knife raised ready

to slaughter the animal, is no better than a murderer. What pain this living soul experiences at this moment. She cries with a bitter wail, because the blessing this *shochet* makes will do nothing to elevate her from her incarnation. On the contrary, she will be cast down even lower than before and she will have "no rest for the sole of her foot" (Genesis 7:8). Woe to such a *shochet*! Woe to the soul he has killed and given over to the hands of her enemies. The result is that people's livelihood is hit, and the little that is available can only be acquired with great toil and exertion. *Shochetim* like these cause the soul to be enslaved by the materialism of the body, and physical lusts and desires gain strength. When the *shochetim* are worthy the soul is elevated and the grossness of the body is crushed and humbled. The body is the seat of animality, folly, darkness and death, forgetfulness, harsh justice and alien ideologies. In their place, *soul* and *form* are elevated. These are the roots of all that is truly noble in man — understanding, light, life, memory, lovingkindness... in short, the wisdom of Torah. Through them the world is blessed with abundance and prosperity (37).

22) A person should always feel contented with what he has. He should take no more from the world than is absolutely essential. He should not live in luxury like so many people do today because of our many sins. People who lack this sense of contentment are referred to in the saying that "the belly of the wicked shall want" (Proverbs 13:25), because they are always in need of something. A man should be contented with what God has given him, and even out of this minimum he should still contribute a portion to charity. This brings about great unification in the worlds above, and the world is blessed with abundance (54:2).

23) The effect of trade and commerce is to cause all kinds of goods and materials to move around from one set of hands to the next. All the complex movements backwards and forwards depend entirely on the sparks of holiness within the objects themselves. There are times when a certain object has to pass from one person's hands to another's and then return to the hands of the first. The determining factor is the Divine sparks

within the objects and their relation with the Divine soul and spirit of the individuals concerned (*Ibid.*).

24) Craving for money puts power into the hands of the forces of wickedness — the domain of Haman the Amalekite, who constantly harries the side of holiness, the vital source of which lies in the wisdom of Torah. In direct opposition to this, the forces of wickedness constantly hunger after money, swallowing the sparks of holiness hidden in the money and rooted in the supernal colors. The more a person breaks his lust for money and draws closer to the wisdom of Torah, the more he releases the holy sparks from the forces of wickedness. The power to achieve this is drawn from the Tzaddikim, who are truly devoted to Torah. They have the power to humble the forces of wickedness and release all the trapped sparks and make of them Torah (56:5).

25) The deeper a person is sunk in desire for wealth, the less his understanding and the shorter his days will be. He will never hear the voice of the Torah, which calls on men constantly to return to God. He will be forced to toil for his living, and it will come to him only with great difficulty. But if he strives determinedly to deepen his understanding and think only thoughts of Torah, ignoring his desire for wealth completely, his livelihood will begin to come to him easily and he will hear the voice of the Torah calling and beckoning. The "voice of the Torah" is the good thoughts which rise constantly in a person's heart with the idea of returning to God. In the end he will be worthy of returning to God in truth (*Ibid.*).

26) The depression which descends on a person when he has to struggle excessively for a living is the "filth of the serpent." All the limbs of the body become heavy, and the vital spirit which pulsates in the body — the very basis of life — is weakened. The weaker it becomes, the heavier the limbs become, and they in turn weigh down the spirit even more. This vicious cycle can actually bring a person to the point of death. The root of the syndrome is the struggle for money, which is the source of anxiety and depression. But when a person sighs with longing for the holy, moaning out of yearning for God, it helps to rally his strength and

revitalize the pulsating spirit within him, bringing new vigor and life. In the end he will attain profound understanding and hear words from Heaven itself (*Ibid.* 9).

27) Anger can be very harmful to a person's livelihood. You should know that when the evil inclination starts tempting you to get angry, at that very moment a flow of blessing is descending from above with a certain sum of money intended for you. The evil inclination wants to thwart this blessing with the anger it tries to provoke in you. This is because anger is so damaging to the flow of blessing. Even a person who already possesses money can lose it if he becomes angry (68).

28) The prohibition against robbery is very serious because a person who robs another robs him of his very children. Even if the victim does not have any children as yet, the robber can bring it about that he never will have. And if he does have children, the robber can cause him such damage that the children will die, God forbid, as a result of his having robbed him of his money (69).

29) One who robs another will end up having all kinds of sexual temptations (*Ibid.*).

30) At times the thief himself can end up losing his wife because of his crime, and at times he can cause the victim to lose his wife (*Ibid.*).

31) A person can come to possess stolen property without even physically stealing it himself. It is possible to rob one's neighbor merely by being jealous of what he has. This is why the prohibition against envy and covetousness is so grave. Through envy alone one can rob one's neighbor of his money and the soul of his sons and daughters, just like an actual thief (*Ibid.*).

32) Giving charity can make amends for any money which has come into one's hands improperly because of envy. But for money which has literally been stolen there is no remedy except to return it to its rightful owner, or, in cases where it is impossible to return it to its owners to devote it to the public good, as our Rabbis explained (*Bava Kama* 94b) (*Ibid.*).

33) If a person finds the money he has to live off is too little for his needs, the best thing to do is to make it into charity. Charity is the

tikkun for material possessions. In the end he will have plenty of money (*Ibid.*).

34) A person who marries a woman for money is a fool and an idiot, as our Rabbis said (*Kiddushin* 72). He will lose whatever intelligence he may have had, and his children will not turn out good (*Ibid.*).

35) The lust for money creates enemies. The stronger the craving, the stronger the enemies become. If the craving becomes excessive, it will create enemies who hate one for nothing (*Ibid.*).

36) The more a person craves for money, the more turbulent and confused his mind becomes. Eventually he turns into a fool (*Ibid.*).

37) When a person is meek and humble no one can "shift him from his place" in the sense of impinging on his livelihood (79).

38) When a person conducts his business with faith and honesty, he thereby fulfills the commandment to "love the Lord your God" (Deut. 6:5) and his income will be sent him without worry and toil (93; 210).

39) Business activity is wholly Torah. Therefore during the time a person spends on his work he should bind his thoughts to Torah alone, and in particular to the laws which are clothed within the activities in which he is engaged (280).

40) A person who fails to bind his thoughts to Torah in the course of his business activities will eventually be punished by having to come before the judges in a law case based on Torah law. The outcome of the case will depend on the degree of his previous neglect. Sometimes the punishment is merely having to undergo the case at all, and the person in question wins his case. But where people have allowed their business activities to diverge too far from Torah teachings, it usually happens that they lose their case (*Ibid.*).

41) The time a person spends working is a time of battle. The battle is against the forces of the Other Side, and the goal is to sift out the sparks of holiness and elevate them. Sifting out the sparks is the main purpose of all business and commerce. One has to be literally perfectly honest. Every word he speaks should be true.

His "yes" should be "yes" and his "no" should be "no." He must also bind his thoughts to Torah. When he is working, only the exterior aspects of his thoughts should be concentrated on the work itself, the inner thought should be bound to Torah. Through this he can sift and elevate many fallen holy sparks. All the worlds are elevated and awesome *tikkunim* are achieved, just as they are through prayer (*Ibid.*).

42) The craving for money is one of the three temptations which flaw and spoil the fear of God which is latent in the heart. But when we celebrate the festival of Pesach with the appropriate honour we can cleanse ourselves of the craving for money and attain true fear, prophetic inspiration and prayer (*Likutey Moharan* II, 1:4,5).

43) A person who wants to provide for those who are dependent upon him must be a person of strength and fortitude, not the opposite. A certain amount of authority and "push" is required in order to earn money (7:10).

44) There is a certain sin* which causes people to fall into debt. A person who is in debt should repent wholeheartedly and plead with God to cleanse him of this sin. The time to do this is when he is in a state of expanded consciousness (Rabbi Nachman's Wisdom 112).

45) When a person has such joy from Torah and *mitzvoth* that he literally dances for joy, his material affairs are elevated (*Likutey Moharan* II, 81).

46) The only purpose in this world is to draw closer to the ultimate goal, which is the World to Come. Whether you have money or you don't, don't worry about it, because if you do you will surely waste away your days, regardless of whether you actually make any money or not. This world is completely deceptive. It constantly makes people think they are gaining, but in the end it is all an illusion — as everybody knows very well at heart. Even if you do become rich, eventually you will be taken away from your money. It is a basic rule that man and money cannot remain together. Either the money is taken from the man

* Rabbi Nachman never revealed which sin.

or the man is taken from the money. In all of human history there has never been a case where a person stayed with his money. It may be hard to achieve very much in serving God. But even if you don't seem to get very far in this, you should still understand that in itself this world is nothing. Your one aim and desire should be to reach the ultimate goal of the World to Come. You should always long to do what God wants. The desire itself is very precious. The main thing is your *will*. Whatever good you can do besides — a good deed here, learning some Torah or saying a prayer there — all the better. Do as much as you can while you can, because the only thing that will be left of all your labor in this world will be your will to do good and whatever holy deeds you were able to snatch in this world while you were here (Rabbi Nachman's Wisdom 51).

47) Keep in mind the words of the Tzaddikim. Don't deceive yourself, and don't let the world deceive you. In this world nobody ends up well. The only good you will enjoy is the good you take with you to enjoy in the eternal world (*Ibid.*).

THOUGHTS & FANTASIES

מחשבות והרהורים

1) Make sure that you don't allow your mind to become *chametz* — leavened. Don't dwell on bad thoughts or desires at all. These thoughts are rooted in the side of death. If they come into your mind, just reject them and push them out completely, because ultimately they ruin the mind and make it impossible to pray properly and experience genuine joy. You should try and avoid even the merest hint of thoughts like this. You should be as carful about it as we are to avoid even the merest speck of *chametz* on Pesach. Evil thoughts are the leaven in the dough, and the law regarding leaven on Pesach is that we must destroy it completely so that it can neither be seen nor found. Purify your mind and empty it of any thoughts like this (*Likutey Moharan* 5:4).

2) A person can't always stop bad thoughts from entering his mind in the first place. But he does have the power to reject them once he becomes conscious of them. This is something very important, because it is the way to make amends for sins he may have committed earlier in his life. Perfect repentance has to balance the original sins exactly, and this is literally what happens here. Before, when he sinned, it was because the temptation entered his mind and he succumbed to it. Now the thought is in his mind again, but this time he rejects it. So don't feel discouraged if you find all kinds of temptations and fantasies continually pressing in on your mind. They are actually providing you with the opportunity to repent and make amends for the damage done in the past. Today you have the power to master your thoughts and temptations. When you do so, the sparks of holiness which fell because of your earlier transgressions are released, and you are able to purify yourself. Your mind and your

voice will be purified and you will find harmony and peace. This peace can bring the whole world back to the service of God (27:8).

3) When a person admits unholy thoughts to his mind, the holiness of his mind is reduced in direct proportion to the space occupied by these degraded thoughts. If you stick a pole in a river bed, all kinds of dirt and filth gather round it. In the same way, all kinds of bad characteristics develop because of these unholy ideas, and the mind is assailed with desires and temptations. In fact all the sins a person does are ultimately caused by the unholy ideas he originally admitted to his mind. To achieve true repentance, you must rid your mind of these thoughts. The mind is the soul, and when a person sanctifies his mind, he elevates and returns everything to its root. This is the essence of repentance (35:1).

4) Unholy thoughts are the "folly of the heart." When a person dwells on such thoughts his heart becomes sullied and the "foreskin of the heart" grows thick. The "void" of the creation is spoiled, and it is as if this person had damaged the whole world. But when he thinks good thoughts, the creation is restored. When a person purifies his heart and expels all unholy thoughts from his mind, thinking only good thoughts, he can bring about real miracles (49:1).

5) A person's entire destiny — for good or ill — depends on the thoughts in his heart. The thoughts and ideas in the heart are the basis of the heart's "inclinations" — the good inclination and the evil inclination. Good thoughts are the good inclination, bad thoughts are the evil inclination (*Ibid.*).

6) When a person expels all the unholy thoughts from his heart and thinks only good thoughts about ways of serving God, then he has founded his strength on the "rock of my heart" (Psalms 73:26) and he will succeed in reaching the level where "my heart is void within me" (Psalms 109:22). He will be able to develop his character to perfection and take on the yoke of heaven with a perfect heart. He will be worthy of true prayer and perfect repentance, and bring about unification in the worlds above and the worlds below. The hidden Torah of the Ancient One will be

revealed, the forces of evil will be destroyed and the forces of holiness will be elevated. Israel will be blessed with vitality, abundance and prosperity (*Ibid.*).

7) All the thoughts which pass through the mind are always expressed in words. At the moment one thinks a thought, "the lips move" (cf. *Yerushalmi Berachoth* 7a). He may not actually feel this, but as the Zohar explains, there is always a movement, however subtle. Every thought that a person can think must be expressed in words, however subtly (66:4).

8) Many people experience very strong mental distractions while they are trying to pray. These can be immoral fantasies or even thoughts about idolatrous worship. There are even cases where people see vivid images of idolatrous objects or else they experience overwhelming temptations the very moment they stand up to pray. They try to push the thoughts out of their minds by tossing their heads from side to side. But the harder they try the more the thoughts press in. This is in the nature of thoughts like these. The more worked up you get about trying to push them out of your mind, the more they insinuate their way in. The best way to deal with them is simply to ignore them. Act as if you were completely unconcerned. Refuse to listen. Carry on with what you were doing — studying, praying, working or whatever. Pay no attention to the thoughts or fantasies at all. Don't keep on looking round to see if they have gone away. Just carry on with what you are trying to do. In the end they will go away of their own accord. But you should understand that this method is only a temporary measure. In the long term the task is to sanctify and purify your body. To achieve this you must go to the Tzaddikim to learn the paths of truth. Thoughts like these will then disappear completely (72).

9) If you allow yourself to be depressed about these kinds of thoughts it simply feeds them with more fuel. It is no good being upset or afraid of them. Just don't pay any attention to them. Try and be cheerful. Elsewhere we discuss the way to be happy always (see *Simcha*). Eventually these thoughts will disappear automatically. Don't keep on testing to see if they are still there. It

won't help if you keep on turning round to look. Just don't pay any attention to them at all (*Ibid.*).

10) The Torah distinguishes between the animals which are pure and those which are impure. The "pure animals" are pure thoughts, and "impure animals" are impure thoughts. The battle between the different thoughts in a person's mind is a battle between the pure and the impure animals. Heaven allows them to carry on fighting because God has great pleasure when He sees a man struggling hard to defeat these "wild animals" (233).

11) The simple fact is that it is impossible for two thoughts to be in the mind at one and the same time. It is therefore an easy matter to rid yourself of bad thoughts by being quite passive. Simply don't think them. Think something else instead — think about Torah or devotion to God, or even about your work, and so on. If you just turn your mind to something else the bad thoughts and fantasies will go away automatically (*Ibid.*).

12) Thought is a very elevated level. One who wishes to think only thoughts of holiness and ascend to the world of thought must be completely silent. Even saying something good and noble would spoil the thought. But even when a person is completely silent, there are still many distractions which confuse the mind. He still has to *purify* his thoughts. The way to do this is through hearing and telling stories of the Tzaddikim (234).

13) Sexual fantasies are the prime source of all impurity. They are as strong a source of pollution as a dead body. Charity gives some protection against these fantasies, but one should never rely on this and permit oneself to talk freely with women. One should say only what is essential. The merit of the charity he gives will then save him from harm (242).

14) There are certain fantasies which derive their strength from a particular husk which is extraordinarily tough. It is very difficult to escape from them. Even if you try to shut your eyes the thought appears wherever you turn. Charity gives protection against these thoughts (*Ibid.*).

15) Whenever you find bad thoughts and fantasies pressing in on your mind, don't be depressed. Try extra hard to turn aside from

them. The effort itself is very precious and brings about a great *tikkun* (*Likutey Moharan* II, 5:7).

16) A person's thoughts are in his power completely. He can turn them in whatever direction he wants. It may be that at times your thoughts run wild and fly to areas you ought to keep away from. It is still within your power to take them in hand, even against their will, and direct your thoughts to the true path. Thought is just like a horse which turns aside from the road and tries to go in the wrong direction. The rider controls the horse with the bridle and forces it to go in the right direction. As soon as you see your thoughts pulling in the wrong direction, take them in hand and bring them back to the right direction (*Ibid.* 50).

17) It is impossible to form any conception of the preciousness of good thoughts — thoughts of Torah and devotion. Out of thoughts such as these there are formed perfect objects which will exist for all time. From this alone you can understand the true evil of unholy thoughts, God forbid (53).

18) You should aim for the level of *Mah* — "What?" This means binding yourself and your thoughts to God at all times in order to draw Godliness over yourself. If you do this, all the battles and difficulties in your life will melt away and everything will go your way. The Hebrew word for "thought" is *machshavah*, which bears the meaning of "think — what?" — *chashov-mah*. That is to say, you must draw *Mah?* into your mind and bind your thoughts to God at all times. The *gematria* of *Mah* is: *mem*, 40, + *heh*, 5, equals 45. This is equivalent to the *gematria* of the name of God when all the letters are written out in full:

Yod	= *Yod, 10*	+ *Vav, 6*	+ *Daleth, 4*	=	*20*
He	= *He, 5*	+ *Aleph, 1*		=	*6*
Vav	= *Vav, 6*	+ *Aleph, 1*	+ *Vav, 6*	=	*13*
He	= *He, 5*	+ *Aleph, 1*		=	*6*
					45

19) You must be very careful about what you think: a thought can literally take on a life of its own (46).

20) Thought is man's highest aspect. It is more elevated than

vision, the sense of hearing, and in fact everything. With thought it is possible to climb ever higher. This is why you must be so careful about what you think (*Ibid.*).

21) Sometimes a thought — a good idea, or a glimmer of perception — can pass through your mind and shine there for a moment and then fly away again. It takes great strength to run after the thought and chase it until you catch up with it (58).

CONTROVERSY & STRIFE — מחלוקת ומריבה

1) You should not allow yourself to be disturbed by the various disputes between the Tzaddikim (as for example the differences of opinion between the Sages of the Mishnah, the Talmud and so on). If a person is troubled by these disputes and states raising all kinds of questions about them, it is a sign that he has allowed some impurity into his mind. It is this internal impurity that is the real source of his doubts. The danger is that his doubts could grow to the point where he becomes permanently separated from the Tzaddikim and their followers, who are the source of true and enduring life. A person should understand that if he finds himself troubled by doubts and questions about the Tzaddikim it is an indication that a flaw exists within himself. If he realizes this, it will help him return to the truth (5:4).

2) You should always make every effort to search out whatever merit and goodness you can find within the Jewish people. Judge everyone in the scale of merit, even those who oppose you and treat you disrespectfully. If you do this you will never be troubled by opposition and arguments. When you seek out the merit of your fellow Jew, you make a precious crown for God studded with beautiful gems (6).

3) If you find yourself in the middle of a dispute, it is very good if you can remain silent and pay no attention to the abuse which people throw at you. When you can hear what is said against you without answering back this is true repentance. It is the remedy for all past sins. Someone who achieves this can truly be said to be wise. He will receive a share in the glory of God and a goodly portion in the World to Come. He will be merged in the figure of the Man on the Throne which is the source of all the judgements

passed on the inhabitants of the world (*Ibid.*).

4) Only the perfect Tzaddik has the strength to fight against the wicked and the enemies of truth. It takes a person who has already rid himself of evil completely to fight this battle successfully. The various character traits are rooted in the four cosmic elements of Fire, Air, Earth and Water. The Tzaddik must be pure in all of them. He must be assured that nothing will make him trip up and sin. Only such a Tzaddik and his followers can fight against the wicked. A person may have cleansed himself to the point that he is entirely free of sin in practice. But if even the mere possibility that he *might* sin remains, he is not a "perfect Tzaddik," and it can be very dangerous for him to try to fight the wicked. They draw their life-force from the Other Side — the "raging stormwind" (Ezekiel 1:3), which has tremendous force at the peak of its power. Only the perfect Tzaddik can descend unharmed into the channel through which the wicked draw their strength in order to break them and humble them and cast them down to the earth (8:5).

5) If you are scrupulous about the mitzvah of *tzitzit* you will be able to stand up against any opposition (*Ibid.*).

6) The people who set themselves in opposition to the Tzaddik are called dead even in their lifetime because they have no share in the holy life-spirit which the Tzaddikim alone draw into the world (*Ibid.*).

7) At times the wicked become so bitter in their battle against holiness that the only recourse is to fight them with the legal apparatus of the non-Jewish authorities. In fact it is a positive duty to do so, and to do the utmost to crush the opposition by this means, even if the cost is heavy. It helps to elevate the sparks of true justice from the domain of the husks and the forces of the Other Side. There are times when God intentionally brings it about that the opposition to the righteous and God-fearing should be so fierce that the only recourse is to the non-Jewish authorities. The whole purpose is precisely to elevate the sparks of true justice from the domain of the husks (20:9).

8) Those who ridicule and abuse the genuinely religious are under

the influence of Torah they have learned from scholars who lack the necessary integrity. These scholars are termed "Jewish devils" (*Zohar* III, 253) because their Torah is "fallen Torah," which lacks the power to guide men along the path of truth and goodness. There is nothing to be gained from such scholars. Anyone who associates with them will turn into an atheist (28:1).

9) One way of developing genuine faith is by offering hospitality to true Torah scholars. When you have true faith it will give you the strength to be untouched by the abuse and ridicule of others (*Ibid.* 2:3).

10) There are people who do not have a good word for anybody. They always look on the bad side of people. The source of their life-force is in the forces of the Other Side, which is called "the end of all flesh" (Genesis 6:13). Such people are constantly trying to make an end of things. They are highly destructive. Their accusations and slander arouse harsh judgements in the world. The fundamental evil here is the abuse of the faculty of speech. Therefore the way to crush and humble these people is by developing the faculty of speech to perfection (38:2).

11) Clapping your hands when you pray helps against strife and divisiveness. Murder and destruction are driven from the world, and peace reigns (44).

12) The deeper a person's understanding the more detached he will be from in-fighting and controversy. The main reason for factionalism and anger is lack of understanding. Torah is the source of all understanding. Therefore the study of Torah brings peace to the world and causes factionalism to disappear (56:3, 6).

13) Immersing in a *mikvah* deepens understanding. It is therefore also a help against factionalism (*Ibid.* 7).

14) When a person is prone to anger, it strengthens his enemies and opponents. One remedy is fasting. Another is taking pleasure in the delights of Shabbat especially the Shabbat meals (57:6).

15) A potent reason for factionalism and quarreling is because people lack sufficient faith in the Sages of the Torah. Someone who finds himself at the center of an argument, with people raising all kinds of questions about him, should take it as a sign

that he does not have sufficient faith in the Sages. He should think about the implications of the argument and use it as a stimulus to help him correct the deficiency in his faith (61:5).

16) There are certain Tzaddikim in particular who could never be said to have less than perfect faith, yet they are still surrounded by controversy. In the case of a Tzaddik such as this the reason for the opposition is that "he bore the sin of many" (Isaiah 53:12) and he has to bear the anguish of this controversy precisely because the rest of the world is lacking in faith in the Sages. The very controversy which surrounds him enables him to correct the flaws in the people's faith in the Sages (*Ibid.*).

17) Another reason for the opposition against these Tzaddikim is that they do not have sufficient faith in themselves. They lack adequate faith in the value of the original Torah concepts which they have developed, nor do they fully believe that God has great joy from their teachings. They have insufficient confidence in their own originality, and as a result their powers grow weaker. This is the reason why opposition is sent to them — to encourage them to repent for their weak faith. Because a lack of faith in one's own originality is also a lack of faith in the Sages. When the Tzaddik repents for this, it gives him new enthusiasm to explore fresh horizons and innovate further, and out of his teachings a book is made. Many holy books of Torah come to be written in this way. As a result disputes and faction-fighting are put to rest and all the harsh judgements are sweetened (*Ibid.*).

18) At the deepest level, the fact that there are disputes between the various Tzaddikim (for example the arguments between the Sages of the Mishnah and the Gemarah and so on) has its root in the concept of the "Empty Void," the mystical concept of the void that was left after the primordial light was contracted. (See *Likutey Moharan* 64 for a fuller discussion of this.) Any real understanding of this concept is beyond the capacity of our human intelligence. Because of this it is wrong for a person to allow himself to be troubled by fundamental doubts through an inability to understand how it could be that there were disagreements between the Sages on matters of Torah. One must

simply have faith that "these and these are the words of the living God," even if we are unable to understand how this can be. We must strengthen ourselves with faith alone (64:4).

19) The more divisions among the enemy, the greater their power of endurance. When they unite, however, they very quickly suck dry the source of their life-force, which is in the waste substances of the brain, and they soon collapse (87:6).

20) The urge to dominate has its source in the blood with which a person has not yet served God. He must see to it that he serves God with every single drop of blood in his body. He must pour forth words of Torah and prayer until all his blood has been turned into words of holiness. Then he will attain peace and his urge to argue and dominate will disappear (75).

21) One who restrains his impulse to take part in disputes will be worthy of being quoted by name for his legal rulings. After his passing he will dwell in both worlds, the World to Come and this world, where his name will still be mentioned. It will be as if he is not dead at all (145).

22) Arguments and in-fighting make it difficult for a person to pray and speak words of holiness. This is why before we begin our prayers we must take upon ourselves the mitzvah of "love your neighbor as yourself" (Leviticus 19:18) in order to draw love and peace into the world. Peace is the root and source of speech (239).

23) Factionalism can cause even truly religious people to start having doubts and questions about their faith (251).

24) A person who is involved in a controversy can be thrown down from his level. He has to be very determined and pray profusely and plead with God not to let him stray from his path because of this (258).

25) When a person is involved in a dispute he should never get up and say that whatever his opponent does to him he will do to his opponent in return. This will only help his opponent achieve what he wants, which is to see his victim suffer. The best thing is to judge his enemies in the scale of merit, and even to do them favors where he can. This is the best way to foil their intentions. In the

end their evil intentions will all come back on their own heads (277).

26) This applies when one's opponents are not good people. But when they are Tzaddikim there is no doubt that their only intention is to benefit him. Their very opposition has the power to raise him up and sweeten any harsh decrees which may have been made against him. This is why they oppose him in the first place. A person must understand that when he is confronted with opposition from Tzaddikim, it is only for his benefit. He must pray to God not to allow him to fall into the error of thinking this is real hostility, because if he does it can arouse genuine opposition from the forces of the Other Side (*Ibid.*).

27) Strife brings poverty. It also prevents people from being healed. Peace brings healing and prosperity to the world (*Ibid.*).

28) When the world is afflicted with wars and bloodshed it can cause the rains to be withheld and bring about high prices (*Ibid.* II, 60).

29) When men abuse the honor of God it causes factionalism (71).

30) The whole world is filled with quarreling. Nation disputes against nation. Every city has its factions. Each household is locked in arguments with the neighbors. Within the household the husband argues with his wife, with the children and the servants. And so on and so on. Nobody thinks about what the ultimate goal of the world is. Every day man dies — because the day that has passed will never come back, and each day he draws closer to the day of his death. How can he waste his time on arguments? Anyone who has any sense should understand this and win long life for himself. Let him not waste his life on quarrels, big or small. He should control himself, hold his anger in check and live peacefully with everybody (Rabbi Nachman's Wisdom 77).

BARRIERS מניעות

1) All the barriers and obstacles which confront a person have only one purpose: to heighten his yearning for the holy deed which he needs to accomplish. It is part of man's nature that the greater the barriers standing in the way of a certain goal, the more he desires to achieve it. When a Jew needs to do something whose purpose is to strengthen his very core, especially when it is something upon which his whole being as a Jew depends — to travel to the true Tzaddik — he is given desire from above. The desire is created through the barrier which is sent to him, and the barrier itself causes his yearning to grow. You should understand, therefore, that there is no barrier in the world that you cannot break if you want to. The entire purpose of the barrier is only to increase your desire. When you achieve the necessary desire and yearning for the holy act you need to accomplish, you will surely succeed in transforming the idea which is in your mind into an actual reality. The barrier itself can bring you to succeed by strengthening your desire to do so (66:4).

2) The greater the goal for which you yearn, the bigger the obstacles and barriers which are sent in order to strengthen your desire. For desire is in proportion to the magnitude of the barriers. From this you can understand that if tremendous barriers spring up on every side as you start to draw near to the Tzaddik, it is an indication of the importance of the goal you wish to achieve. There are always difficulties and obstacles when you try to do anything holy. This is especially true when you want to make the journey to the true Tzaddikim because this is the foundation for everything else. Obstacles appear like at no other time. There are many Tzaddikim. But there is a single point of

truth to be found in their midst. When you seek to draw closer to this point of truth — and everything depends on this — you will find obstacles and barriers springing up and confronting you on every side. You need fierce determination: you must strengthen your desire and will-power in proportion to the greatness of the goal you are aiming for. Then you will succeed in breaking the barriers and attaining your goal. There is no barrier in the world which a person cannot break, so long as he has the desire and will-power to do so (*Ibid.*).

3) Nor should a person try to find excuses and exempt himself. It may well be true that the desire and yearning to achieve something holy are good in themselves, and that even if the barriers prevent him from accomplishing the holy deed in actual fact, it will still be accounted to him as if he had achieved it because his *intention* was good. The Sages did indeed say that "If a person intended to do a mitzvah but was prevented from doing it, it is accounted to him as if he had done it" (*Berachot* 6). This applies to someone who wants to feel that he has at least fulfilled the minimum that was required of him. After all, what could he do? He *wanted* to succeed, but circumstances prevented him! But it is different for someone who does not merely want to feel he has done his duty but actually wants the mitzvah or the holy deed itself. What good is it for him to know that as a special concession it will be accounted to him "as if" he had achieved it because he had the *desire* to succeed? This "as if" will not give him any satisfaction at all. He yearns for the mitzvah itself, he will not be satisfied with a mere "as if." For a Jew, the true goal is to accomplish what he wants and desires in actual *fact* — to transform the thought in the mind into a practical reality. When a person has true desire he can certainly achieve this and break every barrier or obstacle which stands in his way. The only reason they were sent to him was to heighten his yearning. When the desire matches the preciousness of the goal, he can achieve every holy deed that he yearns for (*Ibid.*).

4) There are people who after a whole life time of materialism suddenly feel a strong desire to walk in the paths of God. The

attribute of Judgement then rises up to accuse them. It tries to prevent them following the way of God by creating barriers. The unintelligent person, when he sees these barriers, starts to retreat. But someone with understanding takes this as the very signal that he should draw closer. He understands that God is to be found in the barrier itself — and the truth is that God Himself is indeed hidden in this barrier (115).

5) It may take a lot of effort for a person to break the barriers confronting him when he starts to draw closer to God. Many people experience opposition from their parents or parents-in-law, their wives and so on. But all their effort produces a vessel. Within this vessel he can receive the holiness and purity he will attain thereafter. The greater the struggle one has at the outset, the greater the vessel one forms. In the end he will be worthy of true fear of God, and he will receive abundant blessings and goodness. He will be worthy of giving perfection to the Holy Name of God, because the essence of its perfection is founded on religious awe (185).

6) The way to begin serving God is to imagine there is no one in the entire world except for you. Pay no attention to anyone who puts obstacles in your way, whether it is your father or mother, your parents-in-law, your wife, your children or anyone else. There are certain people who can make things difficult for you through ridiculing you or offering temptations and so on. Pay not the slightest attention to any of them. It is written that "Abraham was one" (Ezekiel 33:24) — Abraham was alone! You must also be alone — as if you were the only one in the world (*Likutey Moharan* II, Forward).

7) People often imagine that the barriers they experience in their efforts to serve God are so great that they will never be able to break them. But this is not true. No one is ever confronted with barriers he cannot break if he really wants to. God only sends a person obstacles that are within his capacity to overcome if he is really determined enough. If he thinks about it carefully, he will realize that the obstacle is really a veil for God Himself. In reality there are no obstacles at all. They are simply an illusion (46).

8) The greatest barriers of all are those in the mind. The heart is slippery. People do not concentrate their entire heart and mind on the true importance of what they need to achieve. For example when someone wants to travel to the Tzaddik and starts experiencing difficulties, if he really concentrated his whole heart and mind on the fact that his entire life and being and that of all his descendants depend on his reaching his goal, nothing in the world could stop him. None of the barriers would be of any significance at all in his eyes. The main barrier is that people are not firm in their own minds. A person may have reached the Tzaddik in spite of all the obstacles. But if some little doubt then arises in his mind and his heart begins to falter as a result, this is the biggest obstacle of all. The same is true of prayer. There are many barriers to prayer. A person may succeed in overcoming all of them and praying as he should. But once doubts about God or about the Tzaddikim arise in the crookedness of his heart, this is the worst obstacle of all. The way to fight it is to cry out to God with a voice which rises from the very depths of the heart (*Ibid.*).

9) The main thing is that your heart should be strong and firm. Then nothing at all will stop you, certainly not material difficulties — financial difficulties or opposition from your wife and children, your parents or parents-in-law, or the ridicule of other people and their attempts to persuade you otherwise. None of these things will have any power at all if your heart is firm and strong in God (*Ibid.*).

10) When a person's heart is firm there is nowhere in the world that he cannot serve God. There is never an excuse to say that in a certain place it is impossible to serve God. When a person's heart is strong, all the places in the world belong to him (*Ibid.* 51).

MIKVAH מקוה

1) Immersing in the *mikvah* is the cure for all troubles. The *mikvah* has the power to purify us from every kind of sin and impurity. The spiritual power of the *mikvah* is rooted in the most exalted levels of wisdom and love (56:7).
2) Immersing in a *mikvah* helps to make it easier to earn a living and receive the flow of blessing. Strife and anger are dissipated and in their place come peace, love, deep wisdom and healing, length of days and the power to arouse men to God (31:2).
3) Immersing in a *mikvah* is not in the least bit harmful. Any doctor who says it is is no doctor at all. So long as the water is not excessively cold, immersing in a *mikvah* is actually very beneficial to the body since it opens the sweat glands, as is known by medical experts (*Ibid.* II, 123).

FESTIVALS & SEASONS מועדי ה'

Shabbat

1) The custom of washing in hot water in preparation for Shabbat is *tikkun habrit.* The same is true of the practice of reading over the weekly Torah portion twice in the Hebrew and once in the Aramaic Targum (*Likutey Moharan* I, 19:5).

2) Shabbat observance is the foundation of genuine faith. All the acts of charity and other good deeds that we do are invested with radiance and perfection only in virtue of the Shabbat, because Shabbat is the very embodiment of faith. Charity has the power to bring an abundance of blessings and holy influences into the world, but they only become manifested in actuality because of the Shabbat. As the embodiment of faith, Shabbat is the fountain of blessings. Shabbat brings everything in the world to its ultimate perfection. Without Shabbat, and the faith it brings with it, all things are lacking. This applies also to our *Da'at*, the understanding we have of Godliness and our knowledge of Torah. True wisdom and the understanding of Torah can blossom only through the influence of Shabbat and of faith (31:2).

3) In order to experience the essential holiness of the Shabbat, namely true faith, it is necessary to observe the Holy Covenant in purity. There is a deep connection between Shabbat and the Covenant, which explains why it is customary to go to spend Shabbat with Tzaddikim. The holiness of the Tzaddikim derives from the fact that they guard the Covenant in purity, in all its aspects. People try to spend Shabbat with them in order to experience the true holiness of Shabbat and deepen their faith (*Ibid.* 3).

4) One should try to draw the holiness of Shabbat into the six working days of the week and sanctify them also. The more the

weekdays are invested with holiness, the more the forces of evil — the "filthy serpent," the "end of all flesh," the "raging stormwind" etc. — are subdued. Through this, speech becomes elevated (38:7).

5) By making a vow and carrying it out immediately you can come to experience the true joy of Shabbat, *oneg Shabbat*. The main joy of Shabbat comes from the food we eat in purity and holiness at the three fixed meals and at other times during Shabbat. It is a mitzvah to eat all kinds of fine foods and special delicacies. Those who truly experience the joy of Shabbat can by their very eating on Shabbat reach spiritual levels which they could only otherwise achieve by fasting. They can conquer anger and reach such levels of understanding that the radiance of God shines in their very faces. All their enemies simply fall away before them (57:4, 6).

6) How precious and holy is the act of eating on Shabbat. It is completely suffused with Godliness without the slightest hint of impurity. The forces of the *Sitra Achra*, the "Other Side," have no share at all in the Shabbat food. Anger is conquered and the force of wild passion is uprooted and cast aside. Love and peace reign supreme (*Ibid.* 5, 6).

7) It is also necessary to give generously to charity. Then you will find a profound peace. The experience of the joy of the Shabbat food, together with acts of charity, brings about peace that "has a mouth." There is one kind of peace that "has no mouth." That is the state of peace existing between people who are nevertheless unable to speak to each other. But peace which "has a mouth" is the state of perfect peace where men talk to one another. For the lips are invested with a wonderful illumination when we eat on Shabbat (*Ibid.* 7).

8) On Shabbat the double portion of bread — *lechem mishneh* — which the Tzaddik enjoys is a double portion of Torah — *mishneh Torah*. Shabbat is a favored time for developing original Torah ideas: "two for every one." Shabbat spreads its influence over all the worlds and sends the light of its radiance to every level, bringing healing to the soul and the body (58:5).

9) The radiance which Shabbat brings into the world stirs men to return to God out of love. When this happens, relief and healing are granted to the righteous in place of the trials and suffering they had to endure previously. People come to see them in a new light, they begin to understand the true greatness and beauty of their souls, and they start to treat them with respect and dignity. In the individual also, the greater his purity — each on his own level — the greater the radiance and splendor that will shine from his soul, and the higher his standing will be in men's eyes. The greater his personal worth and purity, the more he will be able to absorb the teachings which the Tzaddik gives over on Shabbat in all their originality and freshness (*Ibid.* 7).

10) Through observing the Shabbat fittingly, the forces of evil and the *kelipot*, the "husks," are destroyed. The way to reach such a level of Shabbat observance is by making an effort to bring people closer to God and through secluded prayer and meditation before God, examining oneself and bringing oneself to a reckoning for all one's actions (59:1, 3).

11) Shabbat, the World to Come and truth are in essence all one concept. Through it the wicked are brought down and the true greatness of the Tzaddikim and those who are genuinely pious is revealed. When this happens the whole world draws closer to God and men begin to call upon His blessed Name. The faculty of speech becomes perfect. Speech becomes holy and people experience true prayer (66).

12) A person who experiences the holiness of Shabbat can attain true purity — which means to understand his own lowliness and to be so aware of the greatness of Israel that he is prepared to sacrifice his very life for them, as Moses did (79).

13) On Shabbat everyone experiences a certain enhancement of their perception of Godliness, and through this their capacity to give love to their fellow creatures becomes greater. For a person's capacity to give love is related to the degree of his perception. And when he offers love to others, he in turn receives love from Heaven (119).

14) We eat on Shabbat not to gratify our physical appetites, but in

order to open the channels of blessing for the other six days of the week (276).

15) Preparing special delicacies for Shabbat is the main way of honoring the Shabbat. The food of Shabbat is very precious: it has a unique holiness. We partake of Godliness itself. It is good to have ample to eat on Shabbat. This in itself can make up for having desecrated the Sabbath in the past (125; 277).

16) The good deeds and mitzvot which we perform during the six working days of the week lack the power to rise up and go before God until the coming of Shabbat. Then they all ascend and come before God Himself, and He has great delight from them — even from the mitzvot of ordinary people, which may be lacking the proper degree of care and concentration with which the divine commandments should be carried out. As all these good deeds and mitzvot ascend, the path to God is opened wide. It is our eating on Shabbat which actually brings about this ascent (*Ibid.*).

17) "And he begot a son. And he called his name Noah, saying: 'This one will comfort us in our work and in the toil of our hands...' " (Genesis 5:28-29).

Shabbat is called a son — Noah. It brings joy to the highest and the lowest. It brings comfort and happiness to all, and relief from harshness and depression. All the mitzvot which we perform on the six weekdays have a certain heaviness about them. But on Shabbat they are elevated and raised up from this heaviness, and they become suffused with joy. The holiness and joy of Shabbat can also be drawn into the six working days. This comes about through the praise and thanks we give to God, and also when we devote ourselves to the study of Torah law. This is the way to experience the joy of Shabbat on the weekdays also. Then we can have joy in God and perform all the mitzvot in joy even on the six working days. Those who reach this level are granted a vision of the simple unity which underlies all the diverse phenomena of the world. Everything is simply an expression of God's unity. There is nothing more wonderful than to attain this vision. It is something very precious in all the worlds above. Even in God's eyes it is precious (*Likutey Moharan* II, 2:5, 6).

18) The joy of Shabbat is really the gateway to true freedom. Through it you can reach the highest levels in the knowledge of God, free of all distractions and confusion. These levels of knowledge must be founded on genuine fear of God without any hint of foolishness. There are many kinds of fear. When someone is afraid of some earthly power or authority, this is "fallen" fear. Genuine fear of God, which is bound up with the knowledge of God, elevates us from the hold of "fallen" fear (17).

19) You should be very careful to feel nothing but joy on Shabbat. There is nothing to compare with the greatness and holiness of Shabbat. This is explained in many places in our sacred literature, for example the *Reishit Chokhmah*, (by R. Eliahu de Vidas) where the subject is discussed at the beginning of the section on "Holiness." Study this section very carefully. What is written there about the holiness of Shabbat will kindle a burning desire within you to celebrate Shabbat with true joy. For joy is the key to honoring the Shabbat. You must never betray the slightest hint of depression or anxiety on Shabbat. Treat yourself to all kinds of delights — the food you eat, what you drink, your clothes... whatever you can afford. The food of Shabbat is completely holy. It is purely spiritual and filled with Godliness. It rises to a place which is totally different from that of the food of the six working days. Make the effort to feel the joy of Shabbat and you will find true happiness (*Ibid.*).

20) To attain to the holiness of Shabbat is to reach the ultimate in knowledge, which is to reach the boundaries of the unknown (83).

21) Shabbat is one of the names of God. Shabbat is the light of the eyes which illumine the Holy Temple and the whole world. This is why those who observe the Shabbat will have their eyes opened and they will have the power to see into themselves and judge how far they have reached in their spiritual journey. They will be able to repent for all their failings and come to recognize the true greatness of the Creator. They will have the power of vision over the entire universe. They will be drawn to the innermost point of truth — the true Tzaddik and those with genuine fear of Heaven.

Their minds will be opened. It will be as if they are engaged in rebuilding the Holy Temple.
22) Through the merit of Shabbat the homes of Jews are saved from being burned down, God forbid (67).

Rosh Chodesh — The New Moon

1) The force which draws all the worlds to return to God has its root on Rosh Chodesh, the New Moon. On Rosh Chodesh the desire to return to God is felt over the entire creation. Even the sinners in hell cannot escape a certain feeling of contrition. They are drawn a little closer to God and feel a flicker of regret. They are forced to acknowledge the truth and feel ashamed of their wrongdoing (10:9).

The Three Festivals: Pesach, Shavuoth, Succoth:

1) The joy we have on the three major festivals can give us a share in the Inner Light of God. This brings new life to the soul and the mind, through which we gain our perception of God (30:6).
2) The truest joy comes from fulfilling the mitzvot, God's commandments. The more a person forms some estimate of the true greatness of God, the greater the joy he is able to feel with every mitzvah he performs. He begins to realize how privileged he is to perform the will of the Holy One, blessed-be-He, who alone is, was and will be to all eternity. The joy of all the mitzvot we perform throughout the year is collected together, as it were, on the three festivals. This is what makes up the joy of the festival. All the good points of all the mitzvot performed throughout the year are joined together and concentrated in the festival, and the joy becomes truly palpable. If we make an effort to search for the holy joy which is to be found in performing the mitzvot on the other days of the year, then this "festival joy" will be accessible to us every day of the year. But on the actual festivals themselves, the joy is something special. The Torah

itself commands us: "and you shall rejoice in your feast" (Deuteronomy 16:14). The joy of the festivals themselves is made up of the joy of all the mitzvot of the whole year. There are no limits to this joy (*Ibid.*).

3) One of the ways of breaking your pride is by honouring the festivals fittingly and celebrating them with joy and delight, with delicacies and fine clothes, whatever you can afford (135).

4) When you celebrate the festivals fittingly it is equivalent to going to visit your Rav and receiving his teachings. This is true even if you are physically miles apart! It works the other way around also. The more you bind yourself to the Tzaddik, the more you can experience the holiness of the festivals. Through this the forces of holiness are released from the grip of the *kelipot,* the husks, and restored to their true position. The power of evil and the rule of the heathens is thus overturned and destroyed (*Ibid.*).

5) On the festivals we should return to God out of joy. On each of the festivals the world is brought to judgement, as our Sages have taught (*Rosh Hashanah* 16). A time of judgement is a time for returning to God. Through repentance the forces of holiness are released from the hold of the *kelipot* and the final redemption brought nearer (*Ibid.*).

6) When a person is walking along and suddenly slips and falls so that everyone laughs at him and makes him feel embarrassed, it is a sign that he was not as joyous as he should have been on the festivals (235).

7) There are many different ways of honoring the festivals — with fine food and drink, with beautiful clothes, with pure and holy thoughts, with joy and open-heartedness, and so on. Through honoring the festivals you can attain to the knowledge of God and you can draw this knowledge down into the heart, which is the seat of passion and desire. The three main desires which are the root of all others are the desire for riches, the sexual appetite and the impulse to eat. Each one of the festivals has the power to counter one of these desires. Pesach counters the desire for wealth, Shavuot the sexual instinct, and Succot the

impulse to eat excessively. It is because the festivals have these special powers that one should be so careful to celebrate them with the proper respect. This is the way to be freed from these desires. Every Jew has the task of subduing and refining these aspects of his character. When he succeeds, he is open to experiences which are truly prophetic, and he can attain genuine prayer and true healing, and see the sparks of Mashiach. In the end he will come to rule over the angels, which is the very purpose for which the Jew is created and the ultimate destiny of Israel (*Likutey Moharan* II, 1).

8) The festival days cry out, proclaim and reveal the Will — God's Will, which rules over all. There is no such thing as the "inevitability of nature." Every festival commemorates the awesome signs and miracles which God performed on our behalf — all of them contrary to nature. Pesach commemorates the going out of Egypt. Shavuot recalls the giving of the Torah. And on Succot we remember the clouds of glory with which we were surrounded in the wilderness. Through these awesome signs and wonders it was revealed that everything comes about through the Will of God alone. There is nothing inevitable about nature at all. Only you must take care to direct your ear and heart to the holy message which is thus proclaimed. The more carefully you attend to this message the greater the festival joy you will attain. The way to attain this joy is through acts of charity and kindness (see *Tzedakah*). This is why we should give generously to charity before every festival — in order to experience the true joy of the festival (4:6).

Pesach:

1) The days of the month of Nissan are days of repentance like those of Tishrei (49).

2) Nissan embodies the concept of *tikkun habrit*, guarding the Holy Covenant. When you are joyous you can draw the spirit of Nissan, its joy and holiness, into the whole year. Thus you can make amends for abuse of the Covenant, and you will avoid impure experiences by night (*Likutey Moharan* II, 5:10).

3) The Haggadah which we recite on Pesach is a *tikkun* for the Covenant. The reason why it is recited aloud is because the voice arouses *Da'at*, the knowledge of God. So by reciting the Haggadah aloud we can experience a revelation of true *Da'at*. *Da'at* is itself the essence of redemption, because the exile in Egypt came about through the abuse of the Holy Covenant, which brought about the distortion of *Da'at*. The wine of the four cups which we drink on the first nights of Pesach is also a *tikkun* for *Da'at* and for the Holy Covenant (*Likutey Moharan* I, 20:10).
4) When you pray on Pesach you should cry out loud (201).

Counting the Omer and Shavuot:

1) Through the joy we have on Purim, clapping our hands and dancing, we are able to fulfill the mitzvah of counting the Omer properly. Then we are ready to receive the Torah on Shavuot, both the revealed and the hidden Torah (10:8).
2) Each day of the Omer period is associated with a different aspect of the Sefirot. And on that day everything which everyone in the whole world is talking about is purely an expression of the particular aspect with which that day is associated. A person with understanding can hear and recognize this if he pays attention to what people are saying (182).
3) The forty-nine days of the Omer period correspond to the forty-nine gates of repentance, and these in turn correspond to the forty-nine letters in the Hebrew names of the twelve tribes. It is through these letters and gates that we must make our return to God Almighty. The festival of Shavuot is the fiftieth gate. This is the gateway of *God's* "repentance" — when God himself returns, as it were. That is to say, He returns to *us* in love. It is possible to reach all these gates and open them by reciting the psalms. You should be careful to concentrate when you recite the psalms. Then you will be able to reach all forty-nine gates. During the forty-nine days of the counting of the Omer we have to cleanse ourselves of our impurity and return to God. Then

God will return to *us* on Shavuot (*Likutey Moharan* II, 73).
4) When we immerse in the *mikvah* on Shavuot we are connected with the highest levels of God's lovingkindness and abundant mercy, and we can attain awesome levels of perception of God. The illumination which radiates on Shavuot is a supremely exalted level of the Divine wisdom, fine and subtle in the extreme. And this wisdom is in itself an expression of God's lovingkindness and mercy. For love is bound up with wisdom and perception, as is explained elsewhere. It is a wonderful thing to experience the holiness of Shavuot, and in particular the *mikvah* of Shavuot — the *mikvah* of the fiftieth gate — which then becomes the wellspring of holiness and purity for Israel (*Likutey Moharan* I, 56:7).
5) Shavuot is the season of receiving the Torah. It is a time of new vitality. And it is a season that brings healing to the lungs. (The five lobes of the lungs correspond to the five books of Moses.) (266).

The Three Weeks:

1) In time to come, the קינות (*KINoT*) will be changed into תיקון (*TIKkuN*). *Kinot* are the poetic laments which are recited on Tisha b'Av. *Tikkun* is restoration (247).

The Month of Elul:

1) The dominant spiritual theme of the month of Elul is the *tikkun habrit,* the *tikkun* for the abuse of the Holy Covenant. A person who achieves this will find his true partner in life, a partner who will help him in his aspirations rather than fight against him constantly (*Likutey Moharan* II, 87. See also *Likutey Moharan* I, 6 for a discussion of the spiritual meaning of Elul.).
2) Elul is a specially favorable time to attain *Da'at*, knowledge of God. A person can come to know and understand what he did not know before. New clothes are fashioned for his soul and he is released from all troubles (21).

3) Elul is the time to "circumcise the foreskin of the heart" (cf. Deuteronomy 10:16). Only then does a person have the sensitivity to feel real pain in his heart over the sins he has committed. His sensitivity will become so acute that the very hearts of all the drops of seed he cast away will also feel the pain, no matter where they may have fallen. They will all rise up in a great commotion and also return to God (141).
4) Elul is the time most suited to *teshuvah*, the return to God. It is a period of Divine favor, because it was at this time that Moses went up to receive the second tablets and opened a wide path towards God. The key to this path is to understand that God is present in every place and every situation. No matter how far you may have fallen, God is with you there just as much as He is present in the heights of the universe. In fact it is equally important to remember that He is present in the heights, because there are times when a man rises — for example if he becomes wealthy — and then forgets about God. There are even cases of people who have climbed to very high levels of religious devotion only to turn into atheists in the end. You should pray to God not to let you come to any harm as you draw closer to Him. On the other hand, no matter how low you may have fallen, even to the lowest of levels, even to the Ten Crowns of Impurity themselves, you must still bind yourself to God from there. Because His dominion extends over everything (*Likutey Moharan* II, 82).

Rosh Hashanah — The New Year:

1) Anyone who hears the sounding of the Shofar on Rosh Hashanah from a man of true piety can be assured that he will not be afraid of thunder the whole year (5:3).
2) The blasts of the Shofar on Rosh Hashanah revitalize the soul and intelligence of every Jew. Each one receives a new soul and a new level of understanding, each according to his level. This new soul and vision are drawn from the inner countenance of God (35:6).

3) The blasts of the Shofar sweeten the severity of God's judgement (42).
4) The purpose of sounding the Shofar is to arouse men from their sleep and prevent them whiling away their days in slumber. When people are aroused from their sleep, the power of speech bursts forth with tremendous strength. This in turn leads to trust, and those who were barren give birth. Then men are brought to the true fear of Heaven and released from sexual lust and the futility of superficial attractions and the "charm that deceives" (cf. Proverbs 31:30). Instead they attain "fullness of days" in holiness: they learn to lengthen every day of the rest of their lives by adding ever greater holiness and purity. This brings them true spiritual riches and the ability to reach the very heights of contemplation and perception of God. All of this is possible through hearing the blasts of the Shofar from the Tzaddikim, who understand how to accomplish these *tikkunim* (60:9).
5) It is customary to go to the Tzaddik to celebrate Rosh Hashanah. Rosh Hashanah is first and foremost the Day of Judgement. But no matter how great the severity of the judgement and no matter where in the world it threatens, everything is sweetened when Jews gather around the Tzaddik on Rosh Hashanah. With so many Jewish souls gathered together and merged in abundant love, a wonderful joy and delight come into the world (61:7).
6) To explain more about the importance of celebrating Rosh Hashanah with the Tzaddikim, you must understand that the sweetening of harsh judgements comes about when thought is purified and sanctified. This can only be achieved through being attached to the Tzaddik. Rosh Hashanah is the source of the harsh judgements of the entire year. The way to sweeten them is by purifying our thoughts. It is in order to attain sanctity in thought that we journey to the Tzaddikim (211).
7) God gave Rosh Hashanah out of great kindness (*Likutey Moharan* II, 1:14).
8) Who is able to celebrate Rosh Hashanah? He who is worthy

of binding himself to the roots of the souls of Israel (*Ibid.*).

9) The effect of Rosh Hashanah is to strengthen faith. There are great gatherings of Jewish communities everywhere. Especially significant are the gatherings of Jews around the true Tzaddikim. Through these gatherings, all the different facets of faith expressed in all the different souls are joined together in a common whole. They are refined, unified and elevated. The sparks of new intuitions and perceptions flash forth. New levels of understanding begin to develop. The process continues during the Ten Days of Repentance, when we work on ourselves and strive to return to God. The sparks of intuition and perception are embodied in the mitzvah of *tefilin*, which are the "seal of holiness" and an aspect of *tikkun habrit* (see *Tefillin*). Yom Kippur is the climax of the process. The "seal of holiness" is perfected, and the flashes of intuition and perception reach their fullest development. Following this, on Succot the illumination which must be drawn into the world is that of Joy. Through joy we can elevate all the food we eat to prevent it from disturbing our dreams and causing impure experiences at night. On Shemini Atzeret, the Eighth Day of Solemn Assembly, the spiritual work is to bring integrity to the faculty of judgement. If the judges are not honest it can cause unclean occurrences at night. All the *tikkunim* which have been mentioned here are also brought about whenever the followers of a spiritual leader gather at his side. Rosh Hashanah is the main time for such gatherings because the source of the entire process of *tikkun* is to be found then. In fact the very details of the Rosh Hashanah ritual, and in particular the different notes blown on the Shofar, all have the power to bring about these *tikkunim*. Thus the first note we blow, *Tekiah*, has the effect of strengthening faith. The second, *Teruah*, causes new intuitions and perceptions to flash forth. And through the third note, *Shevarim*, we are protected from having disturbed dreams and being corrupt in our judgements. This preserves us from impure experiences at night (5:15).

10) On Rosh Hashanah you must force yourself to put all your

power and strength into your prayers, and you must bind them to the true Tzaddik. The Tzaddik is the real "strong man": through his spiritual powers he is able to offer his prayer in such a way that the prayer itself is on the level of "judgement."

And this is precisely the form of prayer that is necessary on Rosh Hashanah. Through this it becomes possible to extricate from the forces of the Other Side all the holy life—force which they have snatched from the Jewish people and swallowed: all the prayers, the acts of kindness and the wisdom of the Jews... The forces of the Other Side are compelled to vomit them out from their very innards. This is brought about through the strength of the prayers of this "strong man," the Tzaddik. Then the glory of God is revealed in its fullness through the converts who attach themselves to the faith of Israel. Prophecy and true faith enter the world and false ideologies are destroyed. This is a foretaste of the wonderful renewal of the world which is destined to come about in the future. In the new order, the force of nature will be nothing. The world will be governed through the providence of God alone, with miracles and wonders. Then we will be worthy of hearing the sound of the song and the melody which will break forth in time to come. This will be the chief delight of the World to Come (8:11).

11) During the Days of Awe it is a good thing when you can weep profusely like a child. Throw aside all your sophistication. Just cry before God — cry for the diseases of the heart, for the pains and sores you feel in your soul. Cry like a child before his father. Then you will be worthy of a beautiful *etrog*. The more profusely you weep the more beautiful the *etrog* you will have for Succot. (Rabbi Nachman's Wisdom 87).

12) On Rosh Hashanah you must be *wise*. This means that you should be careful to think only good thoughts. Then God will be good to us and give us a good year. On Rosh Hashanah you must be joyous... and on Rosh Hashanah you must weep (*Ibid.* 21).

13) On the first day of Rosh Hashanah people should be very

careful to speak as little as possible. The greater the person the more careful he must be (*Ibid.*).
14) The day before Rosh Hashanah is a good time to present a redemption (*Ibid.* 214).

Yom Kippur — The Day of Atonement:

1) The Day of Atonement contains all days and gives life to all days. On this day the heart is subdued. Our desire is for God alone. All kinds of disputes, spiritual or material, are resolved. Peace comes, bringing happiness and joy (179).
2) Yom Kippur concludes the process whereby the "seal of holiness" is secured and protected (See *Rosh Hashanah* 9).
3) On Yom Kippur we appeal to God to "Forgive!" This cry of "Forgive!" opens up the gate of the holiness of Chanukah, with its theme of the consecration of the Holy Temple (see *Chanukah* 4).
4) There is a custom of referring to the day after Yom Kippur as "the Name of God." This is because the true greatness of God is revealed after Yom Kippur. On Yom Kippur God is reconciled with Israel and forgives them for all their sins. As a simple consequence, all harsh decrees and punishments are lifted — and it is through this that God's greatness is revealed (*Likutey Moharan* II, 66).

Succot:

1) The mitzvah of *succah* can bring us to experience the radiance of God's abundance through *ruach hakodesh*, the spirit of holiness. This experience is a special state of enlightenment granted to certain people when they are worthy of contact with levels of Godliness that transcend the levels of attainment they have reached through their own efforts. For there are levels of Divine wisdom that are granted to people simply through God's beneficence, without their having to work to acquire that level specifically. Indeed man's whole task in this world is to work on

himself until he is worthy of being granted these transcendental levels. This is the true joy of the World to Come (21:3).

2) The merit of the mitzvah of *succah* brings purity of heart. When your heart is pure it is easy to express yourself before God. You will always find new and original words and prayers (156).

3) The *succah* is a *segulah* for having children. The *succah* brings relief from strife and divisiveness. Falsehood is cast aside and truth gains the upper hand. The true Teacher of the age is revealed, and the whole world comes to return to God and "serve Him with one consent" (Zephania 3:9) (*Likutey Moharan* I, 48).

4) Intense prayer, the Land of Israel, and the mitzvah of *succah* are in essence one concept. The three ideas are interdependent (*Ibid.*).

5) A person who is negligent in fulfilling the mitzvah of *succah* closes himself off from the beneficence that God bestows upon *men.* Instead he falls to the level of an animal, receiving only what animals receive. This causes the death of cattle and other animals before their proper time, God forbid (266).

6) A person who fulfills the mitzvah of *succah* fittingly can engage in building without running the risk of being harmed. Building is a dangerous occupation, but the precept of *succah* gives protection (*Ibid.*).

7) From the *succah* comes Torah. Therefore when we enter the *succah* we become suffused with Torah (*Ibid.*).

8) The mitzvah of the four kinds, the *lulav, etrog, hadassim and aravoth*, brings about a relevation of *Da'at*, the knowledge of God. Through the mitzvah of the four kinds we can come to realize how the whole earth is filled with God's glory. We can see Godliness everywhere, even in the languages of the gentiles. People on every level, even the lowest, can come to acknowledge God and draw closer to Him. This mitzvah helps us to bind our hearts to the knowledge of God and in this way to bring the heart under our control. This is what brings us to love God — and through loving God we show the truest love to ourselves.

Then we can rise to receive the light of the love which is in *Da'at*. This is the "hidden light" stored up for the righteous. Through glimpsing it, the hidden Tzaddikim and the hidden Torah are revealed, and abundant peace spreads forth in the world (33).

9) The *etrog* derives its beauty from the true Tzaddik. He is the "head of the house" over the entire world. It follows that if you acquire a fine *etrog* which has all the marks of beauty, you will be worthy of drawing close to the Tzaddik. You will be merged in him and your eyes will be opened. It works the other way also: if you are close to the true Tzaddikim, you will be worthy of a beautiful *etrog*, and in this way you will be able to fulfill this precious and awesome mitzvah fittingly (*Likutey Moharan* II, 67).

10) You should search far and wide for a fine *etrog* that has all the marks of beauty. You must weep and cry on Rosh Hashanah and Yom Kippur to be worthy of such an *etrog*. It is impossible for us to understand the great preciousness and profound holiness of the mitzva of *etrog*. The human mind is simply unable to fathom it. Know that by fulfilling this mitzvah in all its beauty you will be worthy of bringing closer the day when our holy Temple will be rebuilt in splendour and glory. May it be God's will to rebuild it speedily in our days, Amen (Rabbi Nachman's Wisdom 87).

11) For a discussion of Hoshanah Rabbah and Simchat Torah, see *Likutey Moharan* I, 74.

12) Shemini Atzeret brings about the *tikkun* of Judgement. In essence this is a *tikkun* for the holy Covenant (See Rosh Hashanah 9).

Chanukah:

1) Through the mitzvah of kindling the lights of Chanukah we acknowledge the glory of God. His glory is exalted and magnified in the world. Those who were distant from Him are stirred to return. We can attain true fear of Heaven, harmony in

the home and genuine prayer. Strife and malicious slander are banished and universal peace spreads in all the worlds (*Likutey Moharan* 14).

2) Through the mitzvah of kindling the lights of Chanukah we draw down holy *Da'at*, the knowledge of God, upon ourselves. This *Da'at* is "the goodly oil" (Psalms 133:) of *memory*, whereby a person at all times bears in mind that everything in this world, both in general and in particular, has meaning only in relation to the World to Come (See *Zicaron*) (54).

3) The days of Chanukah are days of thanksgiving and praise. Thanksgiving and praise are the essence of the delight of the World to Come. They cause the light of truth to shine: we can pray in truth and learn Torah in truth from the lips of the true teacher, and marriage unions are formed in truth. These three rays of truth send light to all the different facets of *speech* and bring the faculty of speech to perfection. Through this we are able to bring the sanctity and joy of Shabbat into the six days of the week. Then the simple unity of God is revealed. All these *tikkunim* are brought about by the kindling of the Chanukah lights, and the praise and thanksgiving which we offer on Chanukah. How precious it is if you achieve all this on Chanukah and bring about these awesome *tikkunim* (*Likutey Moharan* II, 2).

4) The appeals we make to God to "Forgive us!" on Yom Kippur help us to experience the holiness of Chanukah. The reason is that the theme of Chanukah is the consecration of the Holy Temple (*chanukat Beit Hamikdash*), and on Chanukah we draw the sanctity of the Holy Temple upon ourselves. But it is only possible to do this when our sins are forgiven, as they are on Yom Kippur. The great teaching which the Holy Temple embodies and declares to the world is that "The Lord, He is God:" in all His aspects He is One. This knowledge can free us from the hold of sin. Nowhere is God's love for Israel more clearly revealed than in the forgiveness of sin. When we radiate the holy knowledge of God's unity to our children and pupils in this generation and in all the generations of the future, we can

come to a vision of the transcendental levels of holiness, the holiness which is beyond this world and encompasses it. This vision is a foretaste of the joy of the World to Come. It is through the kindling of the holy oil of the Chanukah lights that we come to perceive these levels and then our very life and sustenance are drawn from the Supernal Will. We can be worthy of receiving an awesome revelation of God's Will and favor at the very time we are eating. We long and yearn and pine for God with a desire that has no limits. But only if you are close to a true teacher who is filled with genuine love can you come to attain these levels on Chanukah. How precious to find such a teacher (7:11).

Purim:

1) Our joy and clapping and dancing on Purim make us worthy of receiving the Torah in its two aspects, revealed and hidden. For the great revelation that came about through Mordechai and Esther was "receiving the Torah." Through this we are able to fulfill the mitzvah of counting the Omer in the proper way. The *kelipah* of Haman the Amalekite (may his name be blotted out) is crushed. The force of pride, idolatry and atheism is broken. Great faith, holy wisdom and true life and length of days are brought into the world. The severity of God's harsh judgements is sweetened, and all the harsh decrees against Israel are revoked (10:8).

2) Purim is a preparation for Pesach. Through the mitzvah of Purim we are protected from *chametz* on Pesach (*Likutey Moharan* II, 74).

MELODY נגינה

1) A holy melody gives strength to the forces of holiness. But the music of the *Sitra Achra,* the Other Side, damages these forces and lengthens the exile. It makes people stumble and traps them like birds in a snare. Be very careful never to listen to this kind of music at all. The musicians and singers who produce it have no religious intentions whatsoever. On the contrary, they only want to make money or become famous. Listening to this kind of music can seriously weaken your devotion to God. But the melodies played by a truly religious, God-fearing musician can be very inspiring. They can strengthen your devotion immensely (*Likutey Moharan* I, 3).
2) Studying the Gemarah at night is a protection against being influenced by the music of the Other Side (*Ibid.*).
3) A holy melody has the power to bring one to the level of prophecy. Music is the foundation of true attachment to God (*Ibid.*).
4) One who sings with purity has kingship and power. He has the power to do whatever he wants. He can give life or death to whomever he wants. But he must be careful to judge all people in the scale of merit so as not to destroy the world. For God desires lovingkindness, and He wants the world to endure (*Ibid.*).
5) When a person achieves moral purity, his voice is also purified. Simply through hearing the sound of his voice singing, God sees which enemy is oppressing us — which of the seventy nations with their seventy languages. Then God saves us from trouble. When a harsh decree is passed against the Jews, God forbid, and one of the nations rises up against us, it is very good to sing the song or anthem of that nation. When our cries and

singing are directed towards Heaven, it arouses God's love. He looks down upon us in our trouble and saves us from the people oppressing us (27).

6) From a person's voice you can tell whether he is powerful or not and to what degree. Everybody has a certain degree of power and influence, and it is recognizable in his voice (230).

7) Music sweetens the harsh judgements. When you sing the words of the prayers in a clear, bright voice, the Shechinah is robed in radiant garments, and this is how the harsh judgements are sweetened (42).

8) Man is endowed with an image-making faculty, which is one of the most powerful forces in his life, because it is through this that he forms his concepts. But because it is linked to the imagination, it is seriously prone to error. Good and evil are mixed up. But music played by a truly God-fearing player for the sake of Heaven has a wonderful power to subdue the wildness of the imagination, and the good is sifted from the bad. Such music has the power to lift you from depression and inspire you with joy. This is the way to develop a good *memory* — which means to remember at all times the goal of the World to Come and to understand the things God sends every day to draw you closer to Him. When you have a good memory, you are free of the deceptions of surface appearances (54).

9) There is a form of atheism from which there is no return. But the melody of the truly great Tzaddik has the power to raise up the souls which have fallen into this (64).

10) The miserable wailing of the songs of the wicked does a great deal of damage because people are easily influenced by them. But when the Tzaddikim sing these songs on Shabbat they elevate and purify them (226).

11) Music has a tremendous power to draw you to God. Get into the habit of always singing a tune. It will give you new life and send joy into your soul. Then you will be able to bind yourself to God. It is especially good to sing on Shabbat and the festivals, and at a wedding celebration (273).

PATIENCE סבלנות

1) To know that everything that happens to you is for your own good is to have a foretaste of the World to Come. The way to come to this realization is through talking out your heart and confessing your sins before a Torah scholar. Through this you will come to understand that everything that happens to you every day of your life is all for your good. Everything springs from the love God has for you. To be serene and patient regardless of what you encounter in life is the highest level of *Da'at*, the knowledge and understanding of God. You must have faith that everything is for your ultimate good (4:1, 3, 4).

2) All physical medicines are bitter, and the same is true in the case of the soul. The soul is healed through bitterness. You may have to overcome many obstacles and endure much suffering in order for your soul to be healed. With physical illnesses there are times when the body becomes so weak that the invalid cannot bear the bitterness of the medicines. The doctors despair of ever curing him and simply abandon him. Similarly, when a person falls under the influence of sin — which is the sickness of the soul — he may be unable to bear the bitterness of the remedy. There may seem to be no hope for him at all. But God is filled with love. When He sees that a person wants to return to Him but hasn't the strength to bear the bitter remedies made necessary by his own sins, then He takes pity and casts all his sins aside to save him excessive suffering. God sends him only as much as he can bear. Many people find that as soon as they try to return to God and follow the ways of the righteous, they suddenly encounter obstacles and hardship from every direction. At times it is impossible to bear the bitterness and overcome the

barriers. There have been cases where people were so discouraged that they fell back into their old ways, God forbid. But a person who truly desires to draw closer to God should have faith that whatever the bitterness or suffering he has to endure, everything is being sent to him out of love. If the suffering were really in proportion to the magnitude of his sins it would have been far greater. He would have been much too weak to bear it and he would have been totally lost. But God in His love only sends as much bitterness and suffering as a person can bear. This much he must bear, and it is certainly within his power to endure it (27:7).

3) A person must be at peace with himself. It is no good if the different aspects of his character are in conflict with one another. He must also achieve harmony in his relationships with the outside world. Regardless of whether things are good or bad, he must always look for God in whatever happens to him. He should not allow himself to be thrown off course by anything. He should have faith that everything he experiences day by day is a favor and a blessing. This applies even to his hardships and suffering. He should believe and know that everything is for his ultimate good. The sole purpose of all of it is to draw him closer to God, if he truly desires it. The same basic principle applies in his relationship with friends. He should love them and be at peace with them regardless of their behavior — even if they make things difficult for him. He should always try to judge them in the scale of merit and find good in them. He must interpret everything in a good light and remind himself that his friend's intentions were not as bad as he imagines. It is very important to strive for relations of love and peace with one's friends and with all Israel. The way to achieve this is through the Torah, which is called "peace", and through the Tzaddikim, who are also called "peace" (33:1).

4) When a person takes his hardship and suffering very badly it is because his power of understanding has been withdrawn and he fails to keep in mind their ultimate purpose, which is wholly good. If he were to concentrate on the true goal and purpose of

life he would see that far from being bad these difficulties have a very positive purpose, because God's intention is only for good. It may be that He wishes to remind him to return to Him, or to scour his sins and cleanse him through this suffering. When he understands that the end purpose is wholly good, he can even come to rejoice in suffering. It is significant that people have a natural impulse to screw up their eyes tightly when they are in pain — as if they were trying to focus on something far away. It is as if by screwing up their eyes they were trying to focus on the true goal — the World to Come, which is good and everlasting. The only way to concentrate on this goal is by averting one's eyes from the folly of *this* world completely (65:3).

5) A person who bears his suffering joyously will achieve new insights in his Torah studies, and when he does it is a sign that he bore his sufferings as he should (*Ibid.*).

6) A person must be long-suffering in all aspects of his character. He should never become angry or irritated over anything. No matter what he has to go through, he should bear everything patiently without being blown off course. He should let nothing make him lose his temper. He should endure everything with patience and simply do his own part to serve God with enthusiasm and joy. The way to achieve this level is through perfect faith, which is attained through the Land of Israel (155).

7) Something you should understand is that however acute your problems and difficulties may be, the very problems themselves always have an angle which in itself offers a solution. It is true that we always hope that God will turn to us in mercy and remove the problems completely. But if you think carefully about the problems themselves you will see that each one has a positive side to it too. If you always look carefully until you find this side of things, you will always be able to bear everything lovingly and nothing will ever disturb you. You will be able to use every experience as a means of drawing closer to God, and through this God will send you help (195).

8) In times of trouble and suffering, it is good to weep and cry before God. Through this we can gain *Da'at*, understanding, and

draw God's providence upon ourselves. The pain and suffering will then be less because the main reason they are hard to bear is that one lacks adequate understanding. It is necessary to understand that everything is under the eye of God and is sent only for our own good (250).

9) The reason why people have to endure opposition and even persecution is to bring them closer to God through this very experience. The more persecution and hardship they suffer the more they must turn to God for relief, because there is no other solution. This is how persecution and suffering bring us closer to God (II, 13).

10) There is no one in the world who does not suffer in one way or another. People have all kinds of hardships and difficulties. It may be the problems of making a living, their health or domestic troubles with their wife and children and the other members of the household. Nobody can escape a certain amount of pain and hardship, because "man was born to struggle" (Job 5:7) "for his days are vexation and pain" (Ecclesiastes 2:23). The only way to escape is to seek refuge in God and His Torah. It takes great patience to bear what one has to go through in life. As our rabbis said, "The medicine for suffering is patience." A wise man said: "For someone without a strategy, the best strategy is patience." All the sages discuss this at great length and warn us that this world is full of suffering and anguish without end. Man was not created to derive pleasure from this world. His task is to labor in this world in order to earn the World to Come. This is why we have to bear everything with patience, in the faith that it is all for our good. "Everything that God does, He does for good." We must take refuge in God and His Torah at all times and plead before Him for mercy. There is no other escape from the afflictions of the world except God, as it is written: "He is my refuge on my day of trouble." Even the lowest of the low can still take refuge in God, because God is to be found in all places, as we have explained at length elsewhere. As soon as a person takes refuge in God, no matter what the experience, it will turn out for good — and the good will be truly enduring (Rabbi Nachman's Wisdom 308).

BOLDNESS עזות

1) One kind of boldness is thoroughly evil. This is the unashamed self-assertiveness of arrogant people. For "the bold-faced will go to hell" (*Avoth* 5:25) and Abraham preferred exile rather than hell as the punishment for the sins of the Jewish people. All other sins are punished with exile, but the penalty for this kind of brazen arrogance is still Gehinnom. On the other hand, there is another kind of forcefulness which is essential for anyone who wants to come closer to God. It is impossible to draw closer to the Tzaddikim and sanctify oneself without it. It entails a certain firmness, determination and initiative. This is the quality the sages referred to when they said, "Be bold as a leopard" (*Avoth* 5:24). The people who oppose those who are truly righteous and who put every kind of obstacle in their way have a brazen arrogance which is "royalty without a crown." Whoever chooses life and truth needs the other kind of forcefulness in order to overcome these obstacles. His opponents have set their jaws firmly against him, and therefore he needs to set himself equally firmly against them. Only with determination is it possible to enter the gates of holiness (22:11).

2) This determination and forcefulness are also necessary in the fight against oneself — or rather, against the brazen arrogance of the body, which is itself so forceful when it comes to satisfying its own desires and has no sense of shame before the Almighty. The arrogance of the body makes it impossible for the soul to come down and draw closer to it in order to communicate something of her own spiritual perceptions. The soul has constant contact with the highest spiritual levels, but the body does not have an inkling of any of this because of its

dogged involvement with its own impulses. One should take pity on the flesh of one's body and break its dogged pursuit of desire. Then the soul will be able to draw closer and give the body a share in her own spiritual visions and perceptions. To stand up to this arrogance of the body requires the other, holy forcefulness and determination. The way to assert the spiritual power of the soul is with holy sounds — the sound of prayer and song, the sound of crying and sighing before God, the sound of the shofar or the sound of the voice of the true Tzaddik, and all the other holy sounds, even the sound of the jingling of coins in a charity box! These holy sounds have the power to break the arrogance of the body (*Ibid.*).

3) But at times a person may be on such a low level and his body so far removed from his soul that even when he groans and cries out to God the body does not hear the sound at all. It is so far removed from the soul that it hears only a confused and indistinct echo. This is because as soon as a holy sound is heard, it arouses the forces of the Other Side, and they are the source of the confused noise. Such a person may even hear the voice of the Tzaddik himself, but he does not hear the essence of his voice, only an indistinct noise, and the arrogance of the body remains unbroken. The body needs to be trained to hear the voice of the soul. It must be pressed into service by performing the practical mitzvot. And to hear the voice of the Tzaddik, the body must be made to participate in practical activities on his behalf. This is the way to train the body to listen to the voice of the sage and to the groaning and crying of the person himself. In the end, the arrogance of the body will be broken (*Ibid.* 7,8).

4) The way to attain this firmness and determination in pursuit of the holy is through joy. Joy and happiness are the main source of strength for one who wants to draw closer to God and serve Him. "For the joy of the Lord is your strength" (Nehemiah 8:10) (*Ibid.* 9).

5) Boldness is essential if you want to acquire Torah. You must be "bold as a leopard" to resist the people who put obstacles in your way. You must not be ashamed if they mock you. The

bolder you are, the more you will find new horizons in Torah. But a person whose boldness stems from arrogance will not discover truly original Torah concepts. The Torah he receives will be drawn from the forces of the Other Side. To be bold in a positive sense in pursuit of the holy is part of the very essence of prayer — and the level of Torah a person attains with his boldness will bring him to a corresponding level of prayer. It takes a certain daring, and even "impudence" to stand before God and ask Him for what we need, including even miracles. A person who feels ashamed when he thinks of God's greatness and his own inadequacies and failings will never be able to open his mouth at all. This is why it takes boldness to pray. The more firm and determined a person is in the face of the opposition, the higher the levels of Torah and prayer he will attain (30:8).

6) The bold have no share in Torah. And only the bold have a share. Those whose boldness is arrogance will have no share. Only those who are bold and determined for the sake of holiness will have a share (*Ibid.*).

7) People may mock at you or put obstacles in your way. But don't allow yourself to be put off by them, and don't become shy and timid. You may think they are better than you or on a higher level. It may even be true and perhaps they really are on a higher level. Even so, as long as your own motive is for the sake of Heaven you must be firm and bold in the face of those who are confusing you and keeping you from the path of life. This is the only way you will attain holiness. Even with the Rav himself you need to be bold. Don't be afraid to talk about anything you need to discuss with him. It is no good to be shy, for "one who is shy will never learn" (*Avoth* 2:6). The reason why some people are closer to the Rav than others is only because they took the initiative and therefore the Rav speaks with them more (171)

ADVICE עצה

1) Everybody has ideas about the way to live. But as far as the great mass of people are concerned, their ideas are all as bad as each other — they're all worthless. Don't pay any attention to their advice. And all the more so, be sure to ignore any guidance offered by wicked people. They are the enemies of truth and the source of everything corrupt and destructive. All they have to offer is the advice of the primordial serpent, which is the antithesis of the Holy Covenant. Anyone who follows it will be covered in filth. He will become alienated from truth, faith and prayer, and he will be unable to come to the Land of Israel. Have nothing to do with their ideas. Bind yourself to the true Tzaddikim and those who follow their ways. Their guidance is the "seed of truth." Through it you will be able to observe the Covenant in purity. You will attain goodness, truth, faith and prayer and be worthy of coming to the Land of Israel (7:3).
2) Observing the mitzvah of *tzitzit*, the fringes, carefully is a protection against the "advice of the serpent." One who fulfills this mitzvah carefully will be guided only by the Tzaddikim (*Ibid.*).
3) Someone who lacks faith in the Sages will never know what he should do: he will always be racked with doubts and he will have no idea what course he should follow (61:1).
4) When a person follows the guidance of the Tzaddikim, it sweetens the harsh judgements, and through this he will be helped and freed from his troubles. But if he fails to follow their advice, he may well come to grief, God forbid, and the responsibility will be his alone, as it is written: "The foolishness of a man perverts his way" (Proverbs 19:3). If a person does

follow the advice of the Tzaddikim, and later on things do not go well for him, he can be sure that this has been sent to him from above (143).

5) Cry from the heart and you will find true guidance. You must cry out to God from the very depths of your heart. The darkness will crack and deep counsel will be revealed. Through this your faith will be strengthened. In the end you will have perfect faith. Healing will come and great goodness will be brought into the world (II, 5:3).

THE EYES עינים

1) Seeing the face of the Tzaddik has the power to lift a person from depression and lethargy and free him of his evil impulses and all their ramifications (4:8).
2) The sexual appetite depends on the eyes. The *tzitzit* are "eyes." The mitzvah of *tzitzit* is a protection and a remedy against immoral impulses (7:4).
3) Falsehood harms the eyes physically and spiritually (51).
4) Be careful not to look at people with an evil eye. The evil eye brings death to the heart of the one who has it. There are several different kinds of evil eye. Some people are filled with envy when they see the success of others. Or there may be different reasons for looking at people with an evil eye. You should be on your guard against this. You must also pray earnestly to God to protect you from being harmed by the evil eye of others. If a person feels he lacks the strength to stand up to the evil eye without being harmed, he must run away in order to escape (54:4).
5) The evil eye is the source of forgetfulness: it impairs the memory and causes one to forget one's purpose in this world, namely to acquire the World to Come. He should remember his purpose every day of his life, and fix all his thoughts on the World to Come, both as a general concept and in relation to all the particular details of his life. But the evil eye kills the heart and it can no longer be directed to the World to Come (*Ibid.*).
6) One with an evil eye will not have a son to survive him after his death (*Ibid.*).
7) You must also guard your eyes against illusions. Their source is in the image-making faculty, which gives rise to fantasy and

imagination. Someone with a good eye must also guard against illusions. Even people with excellent vision can make mistakes when they look from a distance and things appear the opposite of what they really are. This is as true of the mind's eye as it is of the physical eye. For example someone may have the impression that his friend is not being honest or is behaving badly towards him. He may feel resentful in consequence and this can lead to friction. He may *think* that he has the highest of motives for taking issue with his friend. But the truth is that it all stems from an illusory impression. He has been led astray by his imagination, which has caused him to believe things about his friend that were fabricated and untrue. There are many other ways in which the eyes and the mind can veer from the truth because of mistaken impressions. The image-making faculty has the power to deceive even those who have a good eye. You must be extremely careful to avoid mistakes like this. The way to do so is by being careful not to speak badly of other people or even to listen to somebody else's malicious talk. *Lashon hara*, malicious gossip, gives strength to the image-making faculty and the power of illusion, and it damages the power of memory — the power to remember at all times that this world only has meaning in terms of the World to Come (*Ibid* 5).

8) It is good to judge even the wicked in the scale of merit. This is the way to be saved from the evil eye of the wicked. The reason why at times the wicked go unpunished and God raises His judgements far above them is purely for the benefit of the Tzaddik. God Himself judges the wicked in the scale of merit in order to save the Tzaddik from the evil eye of the wicked (55:3).

9) When a person sees the face of the true Tzaddik he can examine himself and see what progress he is making in the various aspects of his character. Then he can repent for all the shortcomings he finds (II, 67).

10) Merely to see the true Tzaddik is in itself a great thing. Admittedly it is even better to hear Torah from his lips. But even just to see him is also very good. When a person sees the Tzaddik and looks at himself in contrast, it brings radiance to

his mind and understanding, and through this he can receive greatness and attain new horizons in Torah, each individual in accordance with the power of his mind. He will achieve true modesty and humility and return to God. This is the enduring life of the World to Come (*Ibid.* 72).

11) Merely to see the face of the Tzaddik can help one change for the better and attain holiness (75).

REDEMPTION פדיון

1) When a person is sick, a redemption is the prerequisite of any cure. Only after the redemption has been made does the Torah give the doctor permission to cure (*Likutey Moharan* II, 3).
2) When a person fills the mouths of the Sages with wine, it is accounted to him like a redemption (I, 41).
3) Rising for the midnight prayer has the same power as a redemption (149).
4) It is a good practice always to give money for a redemption. This is the way to sweeten the power of harsh judgements at all times and be saved from them. Even when nobody in the house is sick and you have no particular problems, it is still good to present for a redemption in order to prevent any problems or sickness, God forbid (*Chayey Moharan, Avodat Hashem* 92).

TZADDIK צדיק

1) Whenever you pray you should have in mind that you bind yourself to the Tzaddikim of the generation. They alone know how to elevate each prayer to its proper place (*Likutey Moharan* I, 2:6).

2) In order to travel the path of holiness it is necessary to break all your bad characteristics. All the different character traits in a person stem from the four basic elements. You must speak out your heart before a Torah scholar and confess all your sins. The Sage will explain and clarify the way you need to go in accordance with the root of your soul (4:8).

3) There are three different stages involved in drawing closer to the Tzaddikim. By working through each stage it is possible to achieve the perfect *tikkun*. The first stage is *seeing* the Tzaddik, which negates the bad characteristics stemming from the mineral and vegetable elements — laziness and its related characteristics on the one hand and evil passions and desires on the other (*Ibid*).

4) The second stage is when one gives *charity* to the Sage. This releases him from the bad characteristics stemming from the animal and human elements — idle pursuits and malicious gossip on the one hand, and pride and its ramifications on the other (*Ibid.*).

5) The third stage is verbal confession before the Sage. It is through this that the Sage can direct you on the path of righteousness in accordance with the root of your soul. This is the most important stage, because through verbal confession you can be saved from everything (*Ibid.*).

6) Each time you are with the Sage you should talk out everything

in your heart. It is through this that you will come to be merged with the *Ein Sof,* and attain the knowledge that everything that happens to you is for your own ultimate good. Before we attain this knowledge, life gives the appearance of being a mixture: some experiences seem good and others bad, and we bless God accordingly. For the good we bless Him as "He who is good and does good." For the bad we bless Him as "the true Judge" But in time to come, when we will understand that all our experiences are only for good, we will no longer make this distinction. We will bless God for everything as "He who is good and does good" (*Pesachim* 50a). To attain this level is to have a foretaste of the World to Come (*Ibid.* 9).

7) When a person confesses before a Sage, all his sins are forgiven (*Ibid.* 3).

8) If you care about yourself, pay no attention whatsoever to the various disagreements between the great Tzaddikim. The fact that the Tzaddikim argue with one another should not be a reason for raising doubts about fundamental matters of faith. You must have faith in all the Tzaddikim. If you find their arguments cause you to have doubts, you should take the very arguments themselves as a personal message directed at you to prompt you to examine yourself and see what you are doing with your life. The doubts you have stem not from their disputes but from something you have done to your own mind. Their arguments are a way of alerting you to the fact that you yourself have harmed your mind with impure thoughts and actions. If you hadn't, you would never have found their arguments problematic in the first place, and you would have had no doubts or questions about the Tzaddikim at all. The purpose of their disputes is to benefit you and to help you remember where you are holding in the world. If you allow yourself to succumb to doubts, they will drive a wedge between you and your own stake in the true life of the spirit, which the Tzaddikim themselves embody. *You* will be the loser, because this is the penalty for abusing the precious drops of your divine intelligence with impure thoughts and deeds, and "None that go with her

return, neither do they attain to the paths of life" (Proverbs 2:19). If you are foolish and fail to understand this you run the risk of becoming completely alienated from the Tzaddikim and you will end up losing your reward in the World to Come. But if you care about yourself you will take these arguments and the doubts they arouse in your mind as a warning to bring you to your senses. You will reflect on your true situation in the world, and you will realize that these arguments have been sent as a test — which you must withstand by paying no attention whatsoever. Use this very test as a way of drawing closer to the Tzaddikim, because any hopes you have of finding fulfillment in life depend upon their guidance. You should understand that the main purpose of all the arguments between the Tzaddikim is only to create a trial for the benefit of those who according to the dictates of strict justice should really be rejected for having abused the drops of their divine intelligence. If they stand up to the trial and ignore the disputes, acknowledging the gravity of their previous wrongdoing, they will be able to draw closer instead of being rejected. Because of their wrongdoing, the only way they can now be drawn closer is by being tested. The truth is that God loves mercy and desires that those who are distant from Him should be drawn closer in spite of their being unworthy. But the only way they can be drawn closer is through being subjected to this test (5:4).

9) Draw close to the Tzaddikim and walk in the paths they guide you along. Follow their teachings, and then the truth will be inscribed within you and you will attain true faith and prayer and be worthy of coming to the Land of Israel and seeing miracles. This is how the redemption will come (7:3).

10) "Make the heart of this people fat, and make their ears heavy, and shut their eyes; lest they, seeing with their eyes and hearing with their ears and understanding with their heart, return and be healed" (Isaiah 6:10). Before a person draws close to the Tzaddik, his heart is fat, his ears are heavy, etc. This means that his heart and ears are shut and his eyes are blind to the truth. He is unable to come to his senses and return to God.

But when he binds himself to the Tzaddikim and follows their guidance, his heart, his eyes and his ears are opened. He sees, hears and understands the truth and becomes worthy of returning to God (*Ibid.* 5).

11) No matter what a person needs or is lacking in life — whether livelihood, health or anything else — it can only be provided through the help of the true Tzaddik and Teacher he is attached to. The reason is that the fulfillment of what we are lacking is through sighing and groaning. The sighs of a Jew are very precious, because through them he draws down the spirit of life and this alone has the power to make up for the deficiency and provide what is necessary. The source of the spirit of life is the Torah, and therefore it can be received only from the Tzaddik, who is totally bound to the Torah (8:2).

12) The enemies of the Tzaddik draw their life-spirit from the prince of the side of the *kelipot*, the husks. Because the *kelipot* and the forces of the Other Side have their own leader whose role is a kind of mirror-image of that of the Teacher on the side of holiness. For "God made the one corresponding to the other" (Ecclesiastes 7:14). The forces of the Other Side have their moment of greatness, because the life-spirit they draw from their leader — the so-called "raging stormwind" (Ezekiel 1:3)— is very powerful when at full force. But this is only for a short time. In the end it is totally spent and exhausted and ravages the body and soul of all who are caught in its hold. That is why they are called "dead" even in their lifetime — because they do not possess the true life-spirit of holiness which is drawn into the world by the Tzaddikim alone (*Ibid.* 3).

13) The Tzaddik hears the sighs of all who are attached to him, for he is the source of the life of each one (*Ibid.* 8).

14) The true Tzaddikim atone for sins, as it is written: "but the wise man will bring atonement" (Proverbs 16:14) (*Ibid.* 4).

15) It is vital for a person's prayer to rise through the gate of his tribe. But it takes great merit to be worthy of this. That is why one must bind one's prayer to the Tzaddik of the generation. He

alone understands how to direct each prayer to the appropriate gate and elevate it (9:2).

16) The Tzaddikim have the power to elevate prayer so that the power and kingship of God is revealed to all the inhabitants of the universe, even to those who are very distant — the wicked and the heathens. The true greatness of the Holy One, blessed-be-He, is revealed when even those who were very distant, even the heathens, come to recognize that there is one God who controls and rules the entire universe. Whenever a person has a problem — for example if someone at home is sick — he should go to the Tzaddikim and ask them to plead for mercy on his behalf. God receives great satisfaction from this, because He yearns for the prayers of the Tzaddikim. The secret of true prayer is known only to the Tzaddikim (10:2-4).

17) Pride is a form of idolatry. But closeness to the Tzaddikim undermines the pride within us and brings us to perfect faith and *ruach hakodesh*, holy inspiration. We can then experience a wonderful joy. We literally clap our hands and dance for joy. The harsh judgements are sweetened and we can attain wisdom, life, length of days and understanding of both the revealed and hidden Torah (*Ibid.* 5).

18) There are people who are very learned in Torah but speak very disparagingly about the Tzaddik. Yet this is also a part of God's plan. He throws a great Tzaddik down into the mouth of this scholar in order that the Tzaddik should be able to release the Shechinah — that is, the *Torah sheb'al peh*, the oral Torah — from its exile in the scholar's mouth. The Tzaddik forms laws out of his words and brings about great and awesome unifications (12).

19) You should search after a Tzaddik who has the power to gather in the souls and elevate them. Then your soul will be elevated with the others and renewed, and through this Torah will be brought down into the world and revealed. You must plead with God again and again to make you worthy of finding such a Tzaddik. He has the power to cleanse you of the blemishes caused by your desires and impulses and actually

elevate them. When a person has a certain lust, the desire itself is a blemish which embitters the soul, as it is written, "she was bitter in her soul" (Samuel I, 1:10) and "her soul was bitter" (Kings II, 4:27). The soul becomes dissipated and does not radiate. It is a "hungry soul" (Psalms 107:9). But by coming to the Tzaddik, a complete *tikkun* can be achieved. The Tzaddik has the power to purify and elevate even a person's negative desires together with his positive, holy yearning, as it is written, "The hungry person He fills with good" (Psalms *Ibid.*). "He will satisfy your soul in drought" (Isaiah 58:10) and "He will renew your youth like the eagle's" — which is to say that all the days of your youth, which were passed in darkness, will be renewed. The wrongs will be corrected and you will be worthy of the name Man. One's body is also elevated and renewed when he comes to the Tzaddik (13:5,6).

20) Each of the different people who come to the Sage of the generation has a certain yearning for good within him. The Tzaddik elevates all these good intentions and renews the souls of those who come to him. It is this that makes it possible for the Tzaddik to reveal the Torah which he teaches when they are all assembled. Every single one of them thus has a share in this Torah, each in accordance with his yearning, and through this his soul is renewed. Each individual must see to it that he works on himself and comes to the Tzaddik with the best intentions and a powerful yearning for God. Then his soul will be renewed with even greater strength. We also heard from the Rebbe that the most important moment is when the Sage is preparing himself to deliver his lesson. This is the time for those who are present to look into themselves and examine their lives and search for the yearning for God which is within them. The Tzaddik will then be able to take each one by the hand and raise him from his present level and renew him for good (*Ibid.*).

21) From this you can understand the tremendous difference between being physically present to hear the Tzaddik teaching and merely hearing about his lesson at second hand. When a person is physically present he actually has a share in the lesson

and his soul is renewed. There are also many other differences, as explained elsewhere (*Ibid.*).

22) Through going to the Tzaddik God's providence is drawn into the world (*Ibid.* 4).

23) The greater the number of souls gathered about the Tzaddik to hear his lesson and receive Torah, the more the breath of wickedness which blows over the earth is curtailed and nullified. The "breath of wickedness" is made up of all the arguments put forward by the atheists when they see that the just suffer and the wicked prosper (*Ibid.* 6).

24) It is a good thing when those who went to the Tzaddik to hear his teachings subsequently give each other encouragement in their spiritual growth and deepen their love for one another. This is a sign that they went to the Tzaddik in the right spirit and their new vitality is for good (*Ibid.*).

25) There are people whose souls are severely damaged. Even when they come to the Tzaddik they are still sunk in all their bodily desires and have not moved away from the profane and closer to the sacred by even a single hair's breadth. It might seem an impossible task to elevate these souls and renew them like an unborn child in the womb. But there is a Tzaddik who has reached the most awesome of levels and who does have the power to elevate even souls which are as severely damaged as these. He can renew them like a newly-formed child growing in the womb. A person who is aware of what he has done to his soul and who wants to take himself in hand and return to God should plead and beg of God to take pity upon him and make him worthy of drawing close to such a Tzaddik. Happy is he who finds such a Tzaddik (*Ibid.*).

26) Only through the Tzaddik of the generation is it possible to attain true awe and love of God. When a person is unable to experience true awe and love, it is because the light of the Tzaddik is hidden from him. It is true that the light of the Tzaddik radiates in all the worlds — and especially in this world. But for this individual there is no light at all because of the intensity of his own darkness. He could be in the same place as

the Tzaddik and even sitting right next to him and still not taste or understand or see the great light which radiates from the Tzaddik and could bring him to attain the true and enduring goal (17:1,2).

27) This is because of his wrongdoing. As a result his divine intelligence has become clouded over with foolishness and bankrupt ideas. He looks at himself as a sophisticated person who needs to raise various questions and entertain doubts about the Tzaddik. All these doubts and questions are completely senseless. His wrongdoing has left his mind clouded and dull and the light of the Tzaddik is hidden from him. This is why he does not have genuine awe and love of God (*Ibid.*).

28) When a person gives charity to the Tzaddikim and to poor people who genuinely deserve it, it restores and clarifies his mind and enables him to see the light of the Tzaddik and thus attain true awe and love (*Ibid.* 5).

29) Everything has a purpose, and this purpose itself serves another purpose, which is even higher. The most important thing of all is the ultimate goal to which everything leads: the joy of the World to Come. This is the final goal of the entire Creation. But no one except the Tzaddikim can in any way conceive of this ultimate purpose. To the extent that a Jew is rooted in the soul of the Tzaddik he too can attain some conception of this goal — depending on how far he has succeeded in breaking his anger with love. If he succeeds, he will come to a level where he can use everything in this world as a means of attaining this goal (18:1,2).

30) There are times when the Tzaddikim refuse all positions of authority and leadership and they are unwilling to guide the world. They attribute their unwillingness to their own smallness, saying they are not fitted to guide the world. But in reality their reluctance is an expression of God's anger and the hiding of His countenance, which comes about as a result of people's lack of faith. But by breaking the force of one's own anger, God's anger itself is sweetened and the Tzaddikim accept positions of

authority. The world then finds a true leader who will guide it with love (*Ibid.*).

31) People ask why it is necessary to travel to the Tzaddik and hear what he has to say directly. Is it not enough to study the *mussar* literature, which deals with spiritual development? In fact there is a very big difference, because someone who hears the Tzaddik himself receives the words of the Holy Tongue in all their fullness, and through the awe which is aroused within him he can subjugate and nullify the basis of all evil, which is the sexual impulse. Then he can achieve purity and observe the Covenant completely. *Tikkun habrit* is the *tikkun* for everything. But one who only hears at second hand, and especially one who merely reads a book, remains far from all this (19:1,9).

32) There is a great difference between one who learns from a book and one who hears from the lips of the Tzaddik himself. In the case of a person who was present to hear the Tzaddik in person, his soul was bound with the Tzaddik when the Tzaddik offered his prayers immediately before beginning the Torah lesson. This person therefore has a share in the Torah that was then revealed. Because the prayer of the Tzaddik brings about a great concentration of holiness in the worlds above, and every prayer which stems from many souls brings about even greater holiness and stirs the Supreme Heart so as to draw an even greater illumination of Torah into the world. Everything depends on the numbers of people present. The evil in those who were present at the time of the lesson is subdued through the goodness in the Sage giving the lesson. He releases them from the power of the forces of the Other Side and brings them into the sphere of holiness (20:4).

33) A person who is present when the Tzaddik teaches Torah in public will be worthy of coming to the Land of Israel and overcoming all opposition and obstacles (*Ibid.*).

34) The Holy One, blessed-be-He, is strict with the Tzaddikim to a hair breadth. If the Tzaddik makes the slightest false move — even no more than a hair breadth — he has no power to draw Torah into the world (*Ibid.* 5).

35) It is not possible to attain perfect faith — which is the basis of everything and the summit of holiness — except through being close to the Tzaddikim. It is the Tzaddikim who foster the authentic faith of Israel among the people of their generation. But the only way to draw close to them is with boldness and determination. There are certain types of people who put up all kinds of obstacles and barriers so as to prevent others from drawing closer to the point of truth. The source of their power is in the arrogant self-assertiveness of the forces of the Other Side. This is why it is essential for whoever wants to overcome these barriers to be bold and forceful in pursuit of holiness. This is the only way to attain holiness. The way to acquire forcefulness is through joy. It is this that gives one the confidence not to feel ashamed and deterred because of other people's mockery and contempt. He must be "bold as a leopard" (Ethics of the Fathers 5:24) against them (22:4).

36) When a person is bound to the Tzaddik he can free himself of the desire for wealth, which is a form of idolatry and death, and then he will be free of the bitterness of the world — all the worries and struggles involved in earning a living and making money. Most people's lives are consumed with such troubles. But the one who is bound to the Tzaddik will have joy. He will be content with his portion, and the light of the countenance of the King of Life will radiate upon him. But the opposite is also true. One who opposes the Tzaddik will fall ever deeper into the desire for wealth, and he will constantly be sunk in all the bitterness which goes with it. His days will be spent in the race for profit. Only through the strength of the true Tzaddik who observes the Covenant perfectly is it possible to be released from anxiety about money (23:2).

37) Man's whole purpose is to gain a perception of God. This is only possible through the help of a truly great Tzaddik. The Tzaddik must be on the highest of levels in order to be able to communicate such perceptions at a level where people can have some grasp of them. One should search hard to find a Tzaddik like this and pray to God earnestly to be worthy of drawing

close to him. The only way to gain any perception of God at all is by means of "contractions," through which the subject is brought down to the level where the mind of man can have some grasp of it. The Tzaddik knows how to present such perceptions in a way that makes this possible. He has the insight to understand how best to introduce the subject and explain all the different things that must be explained in order to enable the individual to grasp it, regardless of his level. Only through the guidance of the true teacher is it possible to reach a perception of Godliness (30:1,2).

38) You must look for the greatest possible teacher. Only a teacher who is on the highest of levels can convey to you a true perception of God in all its radiance. The lesser the person and the lower his level, the greater the teacher he needs. What he needs is a kind of master craftsman who has the skill to clothe the Highest Wisdom — the perception of Godliness — in a form communicable to one as low down and far away as he is. The sicker the invalid, the greater the doctor he needs. So don't delude yourself and say: "It will be sufficient if I find someone simple and upright, respectable and known to be God-fearing. Why do I need to set my sights high and attach myself to such a great Tzaddik? Let me at least make a start by emulating this person here." Many people make this mistake. Don't you. On the contrary, the more you realize how low you are and how far you are from God, the more you need to draw closer to the true teacher. Do not be content until you aspire to the highest of levels (*Ibid.*).

39) We should accept the criticisms of the Tzaddikim submissively, even if they sometimes speak to us in a way that seems abusive. We should realize the great pain they endure because of us. It is obvious that all our wordly activities and everyday talk are evil from their point of view. But even the part of our lives that we would consider the most holy and precious — our prayers and devotions — are also evil as far as they are concerned, mixed up as they are with improper thoughts and other distractions. They are a great strain for the Tzaddikim,

which is why at times they are very abusive in the way they criticize us. We must take their criticisms to heart. Then we will be worthy of God's love, and through this we will have the power to overcome false ideologies and heathen domination and elevate true wisdom and understanding to their proper place so as to attain the perception of Godliness (*Ibid.* 7).

40) The Talmud (*Chagiga* 14b) tells us about the four sages who entered the *Pardes*, the hidden wisdom of the Torah. There are also four corresponding types among those who draw close to the true Tzaddik. Rabbi Akiva entered the *Pardes* in peace and departed in peace. Similarly there is the follower of the Tzaddik who succeeds in learning the true path and follows it to attain perfect righteousness. Ben Azai "gazed and went mad," and Ben Zoma "gazed and died." Similarly there are those who become over-excited in their devotion to the Tzaddik and they can even die or go out of their minds as a result. Nevertheless, even people like this still come into the category of the righteous, of whom it is written, "the righteous will walk in them" (Hosea 14:10). But there is a fourth kind corresponding to "Acher"— (R. Elisha ben Abuyah) who ended up an atheist. So it is with one who becomes alienated from the Tzaddik and leaves him, and ends up as an enemy maliciously slandering the Tzaddik. "Acher", says the Gemara, "uprooted the saplings" — he influenced others to follow his own ideas. The true Tzaddik necessarily has the same powers that the Torah itself possesses: "It is an elixir of life and an elixir of death" (*Kiddushin* 30b). It is in the hands of those who follow the Tzaddik to draw from him what they wish, as it is written, "The righteous will walk in its paths and the sinners will stumble" (Hosea *Ibid.*). One who follows the Tzaddik can receive guidance about the right path to follow and the way to return to God, so long as he truly desires it. But if not, he will find himself on a tortuous path, because there is a basic impurity in his heart. To be sure, he will find in the Tzaddik what *he* wants — namely an excuse to turn to total atheism and be completely separated from God. For "sinners will stumble in them." (31:9).

41) Your devotion to the Tzaddikim and Torah will bring you to love God in all places and all situations, not only when things are good but even when they are bad. You will be at peace with yourself and at peace with the world. Within, you will have perfect harmony. And whatever is sent to you from the outside world, whether it is good or bad it will make no difference to you, you will always find God in it. Love and peace will reign between you and your friends, and in all Israel (33:1).

42) The true Tzaddik is the common "point" that includes all the individual points to be found among the whole Jewish people. This is why it is of fundamental importance to be attached to the Tzaddikim and to talk to them about serving God. The holy point contained within them — which includes and comprehends all the other good points — gives them the power to arouse your heart and send light into your soul. You should also discuss religious matters with your friend. Because every single Jew possesses a unique good point which is not found in any other, and from which his friend can receive inspiration. Each person must receive from every other, as it is written: "and receiving one from the other" (*Targum* on Isaiah 6:3). It is also necessary for each individual to talk directly with his Maker in order for the good point within his own self to be revealed and radiate from his mouth to his heart. This is to destroy the "foreskin of the heart" — the physical lusts and desires. They are called the "shame of the heart," which break the heart of man (34:4).

43) Power is in the hands of the Tzaddik. He can achieve whatever he wants. As our Sages said: "God asks, 'Who rules over Me? The Tzaddik does' " (*Moed Katan* 16b). The power of the Tzaddik is devoted to sending light into the hearts of the Jewish people and arousing them to serve God (*Ibid.* 2).

44) The light of the face of the Tzaddik can give you new intelligence and understanding, and create a new soul in you. Intelligence and understanding *are* the soul. What is the "face" of the Tzaddik? It is the new face of the Torah which the Tzaddik reveals, and this is the source of the new soul and

intelligence one receives from the light of the face of the saintly (35:5).

45) When the Tzaddik reveals Torah he creates new souls in his listeners, each one according to his level and grasp (36:5).

46) It is a very good practice always to give money to Tzaddikim and other pious people for a redemption.* This is the way to sweeten the power of harsh judgements at all times and be saved from them. Even when one has no specific problem, God forbid, it is still always good to give money for a redemption in order to sweeten the harsh judgements and avoid the onset of any problem (*Chayey Moharan, Avodat Hashem* 92).

47) When one "fills the throats of the learned with wine" it is the equivalent to presenting a redemption, and the harsh judgements are sweetened (*Ibid.*).

48) When a person has faith in the Torah Sages and believes that everything they say and do is far from being simple and straightforward but contains deep secrets, this brings about the sweetening of harsh judgements (42).

49) When a person makes a beautiful garment for a Tzaddik, it sweetens the harsh judgements (*Ibid.*).

50) It is a fundamental principle that one should have faith in the Sages and be punctilious in showing them the honour and reverence due to them. Even if he has the impression that they are acting contrary to the Torah, he should still have absolute faith that they are really acting in complete accordance with the Torah. Because the Torah was entrusted to the Sages of each generation to interpret in accordance with their wisdom. That is why one must cast aside one's own pretensions to intelligence and understanding and rely on the Sages alone (57:1).

51) The cure for every disease is dependent upon the Torah. Now the Torah has been entrusted to the Sages, and we have been commanded to listen to them and not to turn aside from their words either to the right or the left. Anyone who derides the words of the Sages and refuses to believe in them because he

* See *Pidyon*

thinks they are in conflict with the written Torah will be afflicted with a disease which has no cure, and he will die from it (*Ibid.*).

52) The remedy for someone who has lost his faith in the Sages is to make a vow and fulfill it immediately. Through this his faith in the Sages will be restored and he will be healed, and the light of our forcfathers, Abraham, Isaac and Jacob will radiate within him. He will be able to experience the true delight of the Shabbat, which is to eat the Shabbat food in holiness. This is the way to break the force of one's anger and humble and overthrow all one's enemies and opponents. The stronghold of the forces of the Other Side will fall, the Mashiach will come and the stronghold of holiness will be rebuilt (*Ibid.* 2).

53) The true Tzaddik is "Moses," who was himself the embodiment of the three forefathers, Abraham, Isaac and Jacob. The Tzaddik is thus the channel for the influx of the three kinds of blessing which come into the world: "the well," "the cloud of glory" and "the manna" — drink, clothing and food, respectively. The Tzaddik constantly fights God's wars, because he struggles against the husk of Amalek, the negation of the Holy Covenant and the source of all impurity. It is the Tzaddik who humbles Amalek and all the other enemies who pursue those who are weak among the Jews. The Tzaddik gives these Jews strength and helps them to start serving God and purify themselves. The Tzaddik himself receives a double share of blessing — the two loaves (*lechem mishneh*) of Shabbat, which means the double share of original Torah teachings (*mishneh Torah*) which the Tzaddik gives over on Shabbat — "two for every one." This brings healing to all in both body and soul, and the world is aroused to return to God out of love. Healing comes to the pious, and people begin to respect them. Then there is a share for everyone in the original Torah teachings — the hidden Torah — which the Tzaddik reveals on Shabbat (58).

54) When you have faith in the Sages, your mind will be purified and your intellect clear. You will be able to derive a personal lesson for yourself from everything you learn in the Torah and develop the right habits and practices in serving God. You will

know how to act in every situation, and you will be able to guide all who come under your influence. But those who lack faith in the Sages must suffer the torments of the flesh — the "superfluities." Stinking vapors rise up to their brains and distort and confuse all their thoughts. Far from being able to learn the right way to live, all their Torah studies give them the exact opposite of the truth. They never have a clear idea about anything. They are constantly afflicted with doubts and pulled in all directions at once. When a person has no faith in the Sages, his heart becomes as filthy as a privy, all his thinking is warped, and he never knows how he should act in any situation (61:1).

55) The obstacles and difficulties which a person encounters from others are sent to him because his faith in the Sages is weak. It may be that he does not fully accept that the great Tzaddikim were the true Sages, and he regards their holy words and writings as being at best of merely incidental interest. He may even go as far as to make fun of them and scoff. The weaker his faith, the greater the obstacles and difficulties he will have to encounter. Their purpose is to rouse him to reflect. One should realize that one's problems and difficulties are in exact proportion to one's lack of faith in the Sages. Accordingly he can learn from them to what extent he needs to strengthen his faith. Then he will see the true significance of their writings and understand that all of them are necessary. He will be cleansed of the filth in his heart and learn the right way to lead his life. The bitterness of his life, with its pressures and problems, will be sweetened, and all the harsh judgements will be softened (*Ibid.* 5).

56) Every time you visit the Tzaddik, see to it that you come to him afresh. It is no good if this visit is exactly the same as the last — as if it were merely the second visit in a series. When you come to him now it must be a unique occasion. Always begin everything afresh. The main thing is the beginning (62)

57) You should understand that the Tzaddikim have different ways of relating to their followers at different times. Sometimes the Tzaddik may draw very close to people, but to others he

conceals himself and makes himself very distant. He may not merely keep himself apart and remain way above them, making it impossible for them to draw closer. At times it can even happen that questions and doubts are raised about him, and his followers become confused and uncertain about the way he treats them. But this is all for their benefit. Don't be put off by it — it is all for your own good (63).

58) There is a certain meadow in the worlds above in which all the souls are nurtured. These souls depend upon the master of the field to labor in order to restore them. One who wants to take pity on his soul should pray and plead with God all his life to be worthy of drawing close to this Tzaddik — the master of the field — who watches over each one in order to bring him to the ultimate goal, which is absolute unity and perfection (65).

59) To be present at the moment when a Tzaddik leaves this world is a very great thing even for someone who is not one of his pupils. At such a moment there is a great and powerful revelation, which is for the good of all who are present, making them worthy of long life. But the pupils of the Tzaddik themselves receive a supremely powerful revelation — so much so that at this moment they can receive a double share in the soul of their teacher, as long as they are as closely bound up with him as branches on a tree. The bond must be so strong that even when they are distant from him they can still sense when he is making progress and when he is having setbacks. With his double share in the spirit of the Tzaddik, it can happen that the pupil has an even greater power to pray with intensity and work wonders than his teacher. Even so, all his power comes from the soul of his master (66:1).

60) One should try very hard to be with his teacher at all times. This will make it possible for him to receive a double share in his teacher's spirit (*Ibid.*).

61) The true greatness of the Tzaddikim and their followers will only be revealed in the future, on the great and awesome day of judgement. The whole world will then see their greatness and radiance — happy are they and happy is their lot. How great is

the good stored up for them. The whole world will then witness the fall of the wicked — for this will be the great Day of Judgement, when each individual will be brought to judgement for every detail of every action in his life. Nothing will be passed over, because God forgets nothing. Then the world will see the difference between the righteous and the wicked — between those who were worthy of drawing close and binding themselves to the true Tzaddikim and those who fought and opposed them. The whole world will then turn to God, even the nations of the world, and all will call upon the name of God. When a person prays truthfully to God alone with no ulterior motives (for example to impress men with his intense religiosity) then he can have a foretaste of the World to Come even in this life. He will witness the fall of the wicked even in this world, and all will be forced to return to God. Through this the holiness of speech becomes perfected, which makes it possible to bring things from potentiality to actuality — that is, to achieve all the holy tasks one yearns to accomplish (*Ibid.* 3).

62) It is through the Tzaddik that we draw "cool waters" to revive the soul when it is weary. Then we can be worthy of praying with all our heart, as it is written, "*All* my bones will say, Lord, who is like unto Thee?" (Psalms 34:10). This is true prayer. The difference between hearing Torah from the Tzaddik himself and merely learning from a book is that one who hears the Tzaddik himself receives from him the "cool waters" which revive the soul. But one who merely learns from a book does not always know how to restore his soul when it is weary (67:8).

63) The true Tzaddik has a kind of gravitational power to draw the whole world closer to God and His Torah. Why is it then that people are far from the Tzaddik instead of being drawn to him? The reason is because there is a counter force which works against the pull of the Tzaddikim. For there is a class of men whose words and deeds create a barrier which keeps people far from the Tzaddik. The main strength of this counter force lies in people's pride and pretensions. They believe it will bring them to indignity and disparagement if they draw closer to the truth.

One who desires the truth has to lower himself and remember his own insignificance. He has to consider everything that has happened to him since he came into the world and think of his failures and shortcomings. When a person genuinely feels his own smallness the truth will be revealed to him. The gravitational draw of the Tzaddik will prevail over the countervailing force, and he will be drawn to the Tzaddik with tremendous enthusiasm (70).

64) The smaller a person makes himself, the greater his "drawing power" — his power to draw the Indwelling Presence of God down into the world until He dwells with us. The same applies if he wants to draw blessings down upon Israel. And similarly, the smaller a person makes himself, the closer he is to the drawing power of the true Tzaddik (*Ibid.*).

65) One who gives charity to a truly humble Tzaddik is blessed immediately (*Ibid.*).

66) It is very difficult for one when he is famous (71).

67) There are certain Tzaddikim who take afflictions upon themselves of their own accord for the sake of the Jewish people. Because of this they receive a very exalted spiritual blessing (*Ibid.*).

68) Even one who prays and studies constantly can never know how to serve God except if he is close to the Tzaddik (76).

69) There are times when the Tzaddik talks to people about secular topics, and this is very beneficial for them, because the secular conversation of the Tzaddik has the power to give them a connection with true Wisdom, namely Torah. There are certain people who are so far from Torah that it is not possible to draw them closer with words of Torah as such. The only way is through worldly conversations. The Tzaddik uses them as a garment in which to clothe and veil his Torah teachings. And at times the Tzaddik himself can sharpen his mind and freshen himself with this kind of conversation (81).

70) The opposition which the great Tzaddikim endure enables them to draw down blessings without stirring up the Accuser (88).

71) The fact that it is necessary to visit the Tzaddik in person and that learning from books is insufficient is actually mentioned explicitly in the Torah (Exodus 17:14ff.) "And the Lord said to Moses: Write this as a memorial in the book and place it in the ears of Joshua." Moses was to *speak* with Joshua face to face, because the important thing is to *hear* the words from the lips of the Tzaddik himself. The Midrash comments on Moses' words to the Children of Israel, (Deut. 9:1) "Hear O Israel, you are to pass over the Jordan this day." What made him say to them '*Hear* O Israel' now? The Rabbis explained it with a parable about a king who gave his bride two pearls. When one of them got lost the king said to her, "You have lost the one. Make sure that you guard the other." God's "marriage" with Israel was sealed with Israel's declaration of "We shall do, then we shall hear." When the Children of Israel made the golden calf they lost the "we shall do." Therefore Moses said to them, "You have lost the 'we shall do.' Take care that you guard the "we shall hear" — "Hear O Israel." No book has the power to move a person like the words he hears from the mouth of the Tzaddik himself. This hearing is the "we shall hear" which Israel still has (120).

72) The basis of everything is to be bound to the Tzaddik of the generation completely and to accept everything he says as correct, whether it is a major or a minor thing. One must turn neither right nor left from what he says, but simply abandon his own ideas as if he knows nothing except what he receives from the Tzaddik. So long as a person retains even a residue of his own independent way of thinking he has not attained fulfillment and he is not truly bound to the Tzaddik (123).

73) When a person simply believes in the Tzaddik and draws closer without even receiving anything from him, this in itself is very good because his very faith and closeness have the power to consume the evil within him and convert it to the very substance of the Tzaddik himself. The one condition is that his intention should be for the sake of Heaven. Somebody who goes to the

Tzaddik for some other reason will never gain anything from the relationship (129).

74) Being close to a Tzaddik breaks one's pride. The test of whether someone is truly close to the Tzaddik is whether he is humble or not (135).

75) One who is bound to the Tzaddik can experience the true sanctity of the festivals, and through this the dominion of holiness is elevated from the husks and the forces of evil thrown down (*Ibid.*).

76) You should love the Tzaddik with a perfect love until your soul is bound up with his and your love for him will replace the love of women: "Wonderful was thy love to me, passing the love of women" (II Samuel, 1:26) (*Ibid.*).

77) The Shabbat one spends with a Tzaddik is like a fast (167).

78) A man's task in life is to rid himself of the spirit of folly which clings to him and fills his heart. When he is bound to the true Tzaddik and loves him with a spiritual love, he will soon rid himself of the spirit of folly and break the stubbornness of his heart (177).

79) One who has genuine faith in the Tzaddikim will constantly witness great wonders from them — because the true Tzaddikim are full of wonders. Someone who believes in them and pays attention to their words will find that everything that happens subsequently was already hinted at in what they said (186).

80) Before a person emerges into the air of this world he is taught and shown everything he will have to accomplish in this life. But as soon as he enters the air of the world, he immediately forgets it and everything is lost. That is why he must journey to the Tzaddik — to search for what he has lost. Because everything that all the inhabitants of the world have lost is to be found with the Tzaddik (188).

81) All the words which are spoken against the true Tzaddik and his followers are actually beneficial both materially and spiritually (181).

82) When a person hears something said by the true Tzaddik, and especially when he sees him at the moment he says it, he

receives something of the inner life and wisdom and soul of the Tzaddik. But he must beware of forgetfulness, because if he is not careful he will forget it all. If he tries to remember the words of the Tzaddik exactly as he said them and then repeats the lesson one hundred and one times in order to fix it in his mind — and if when he tells anyone what the Tzaddik said he tells them in the name of the Tzaddik and sees the image of his face before him — then it is as if the Tzaddik himself were saying the words. But this is true only when the memory of the experience is genuinely very strong (192).

83) When a person hears an original Torah teaching at the moment the teacher reveals it for the first time, he will remember it well. But if he does not hear it from the teacher himself, or even if he hears it from him later and not when it was first said, he can easily forget it (*Ibid.*).

84) The righteous are persecuted by the wicked and suffer pain and anguish as a result. But this is something brought about by God in order to bring the righteous man to reflect on himself and examine his deeds. The wicked turn out to be guardians preventing the righteous from falling into materialism (208).

85) The opposition which confronts the Tzaddikim is really an advantage because it acts as a cloak against their being revealed and avoids unnecessary attention. The opponents of the Tzaddikim themselves would dearly like to cover them up completely and get rid of them altogether, God forbid. But God does not abandon them or deliver them into their hands (*Ibid.*).

86) It is impossible to achieve a clear mind and pure thoughts except through being bound to the Tzaddikim. This is the main way in which harsh judgements are sweetened. This is why it is essential to be with the Tzaddikim on Rosh Hashanah (211).

87) The ability to speak derives from one's bond with the Tzaddikim (212).

88) Even those who are far from the Tzaddik receive vitality and radiance from him (224).

89) Stories about the Tzaddikim, their lives and achievements have a wonderful power to purify a person's thoughts and

sweeten the harsh judgements, releasing him from all his troubles. But the only people who can really tell stories about the Tzaddikim are those who know how to distinguish between light and darkness — that is, between stories about the genuine Tzaddikim and those about wicked men and liars. The way to achieve this is through the Land of Israel (234).

90) The true Tzaddik is the source of all blessings. Therefore whenever a person is far from the Tzaddik, his own blessing comes to him only with great difficulty. There are even cases where a person can die because of money that comes to him, and the money itself may still be lost instead of being inherited by his children. All this is because of his distance from the Tzaddik (240).

91) Stories about the great Tzaddikim have the power to move a person in his very heart and kindle a flame of passion for God. Many of the greatest Tzaddikim have said that their main awakening came through stories about the Tzaddikim, which made their hearts burn for God and gave them the encouragement to struggle with their devotions until they achieved what they did. Happy are they (248).

92) It is impossible to gain any true conception of what the Tzaddik is in himself. He is totally beyond our grasp. It is only through seeing his followers that one can gain some understanding of his awesome greatness. When one sees that they are men who have achieved great things and who follow God's path in truth, then one can understand the greatness of the Tzaddik himself (140).

93) Whenever you need guidance you should turn to the true Tzaddik. The harsh judgements will be sweetened and the help you need will come in the end (143).

94) The Tzaddik has total control over his inclination. Even in what is permitted to him he holds his desires in his hand. He lives for ever, even after death. For him there is no difference between death and life (144).

95) Only with the help of the true teacher is it possible to attain perfect faith and observe the Covenant completely, guarding

one's mind in holiness and purity. This will bring protection against impure experiences at night, and one's sleep will be pure and holy. The only way to purify the five senses is by coming to the Tzaddik. By seeing the Tzaddik, the sense of *sight* is purified — because simply to see the Tzaddik with one's own eyes is a great thing. The sense of *hearing* is purified when one listens to the guidance of the Tzaddik. One may have to go through many difficulties before reaching the Tzaddik — and without them it would be impossible to come and draw from his holy wisdom. All the difficulties have the effect of purifying the sense of *smell.* One's sense of *taste* is purified when one tastes the pleasantness of the Tzaddik's words. And his sense of *touch* is purified through all the expenses he has to meet from his own pocket out of the fruits of the labor of his hands in order to reach the Tzaddik. The main time for the followers of the Tzaddik to gather at his side is on Rosh Hashanah, and it is then especially that the five senses are purified (*Likutey Moharan* 5:15).

96) How great is the love that the true Tzaddik shows to Israel. His love is *true* love, because his mission is to bring them to acquire holy wisdom and attain a perception of God. Then they will understand that "The Lord, He is God" (I Kings, 18:39) and emerge from sin. There is no love greater than this, because Israel is the Holy People, and they are unable to bear the burden of sin for even a single day. The Tzaddik understands the true greatness of Israel's holiness and the subtle spirituality of their essence. He understands how totally distant they are from sin. Indeed, the Jew has no connection with sin whatsoever. That is why the Tzaddik is willing to sacrifice himself completely in order to release the Jewish people from sin, pleading with God to forgive them. The Tzaddik kows how to show love without in any way harming the person who receives it and without giving love to those upon whom it is forbidden to take pity. The Tzaddik must also strive to leave a legacy of his wisdom for all the generations to come. His ultimate perfection after he leaves the world depends upon this. For even if the Tzaddik were to ascend to the highest realms after his passing, he would be short

of perfection if he only dwelled above. It is necessary for the Tzaddik to radiate even in the lowest realms. He must see to it that he leaves behind him a *son* and a *pupil* who have received his holy wisdom and who will radiate it to the world in each generation until eternity.

The Tzaddik understands the best way to talk to each person individually. He knows how to make a fence to his words — to be silent where silence is called for — in order to prevent his listeners raising questions and seeking answers in areas where it is forbidden to enter. The Tzaddik has the power to send light to those who "dwell above" and also to those who "dwell below." To those who "dwell above" and have achieved high levels, the Tzaddik shows that they really know nothing about the Holy One, blessed-be-He, for "What knowest thou? What have thy searchings achieved?" (*Zohar Bereshith* 1b). It is different with those who "dwell below" and who are sunk in the very earth itself — in degradation and despair. The task of the Tzaddik with them is to show them that God is still with them at their very side. The Tzaddik must fortify them and save them from despair.

The Tzaddik brings all the worlds together, causing the highest to merge with the lowest and the lowest with the highest. He sustains them all through the greatness of his strength, and thus draws down blessings from the source of Desire. Any "man of strength" can receive these blessings through the Tzaddik, and then, when he is eating, he will receive an illumination of Desire — a longing and yearning for God which is so powerful that he doesn't even know what it is he desires.

The only way to achieve anything spiritually is with the help of the Tzaddik and his followers, who draw from his holy wisdom. Think carefully about your life and your purpose and see to it that you take care of your own best interests. You must beg and plead before God with "threefold tears" to let you be worthy of finding the truth and finding a true guide who has genuine love and who will release you from your sins and lead you to the spiritual goals we have mentioned (*Likutey Moharan* II, 7).

97) There are things which the true teacher only hints at to his pupils with his hands. Because certain things cannot be explained directly, they can only be conveyed with hints. It is through these gestures with his hands that the Tzaddik draws down the influx of blessing (*Ibid.* 10).

98) The true leader of each generation always possesses the spirit of prophecy. Even in our times, when prophecy has ceased, the Tzaddik necessarily possesses a form of holy spirit which the rest of the people do not have and which is equivalent to *ruach hakodesh* and the prophetic spirit. It is this prophetic spirit of the Tzaddik which makes it possible to purify the image-making faculty, which is the source of imagination and illusion, in order to distinguish what is imaginary from what is true and attain perfect faith. Everyone must do his utmost to search after such a leader and draw close to him in order to attain this faith. Because faith is only complete to the extent that one has cleansed oneself of illusion and falsehood. Genuine faith is the belief that God perpetually renews the work of Creation and that He created the world and brought it into existence out of absolute nothingness. The secret of the world's renewal can never be understood intellectually. It can only be grasped through faith — the faith we receive from the true Tzaddik. Do not deceive yourself and think it is easy to find such a guide. You have to hunt and search and pray to God and beg Him to make you worthy of discovering a guide who will help you attain perfect faith. Because there are false leaders too, and when people follow their guidance they absorb false ideologies and mistaken beliefs. When a person finds a true guide and attains perfect faith, he will be worthy of experiencing the renewal of the world that is destined to take place in time to come, and he will hear the melody and song which will be sung in the future when God renews His world. This is the melody which will be played on seventy-two strings. It is the source of all the goodly scents in the world, and of true awe. This melody is the essence

of the reward of the Tzaddikim in time to come. Happy is the one who is worthy of this (8:7, 8, 10).

99) Being close to the Tzaddik thwarts the power of the corrupt serpent. But false leaders strengthen it, God forbid (*Ibid.* 8).

100) The true Tzaddikim have the power to lift depression and heaviness from the hearts of the Jewish people. Only then can their hearts burn with passion for God. But at times a person's heart can burn too strongly for God. This is also not good. This is caused by the "raging stormwind" (Ezekiel 1:3) which is also called "Destruction." The Tzaddikim have to watch over this and subjugate the "raging stormwind," in order to ensure that the intensity of passion is not excessive and that each Jew tempers his passion for God and keeps it within bounds (9).

101) There is a paradox which arises from the very fact that there are Tzaddikim who have reached the most awesome levels and who at times make extraordinary statements and even appear to boast. And indeed they *are* capable of formidable feats: they have the power to serve God with everything in the world, even when they eat and drink and so on. There are Tzaddikim who can achieve a redemption through their eating alone. The paradox is that just because there are Tzaddikim like these, there are also *false* Tzaddikim who vaunt themselves and push themselves forward as if they were able to achieve similar feats. Some of them are even leaders and they deceive people into thinking there is nothing they cannot do. Because of the fact that there really are true Tzaddikim who do have these powers, the false Tzaddikim seem to bear some resemblance to them, just as the ape bears a certain resemblance to a human. These false Tzaddikim are the "false prophets."— But in reality they are a benefit to the genuine Tzaddikim. The reason is that there are people who make charitable donations and yet they are thoroughly wicked and adulterous. Their charity would harm the true Tzaddik. So it is good for him that there are false Tzaddikim to whom people like this can give their charity. God tricks these people into making their donations to the false

Tzaddikim and thus the true Tzaddik is saved from their charity (15).

102) The true Tzaddik receives the speech of his holy lips from those who give charity (*Ibid.*).

103) Don't be worried or disturbed if you find you have various doubts and questions concerning the true Tzaddikim. The Tzaddikim resemble their Creator. Just as there are necessarily questions and problems concerning the Creator — and none of them can in any way detract from His greatness — similarly there are also necessarily questions and problems concerning the Tzaddikim (52).

104) The higher the level of the Tzaddik the greater his ability to keep in touch with the world — to watch over it and understand it. This is the opposite of what people suppose. They imagine that because the Tzaddik is so great he must be remote from the world (58).

105) The Tzaddik repents on behalf of Israel. Therefore the closer people are to him the easier it is for them to repent and return to God. Because the Tzaddik repents for them (66).

106) The true Tzaddik is the pride and glory and delight of the whole world. He is, as it were, the "Master of the House" over the whole world, and the "Master of the House" over the House of God, which is the Holy Temple. The Tzaddik sends light into the Holy Temple and the whole world — because he *is* the light and splendor and glory of the world. When the Tzaddik becomes revealed and magnified throughout the world, the Name of God is thereby glorified. The greater the name of the Tzaddik the greater the glory of God. Whoever is truly merged with this name, which is the glory and splendor and true delight of the whole world — whoever draws close to the Tzaddik and is subsumed under his name — through this, his eyes are opened and he can begin to examine himself and see where he stands in the various facets of his character. Then he can return to God and cleanse himself of all his evil characteristics. He will be worthy of perceiving the greatness of the Creator and of looking at the whole world with clear vision, because his eyes and his

mind are opened by the true Tzaddik, who sends light to the whole world (67).

107) On the other hand, when the name of the true Tzaddik becomes concealed and removed from the world and fame and prestige go to a false leader who does not have the Name of God within him at all, then God Himself is diminished and concealed, as it were, because of this. All kinds of occult religions spring up as a result — cults which depend upon the forces of darkness. The world is visited with terrible afflictions and conflagrations, and the very light of our eyes is withdrawn. It is as if the Holy Temple were in ruins and ashes and the precious Children of Israel were tossed out into the street. This was the lament of Jeremiah: "How is the gold become dim. The hallowed stones are poured out at the head of every street. The precious sons of Zion, comparable to fine gold. How are they esteemed as earthen pitchers, the work of the hands of the potter?" (Lamentations 4:1,2).

The remedy is to rise every night at midnight to mourn over the destruction of the Holy Temple. The main thing is for each person to weep and mourn over his own sins, because they are the obstacle holding up the rebuilding of the Holy Temple, and because of them he is regarded as if he himself had destroyed it. Perhaps in his first incarnation he was indeed one of those who was responsible for the destruction of the Holy Temple. When a person rises every night at midnight to mourn over this, he will be regarded as if he was one of those who are making every effort to rebuild the Holy Temple, and this will bring a remedy for all the ills we mentioned above (*Ibid.*).

108) The true leader of the generation must be a Tzaddik on the highest of levels. He must be separated from sexual desire to the utmost degree and in absolute holiness. Then he is worthy of being the leader of Israel, and he merely has to look into the soul of each Jew for it to radiate and shine. This is how the Tzaddik can give every Jew a share of true greatness, each in accordance with the radiance of his soul, and then each one is able to innovate and create new and original concepts of Torah.

He too can sanctify himself and separate himself from sexual desire. Then it is possible to attain a genuine sense of shame and thereby repent and return to God. This will bring true humility, which is the enduring life of the World to Come. But when Israel is without such a leader, God forbid, then the whole world falls into confusion. Anyone who wants to can push himself forward and assume the leadership — which is what we are seeing today because of our many sins (72).

109) The sign of a person who has been to the Tzaddik is that he has a sense of shame and humility. This comes from having heard words of Torah from the lips of the Tzaddik. For the Torah which a true Tzaddik teaches inspires a sense of shame which is the source of genuine repentance, and it is through this that one attains true humility (*Ibid.*).

110) Simply to look at the face of Tzaddikim is a very great thing. How much more so when one is worthy of speaking to him, and even more than this, when one hears Torah from his lips. But simply seeing him is very good in itself (75).

111) Happy is the one who is worthy of drawing close to a true Tzaddik in his lifetime — happy is he and happy is his lot! Because afterwards, when he is dead, it will be hard indeed to draw close. The Evil One has made it his mission to confuse the world. Today's young people have an unparalleled yearning for God the like of which was never seen in earlier times. But they do not know who they should follow. You must plead with God to be worthy of drawing near to the true Tzaddik (78).

112) The only reason why a person is sent into this world is to reach the true goal. The soul is unable to achieve this goal, namely to know and acknowledge the Creator, except by coming into this world. And in this world it is impossible to attain that goal except through the help of the true Tzaddik, the Moses of the generation. This Tzaddik has the power to use every creature in the world in order to enlighten us and give us an understanding of the ultimate goal. In our time we are fully aware that our level is very low and that none of us has attained spiritual beauty. But even we can still find enlightenment

through the strength of the true leader, and he has the power to bring us to our goal. You must plead with God and beg him with "threefold tears" to take pity on us and send us a true leader and a faithful shepherd who will give us true wisdom and perception using everything in the world to do so. In the end we will be able to attain the goal for which we were sent into the world (39).

113) There is *chametz* — leaven — in a person's heart which induces him to have doubts about the leading Sages of his time, deciding that "This one is all right, that one is no good," etc. But through *tikkun habrit* this leaven is expelled from the heart (83).

114) Everything in the entire world — every object and every idea has to be bound to God. Whoever fails to do so is the "whisperer" who "separates familiar friends" (Proverbs 16:28), because he separates the Leader of the world from His creation. This is the cause of the blemish of the moon and the exile of the Shechinah. No matter where a person is or what position he finds himself in he must bind his mind to the Torah and to God from that very place. It is possible to achieve this through the true Tzaddikim, because when they talk about worldly matters they do so in a way that binds everything to God. The everyday conversation of the Tzaddik is very precious. It has the power to bind everything to God, even those who are very far. The harsh judgements are annulled, guilt is transformed into merit, and all is light and perfection (91).

115) It is written of the future: "To grasp the ends of the earth and shake the wicked from it" (Job 38:13). But somebody who is close to a true Tzaddik will hold onto him firmly, and he will be left in his place without being cast off with the wicked (Rabbi Nachman's Wisdom 22).

116) The pity one should have for the souls in the World to Come is unimaginable. Because there are souls which are left literally naked. They cry out bitterly but there is no one to take pity — for pity will not help them. But one who is close to the

Tzaddik can run to him and receive clothing for his soul (*Ibid.* 23).

117) It is impossible to imagine the greatness of one who is worthy of giving charity to a true Tzaddik (*Ibid.* 24).

118) One who speaks against the Tzaddik is actually speaking against God and is called an "atheist" (*Ibid.* 38).

119) One who ignores the words of the Sages can go mad because of it (*Ibid.* 67).

120) If a person is not bound to a true Tzaddik, all his devotions are nothing but twisting and turning and pretending to be something he isn't — as if an ape were pretending to be a man. Service of God is nothing without the true Tzaddik (*Ibid.* 111).

CHARITY צדקה

1) You should give to charity before you pray. This is the way to avoid the extraneous thoughts which come to a person while praying. You will be able to pray properly without straying to the right or the left. You will order and measure your words in the scale of justice (2).

2) Giving charity to Torah scholars will protect you against time-wasting and malicious gossip. It will also save you from pride and all related character defects. Giving charity is a protection against poverty and will make you wealthy (4:8).

3) In order to break your appetite for riches you must give charity. The harsh anger which hangs over the world will be dissipated, and God's providence will be drawn over the whole world. Through giving charity the force of love and kindness is brought into the world; the Messiah is revealed, and the Holy Temple, which is itself the revelation of the knowledge of God — rebuilt. The unification of the Holy One, blessed-be-He and the Shechinah then becomes complete. Through this we will become worthy of the new revelation of Torah which is destined to come about in the future. The upper and lower chariots are restored, and it is accounted like an offering of incense (13).

4) Through giving charity to the true Tzaddikim and to poor people who genuinely deserve it, converts are made. Through this one attains perfect wisdom and becomes worthy of seeing the light of the Tzaddikim. This is how to achieve the love and fear of Heaven (17:5).

5) When a person gives charity to the true Tzaddikim and to poor people who genuinely deserve it, it is as if he gave charity to many, many Jewish souls (*Ibid.*).

6) This kind of charity enables all the goodness which is held captive amidst the heathen nations of the world to be brought back to mind and be remembered. This goodness is all the sparks of Jewish souls which have fallen into exile, and because of the length of the exile they have forgotten their true worth. Giving charity enables these souls to remember what they really are and how they have fallen from heaven to earth. They start to take pity on themselves, and long and yearn to be restored. Because the real essence of the soul is *beyond* all the worlds — for "Israel arose in His thought first" (*Bereshith Rabbah* 1) and "the Holy One, blessed-be-He, consulted with the souls of Israel when He created the world" (*Ibid.* 8). But now these sparks are trapped in exile, and they are in danger of being destroyed and going to waste, God forbid. But when they remember their own exaltedness they repent and their holiness is restored. If you think about all this carefully you will see for yourself how far you need to take care of yourself and have pity on yourself and your condition, considering the true preciousness of your soul. You should say to yourself: "Am I not from the seed of Israel, who are above all the worlds? What have I come to? Who knows what will be in the future? Is the Evil One trying to destroy me, God forbid?" Think deeply about this, and you will be so overwhelmed with the desire to do something for yourself that you will try with all your might to return to God (*Ibid.* 6).

7) When a person gives some of his money to a poor person who genuinely deserves it, it is a *tikkun* for *all* his money. The "supernal colors" are revealed through his money — this is the main revelation of the greatness of the Creator. The husks are thereby broken and humbled — namely the fantasies, desires and distractions which rise up against a person every time he has to climb from one level to the next and which range themselves against him to prevent him entering the gates of holiness. Giving charity makes it possible to break the husks and rise from level to level (25:4).

8) Charity is the comprehensive *tikkun* for business activity. With every step a person takes as he goes about his business,

with every word he speaks and every ounce of strength he puts into his work, he should have it in mind that his only goal is to give charity from the money he earns (29:9).

9) Giving charity expands and elevates the mind, and this brings blessing and livelihood (*Ibid.*).

10) Through giving charity one can come to speak words which radiate with the wisdom of Torah (*Ibid.* 10).

11) Acts of charity and lovingkindness have the power to undermine alien ideologies and release us from the burdens of worldly authorities, and we can achieve a perception of Godliness (30:7).

12) When the Sages criticize us and point out our faults, we should accept their criticisms submissively, even if at times they are expressed in a derogatory way. Through this we will be worthy of performing acts of charity and lovingkindness (*Ibid.*).

13) All the heavenly constellations are directed and governed by *tzedakah*, charity. It is through charity that all blessings flow into the world. But only on Shabbat are the blessings perfect. Shabbat is the embodiment of faith. The main significance of charity is that it is an expression of faith. This is why the true radiance of the light of charity and its perfection are seen only on Shabbat — the embodiment of faith (31).

14) One should give charity before going on a journey. Then he will be saved from any obstacles and troubles on the way (*Ibid.*).

15) The central aspect of any fast is the charity which the person who is fasting gives. Fasting and charity make it possible to subdue the body as against the soul, substance as against form, folly as against wisdom. One emerges from darkness to light, from death to life, from animality to the level of Man. The force of alien ideologies and all other false and foolish idea-systems is broken, and the wisdom of Torah, which is the true wisdom, comes into its place. The hold of forgetfulness is broken, and in its place comes memory. The harsh judgments and darkness are dissipated, and love is brought into the world (37).

16) Charity given for the Land of Israel is greater than charity for other causes. When you give charity for the Land of Israel

you become included in the air of the Land of Israel, which is holy breath without the taint of sin. Harsh judgements, darkness, forgetfulness and folly are banished from the world (*Ibid.* 4).

17) You must aim to be contented. You must be contented with just as much as is essential for you to take from this world. And even out of that you must still devote a portion to charity. The effect of this in the upper worlds is to bring about a great unification, and abundant blessings are brought into the world (54:2).

18) Charity for the Land of Israel can save you from distracting thoughts while you are praying. Your mind and thoughts are clarified and purified. This is *tikkun habrit* (44).

19) Charity brings abundant peace (57:7).

20) Acts of charity bring blessings of love into the world. The honor and majesty of the forces of holiness are released from the husks and the Other Side. The lust for food is broken. The prestige and power of those who are arrogant and self-assertive is broken, and honor is returned to the true leaders (67).

21) During the morning service, when you reach the words "And You have dominion over everything" (Chronicles I, 29:12) you should give to charity. The reason for this is to elevate glory and dominion from the forces of the Other Side and return them to the side of holiness (*Ibid.* 7).

22) When a person gives charity, it is a *tikkun* for *all* his money. This way it will stay with him, and his livelihood will be sent in abundance (69).

23) One who gives charity to a Tzaddik who is truly humble is immediately blessed (70).

24) Giving charity in secret is a *tikkun* for a wasteful emission at night (83).

25) Charity saves from sin (116).

26) Through charity comes wisdom (119).

27) A *segulah* for epilepsy, God forbid, is to distribute charity to the poor. In the Hebrew words of the verse: "He hath scattered abroad, he hath given to the needy" (Psalms 112:9) the first

letters of each word, Pizar Matan La-evyonim, spell out the word NoPheL, which is the word for epilepsy (201).
28) The charity you give to Torah scholars is something great and precious. No sin can extinguish this merit (204).
219) The Sages ordained that we should give between a tenth and a fifth of our income to charity. This tithe has the power to save us from our enemies (221).
30) The tithe we give to charity brings us contentment (*Ibid.*).
31) Charity protects against immoral fantasies (242).
32) Charity is a remedy for immorality. But it is important not to give money to a poor person who is undeserving because this only makes things worse. One must beg God to make him worthy of finding poor people who deserve to be helped (264).
33) The merit of those who support the Torah and give money for Torah scholars is very great indeed. This money makes it possible for them to devote themselves to Torah, to give birth to new legal rulings and to open up new horizons in Torah. Those who gave the money therefore have a share in the Torah which was born and revealed through their help. Whatever they gave to the Torah scholars and whatever they themselves went short of as a result, will all be made up to them later on, by means of the new Torah concepts which came into being through their help.Revelations of Torah bring an influx of love into the world which completes all that was lacking. Those who support Torah scholars will be rewarded with the delights of the World to Come (II 2:2).
34) It is speech that gives man his uniqueness. The roots of speech lie in charity. The instinct to give charity and show lovingkindness is peculiar to man. It is in the nature of Man, the Speaker, to show kindness to his fellow creatures. When a person fails to act kindly and charitably it is a stain on the faculty of speech and he cannot be defined as a Man (225).
35) When we give charity, the main task is to break our instinct to be cruel and turn it in to lovingkindness in order to give generously. When a person who is kind by nature gives charity purely out of instinct, it cannot be called an act of service of

God. In order to fulfill the mitzvah of charity in the proper way, one must first experience the battle of breaking his natural instinct to be cruel and turn it into love in order to give to charity (II, 4:1,2).

36) Charity has the power to widen the entrance to holiness. When a person wants to embark upon a certain path of devotion, he first needs to make an opening in order to enter his new path. This is why all beginnings are hard. But giving charity makes the entrance wider (*Ibid.* 2).

37) Any act of charity is very hard and heavy at the beginning. But the effects of charity are great beyond measure. The body has many needs — even the essentials, like food, drink, clothing and shelter are very demanding. They are all a distraction from one's religious devotions. But charity has the power to break all these obstacles because it opens up the channels of God's blessing and love to the point where one has no need to work at all in order to have what he needs to live. All his work will be done by others, leaving him free to devote himself to the service of God (*Ibid.* 3).

38) Charity is the remedy for the damage caused when the elders of the generation do not lead their lives as they should. Through remedying this, it is possible to strike at the very roots of materialism — the idea that everything in the world is dominated by the laws of nature. Then we can hear the message of the three festivals, Pesach, Shavuot and Succot: that everything takes place only through the will of God. Each of the festivals recalls the miracles that were brought about for us — miracles transcending nature. To be aware that God's will transcends the laws of nature, is to experience the joy of the festivals and attain to the fear of Heaven.Fear of Heaven is the channel for receiving blessings so abundant that you will have not have to work at all, to have what you need to live (*Ibid.* 9).

39) Charity is the remedy for all wounds (*Ibid.* 12).

40) The true Tzaddik receives the words of his holy lips from those who give charity (II, 15).

41) Zealousness for the Lord of Hosts is accounted as an act of charity (65).

42) You must learn the thirteen Divine attributes of lovingkindness — learn them in order to fulfill them in practice. You must cultivate the quality of love and do as many kindnesses as you can for other people. When we strive to fulfill each of the thirteen attributes of love, the thirteen supernal attributes of love are aroused, and the destructive angels brought into being through sin are humbled. Our own acts of kindness arouse God's forgiveness, and He passes over our sins one after the other (Rabbi Nachman's Wisdom 89).

TZITZIT ציצית

1) The mitzvah of *tzitzit* is a safeguard against immoral temptations. The *tzitzit* have the power to protect us from the "suggestions of the serpent" — the negative ideas of those who are far from God's service and who put obstacles in the way of people who want to draw closer to the truth. Then it becomes possible to follow the guidance of the Tzaddikim and their followers, who are the "guardians of the Covenant." This is the way to find truth and faith, to become worthy of true faith and of coming to the Land of Israel and witnessing miracles. Then the redemption will come. Whatever one needs will be given in abundance, and in his study of Torah he will be able to understand whatever he learns.Because of the greatness of the mitzvah of *tzitzit* you should be very careful to perform it properly. When you wrap yourself in the holy *tallit* and recite the blessing, have in mind that you would like to be worthy of achieving all these goals (7:4).
2) *Tzitzit* is the embodiment of the *ruach chaim,* the life-spirit which animates everything holy. In the merit of this mitzvah we will be provided with whatever we may be lacking. When a Jew is in need of something and sighs with a deep breath, he draws his breath from the life-spirit of Torah, which is the source of creative power and can therefore provide whatever is lacking. The sighs and groans of a Jew who yearns for holiness have the power to curb the life-spirit which gives vitality to the husks and which is called *ruach seara* — a "raging whirlwind" (Ezekiel 1:4). In this way it is possible to shake off the evil in one's character and leave only the good. The wicked will be crushed and cast down to the earth (8:8).

3) The mitzvah of *tzitzit* is a manifestation of the sovereignty of God.Through it, the supremacy of the forces of the Other Side is crushed. But the Jewish people, who are bound to the side of holiness, receive all their vitality from there and draw down abundant blessing and wealth without end (49:7).
4) If you are careful about the mitzvah of *tzitzit* and perform it properly you will be able to achieve true prayer and return to God whole-heartedly.The harsh judgements will be sweetened, and the secrets of Torah will be revealed to you (*Ibid.*).
5) Every day God sends hints and messages to each person in order to draw him closer. One should strive to expand his mind in order to understand them. On the other hand there is a certain limit beyond which it is forbidden to delve and speculate on the meaning of these hints. It is dangerous to overstep this limit. The mitzvah of *tzitzit* creates the necessary frame within which the mind must work. This explains why we put on the *tzitzit* before we lay the *tefilin*. First it is necessary to erect the frame so as not to go beyond the boundary. Only then is it safe to expand the mind so as to understand the hints God sends. This understanding is embodied in the *tefillin* (54).

HOLINESS קדושה

1) The essence of the holiness which every person must strive for is to observe the Covenant in purity. The way to achieve this is by sanctifying the way you speak. You must speak only words of holiness and keep yourself from any lapse into language which is not holy. Then whatever you say will be in "the Holy Tongue," and through this you will achieve the holiness of the Covenant (19).2) You must sanctify your mouth, your nose, your eyes and your ears. You must guard your mouth against words of falsehood and anything else which falls short of holiness. You must develop your fear of Heaven in order to sanctify your nostrils. Your ears will be holy when you believe in the Sages and listen to their words. And you must close your eyes and shut out anything which is not good for you to see. The sanctity you attain will bring you perfect understanding, and you will have wisdom, which is God's blessing, and *ruach hakodesh*, the holy spirit. Another way of sanctifying your nostrils, is if you are humble and patient and do not burst out in anger if someone insults you (The Hebrew expression for anger is a "burning in the nostrils"). The way to sanctify your ears is to be one who is "faithful in spirit and concealeth a matter" (Proverbs 11:13) — he is careful not to reveal a secret which there is no need to reveal (21).

3) One who is prepared to sacrifice himself for the sake of sanctifying God's Name will attain peace, and through this the ability to speak holy words of Torah and prayer and to bind the thoughts in the mind to the words which the mouth is speaking. In order to pray with devotion, have in mind that you are willing to sacrifice yourself entirely in order to sanctify God's Name. To

achieve perfect prayer, you must pray with a spirit of total self-sacrifice (80).

4) It has been proved many times that even the most worthless of Jews, even the sinners of Israel are prepared to sacrifice themselves for the sanctification of God's Name if someone tries to force them to violate the Torah. Each day you should remind yourself that you would be ready to give your life to sanctify God's Name. This is the essence of Israel's holiness. You will then attain peace and be able to pray with true devotion (*Ibid.*).

5) When you recite the Shema you should say the words in a spirit of total self-sacrifice for the sake of God's Name. Picture in your mind the four death penalties imposed by the Beth Din — stoning, strangulation, burning and the sword. You should imagine every detail so vividly that you can literally feel the pain of dying. Thought has a very great power. By imagining yourself dying you can literally come to feel the pangs of death. But be careful not to dwell on these thoughts for too long, because otherwise your soul could literally leave you, God forbid, causing premature death (195).

6) Self-sacrifice for the sake of God brings unity to the worlds above (260).

7) There are certain Tzaddikim who have a very great name and who are known very widely. Yet people hold them in contempt and talk against them. They suffer mercilessly because of this, but it is something they take on themselves in order to sanctify God's Name, and because of it they can save thousands of Jewish souls from slaughter and death, God forbid (*Ibid.*).

8) Each person has something in his life which is more of a barrier for him than anything else. This is precisely the barrier he has to break in order to serve God. This is his task in life. It is his own way of sacrificing himself. Someone who is very afraid of dying must be more ready than anyone to give up his life to sanctify God's Name (Rabbi Nachman's Wisdom 57).

WILL & DESIRE רצון וכיסופין

1) The soul of the Jew is actually formed through the yearning and desire which he feels for God and his good intentions to serve Him. No matter what his level, each individual has a desire to reach a higher level. It is through this yearning that his holy soul is formed (31).

2) But in order for his soul to come from *potential* to *actual* existence he must express his yearning and longing in words. This is the means by which he will make his desire into a reality and accomplish what he wants. This is why it is so important to speak to God every day and articulate your desires and good intentions with your lips. You should speak about your inadequacies and shortcomings and how you yearn for God to help you in them. You should plead with God. Beg Him to take pity on you and satisfy your yearning and longing for Him. This is the way to succeed in making the potential into an actual fact and achieving what you need to accomplish (*Ibid.*).

3) The letters of the written Torah are without vowels. It is through speaking them aloud that we give them a shape — whether for good or for evil. The yearning which a person has for goodness — for God — gives shape to the letters of Torah for good. The Torah becomes an elixir of *life*, and such a person brings good into the world. Conversely a person's bad desires give the opposite shape to the letters of Torah, and for him it becomes an elixir of death, for "sinners stumble in them" (Hosea 14:10). This brings evil into the world (*Ibid.*).

4) The yearning and longing for something holy are themselves very precious. They are the means by which the soul is brought into being, and it reaches completion through speech. The soul

that is thus created can even enter the body of a wicked person and bring him to return to God. On the other hand the desire for something evil can cause great damage. The soul that is brought into being by evil desires can at times even find its way to a Tzaddik and this can cause him to sin, God forbid (*Ibid.*).

5) A person may be totally unable to study Torah — whether because he is an ignoramus or because he is without a book, on a journey or in the desert, etc. But if his heart burns with desire and yearning to learn, the very desire and longing he has are "learning from a book" (142).

6) When a person has any desire except to do what God desires, it gives strength to the forces of the Other Side. A man must nullify his own will to the point where he has no will and desire for anything except what God desires — whether that he should have wealth and children or not, God forbid. It should be the same with everything else he wants. He should desire only what God desires. This makes God alone the King (177).

7) The main thing is the will and desire. It may be true that everyone wants to serve God. But not all desires are equal. There are many gradations and distinctions. Even in one and the same person at different times and even from moment to moment there are all kinds of differences. The main thing is that a person should have the desire and the longing. He should yearn for God... and meanwhile pray... and learn... and carry out the mitzvot (Rabbi Nachman's Wisdom 51).

HEALING רפואה

1) A person who is sick can be helped by looking at the *tzitzit* (7).

2) A woman who loses a lot of blood and has no set period can be harmed by wine. Nevertheless, the cure for her is wine which a true Tzaddik has looked at (29).

3) Understanding brings peace, and peace is the source of healing. Therefore the remedy for sickness is devotion to Torah, which brings wisdom and the knowledge of God (56:6).

4) Immersing in the *mikvah* brings understanding and therefore healing (*Ibid.* 7).

5) It is best to rely only on God. Someone who does not, has no option but to devise all kinds of complicated methods of trying to get what he needs. If he is sick, for example, he may have to look for all kinds of special drugs and medicines, and often the ones he needs are not available where he lives, while those which are available are useless for his condition. But the goodness of God reaches everywhere. God has the power to cure all wounds and illnesses. He is always available. If you are ill, you should rely only on prayers and supplications. They are always available, and they will certainly help. If you depend on doctors and medicines you will have to do a lot of searching because you will have to look for the right doctor with the right medicines. And it is usually impossible to find them, because doctors do more harm than good (14:11).

6) When a person has no faith in the Sages there is no cure for his malady. The remedy is to make a vow and fulfill it at once.

This will restore his faith in the Sages, and then he will be completely cured (57:2).

7) Sweating is a cure for fever (263).

8) The main cure for any illness depends on a redemption. The Torah only permits the doctor to heal after the redemption has been made. The redemption is necessary in order to sweeten the harsh judgements. Only then can the doctor help to cure the patient, not beforehand (II, 2:3).

9) Charity is a cure for all diseases (4:12).

10) There are people who suffer from the most terrible illnesses, God forbid. They are all caused by their inadequate faith. When faith is lacking, it can bring on the most terrible afflictions which can be cured neither by prayers nor through the merit of the Fathers. Even cries and groans of distress will not help, though in other cases the cries of the sick awaken God's pity. But when faith is lacking even this doesn't help. The only answer is to cry out from the very depths of the heart. This will restore one's faith and bring healing.

11) Anyone who wants to take care of himself should keep well away from physicians and doctors. They are notorious for the damage they cause (Rabbi Nachman's Wisdom 50).

12) Reciting psalms can help cure someone who is sick. But it needs strong trust in God, and then He will send help and the patient will be healed and rise from his sickbed (Rabbi Nachman's Wisdom 98).

JOY שמחה

1) Seeing the face of the Tzaddik can give you joy and enthusiasm (4:8).
2) You should feel so happy when you do a mitzvah that you don't do it merely to receive a reward in the World to Come. You want God to send you *another* mitzvah, and this will be the reward of the first one, because your joy is in the mitzvah itself. Someone who attains this degree of joy will be able to know what decrees have been passed against the world, whether the decree has been sealed yet or not, and against whom judgement has been passed. And through this he will know how to pray for the world, because after the decree has been sealed the Tzaddikim have to clothe their prayers in story form (5:2).
3) If you pray with intensity and with great awe and love you will be able to experience this joy (*Ibid.* 3).
4) When people dance and clap their hands the harsh judgements are sweetened (10:1).
5) It takes determination and boldness to press forward in your quest for holiness in the face of all the obstacles created by arrogant people. The main source of strength is in joy: "For the joy of the Lord is your strength" (Nehemiah 8:10) (22:9).
6) The way to come to joy is through Torah and prayer. The main thing is prayer. You should always pray to attain the level that is hidden from you. And when it is revealed, you should pray to achieve the level that is still hidden. This is how to rise from level to level. It is the way to find joy, which is the source of spiritual strength. You need to be strong in order to draw closer to the true Tzaddikim. They are the epitome of holiness, and with their help you can develop perfect faith (*Ibid.*).

7) Joy is the "radiant countenance," "truth" and "faith." Depression is a form of idolatry. It is a "dark countenance" and "death." How joyous we are depends on our purity and how close we are to the true Tzaddikim, who are the joy of all Israel. If you are joyous you will be able to bind yourself to God and "see the pleasantness of thc Lord" (Psalms 27:4). The light of the countenance of the King of Life will radiate upon you (23).
8) Through carrying out the mitzvoth in joy it is possible to reach the ultimate goal of all things. For there is a light which is beyond "soul," "spirit" and "breath." This is the Light of the Infinite, which it is possible to "reach, yet not reach." Happy is he who chases after his thoughts in order to reach such a vision (24).
9) The joy of the mitzvot is the perfection of holiness. It has the power to free all the vitality and holiness which have been caught in the husks and to elevate them. The Shechinah itself is thus released from the *kelipot* (*Ibid.*).
10) Don't be depressed. The root of depression is in the husks, which are at war with all that is holy. They are the epitome of severity and harshness. Whenever depression takes grip, the Shechinah, which is the joy of Israel, goes into exile. The strength of the forces of holiness and the destruction of the *kelipot* depends upon joy (*Ibid.*).
11) We are taught that the incense which was burned in the Holy Temple had the power to free the holy life-force from the husks and elevate it, thereby spreading joy. Because of this you should recite the passages in the prayer book which deal with the daily incense offering with great concentration (*Ibid.*).
12) It is a wonderful thing when people dance for joy for the sake of a mitzvah! There are times when it is a mitzvah to drink wine — on Shabbat and Yom Tov, or at a wedding or other religious celebrations. If you drink on such occasions your intention should be for the sake of Heaven. Drink moderately and not to excess, and with the purpose of experiencing the true joy of Israel, which is to rejoice in God, who chose us from all the nations. As your joy begins to radiate, it will spread to your

legs and you will literally start to dance for joy. This will banish the forces of the Other Side, which grip the legs. The force of severity and harsh judgements will be broken, and then you will be able to receive blessings. The fire with which we dance is "a fire offering, a sweet savor to the Lord" (Numbers 28:8). But when one dances in the heat of the evil inclination, it is a "strange fire" (Leviticus 10:1) and the wine which he drinks is the "wine of drunkenness," which gives a hold to the forces of the Other Side. But dancing with holy intentions has as much power to sweeten the harsh judgements as a redemption. (41).

13) Man's image-making faculty is the source of all temptations. It is one of man's animal aspects. If it becomes dominant, it is because of depression, which is a "broken spirit, an evil spirit." Forgetfulness gains a hold, and one forgets one's purpose and fails to bear in mind the reality of the World to Come, both as a general concept and as one which gives memory to every detail of the day. We have to fight back. We should aim to be constantly happy so as to break the power of the image-making faculty. Then we will be able to remember the World to Come every day and at every moment (54:5).

14) The music of one who is truly God-fearing can help you to be happy. It has the power to break the force of fantasy. This will sharpen your memory: you will be able to center your thoughts on the World to Come and to understand the hints which God sends you constantly each day in order to draw you closer to Him. Music and joy can inspire you with the spirit of prophecy — *ruach hakodesh*, the holy spirit (*Ibid.* 6).

15) Music and joy can help you to pour out your words like water before God. When you are constantly happy it is easy to express yourself in words before God and meditate well (*Ibid.* 6).

16) If you are joyous, it will bring you to new horizons in Torah. Joy is a vessel with which to draw upon the wellsprings of the Torah's vitality and freshness (65).

17) The holiness of the Land of Israel has the power to break the force of anger and depression (155).

18) A person who examines and judges himself over everything

he does thereby frees himself from the harsh judgements which were weighing upon him. He will be so happy that he will literally dance for joy. But when a person is under the weight of some harsh judgement, it is hard to dance (169).

19) The main reason for immorality is because of depression. The way to be pure is through joy. If you are happy, God will help you to keep yourself pure (*Ibid.*).

20) Crying is good if you cry out of joy. Contrition and regret for your sins are also good if they stem from joy — in the sense that you experience the joy of God's presence so intensely that you feel sorry for ever having rebelled against Him and you burst into tears out of joy (175).

21) When you confess your sins, you must specify each sin exactly. You should confess about everything you did, and the confession must be in words. Thinking alone is not enough. You must also go into all the details. Many people have a lot of barriers against this. The way to overcome them is through the joy of fulfilling mitzvot. When you go to a wedding or some other happy occasion you should work yourself up into such a mood of joy that you dance and dance. When you are happy it is easy to confess, and it will make amends for all the damage you did with your sins (178).

22) Fasting brings joy. The more you have fasted, the greater the joy (*Ibid.*).

23) Be very careful not to fall into depression and lethargy. They are the "bite of the serpent" (189).

24) When you are happy, it gives strength to the angels who receive the blessings contained within the food you eat, and it humbles the evil spirits, preventing them from sapping more energy than they should from the food. This gives protection against the impure emissions which can sometimes be caused by eating if the holy angels lack the necessary strength. The source of their strength is in joy (II, 5:9,10).

25) If you put so much effort into a holy task that you literally sweat you will be able to experience true joy (6).

26) Depression is like a sediment which covers the heart of the

Jew and stops it from burning with passion for God. But the true leaders blow with their holy spirit until they remove this sediment of depression and kindle the hearts of Israel with passion for God (9).

27) When a person is depressed, his intellect and his mind go into exile. This makes it very hard for him to concentrate his mind on *teshuva*, returning to God. The main reason why people are far from God is that they do not stop to consider what the main purpose of their existence is. But when someone is happy his mind becomes settled and he is able to understand things clearly. Joy is freedom. When a person fills his mind with joy, his intellect becomes freed from its exile. He can control his mind and intellect however he wants so as to concentrate on his goal and return to God (10).

28) Once a person decides to be pure and devote himself to serving God it is a very big sin if he allows himself to be depressed. Because God hates depression (48).

29) Try to be as happy as you possibly can. Search for your good points in order to make yourself happy. If for nothing else, you can be happy with the thought that you are a Jew and God did not make you a non-Jew. If you genuinely realize the true implications of this you will find joy without limits. And nothing will be able to spoil it, because God Himself made it so. Get into the habit of saying out loud and with all your heart: "Blessed be our God who created us for His glory and separated us from those who are in error etc." No matter what you may go through you will always be able to take heart from this and be happy all your life. There may be times when the only way to make yourself happy is by doing something silly or making jokes. There are so many troubles that people have to go through physically and spiritually — trying to make a living, etc. etc. — that in many cases the only way they can make themselves happy is by doing something silly and acting a bit crazy. The whole vitality of body and soul depend on being happy. And in the worlds above as well great unifications are brought about through the joy of the spirit (*Ibid.*).

30) It is a great mitzvah to be happy at all times. Be determined to keep away from depression and aim to be happy constantly. Happiness is the remedy for all kinds of diseases — because many illnesses are caused by depression. You must be resourceful in order to make yourself happy. Often you must do something a little bit crazy in order to make yourself happy (24).

31) Try hard to turn your very depression and worry into joy. If you really set your mind to it, you will easily find that even amidst the worst troubles and suffering there is an opening which you can use to convert all the depression into joy. True joy is when you drag your darkness and depression even against their will and force them to turn into happiness (23).

32) When someone is happy all day it is easier for him to spend an hour or so with a broken heart, talking to God and pouring out his heart like water before Him. After a broken heart comes joy. The test of whether your heart was really broken is if afterwards you feel joy (Rabbi Nachman's Wisdom 45).

33) You should constantly center your thoughts on contemplating the root of all things. This is the source of all that is good and all joys. You will feel an overwhelming joy, because when one contemplates this root — which is wholly good — then everything good and joyous is merged into one and radiates with abundant light (II, 34).

34) What a great thing it is when you study Torah or carry out a mitzva with such joy that you literally dance for joy. This is the remedy for saying something bad. You will be blessed with wealth and children and your faith will be strengthened (81).

35) To find true joy is the hardest thing of all. It is harder than all other spiritual tasks. You must literally force yourself to be happy all the time. Put all your energy into it. Use every kind of ploy. Often the only way is by literally doing something foolish or childish (Rabbi Nachman's Wisdom 20).

36) Most important of all, you must be happy while you are praying. Be sure always to pray with joy. The same applies to carrying out the mitzvot. You should be especially joyous on

Shabbat and Yom Tov. Even on weekdays it is a great mitzvah to be happy always (*Ibid.* 155, 299).

37) Depression can make a person forget his own name (43).

38) Someone who is himself happy can give heart to somebody else. It is a great thing to bring joy to the heart of your fellow Jews. Most people are full of pain and worry and all kinds of troubles, and they find it impossible to speak out what is in their hearts. Someone who comes with a smiling face can literally give them fresh life. This is a very great thing. When you make another person happy you are literally giving new life to a Jewish soul (*Ibid.*).

39) Joy gives protection against the death of little children (*Ibid.* 34).

PEACE שלום

1) The gateway to Torah is through humility and meekness. Torah has the power to draw penitents and converts closer to God, and this is how the glory of God is exalted and magnified and the fear of God spreads throughout the world. This brings peace (14:2-5).

2) There are two kinds of peace. There is the peace "in one's bones" — in oneself. This is the first priority, because at times a person has no peace in himself, as it is written: "There is no peace in my bones because of my sin" (Psalms 38:4). When a person develops genuine fear of Heaven he can attain peace within himself. Through this he is able to pray. And prayer leads to the second kind of peace — *universal* peace, when there is peace in all the worlds (*Ibid.* 8).

3) The leaders of the generation, who give criticism and guidance, bring abundant peace into the world. They also make peace between Israel and their Father in Heaven (22:1).

4) As peace spreads in the world the whole world can be drawn to serve God with one accord. Because when men are at peace with each other they talk to one another and together they can think about the purpose of the world and all its vanities. People then talk to each other about the realities of life — that in the final analysis, when a person dies, nothing remains of him except whatever preparations he has made for the eternal world which awaits him after death. Neither silver nor gold accompany a man after his death... When people understand this they will abandon their illusions and their idols of silver and aspire only to God and His Torah. Their only aim will be to serve God and seek out the truth. But when there is no peace in the world, and even

worse when there is strife and dissension, men are not open with one another and they never discuss the purpose of life. Even when somebody *is* open about it his words fail to enter the hearts of other people, because people are not interested in finding out the truth, all they want is to win the argument: they are aggressive and full of hatred and jealousy. When somebody wants to win an argument his ears are not open to the truth. The main reason why most people are so far from God is because of the divisiveness and strife which are so widespread today due to our many sins (*Ibid.* 6).

5) Moral purity leads to peace (*Ibid.* 6).

6) The search for peace must be twofold: within the Jewish people as a whole and within each individual himself. Each person must resolve any conflicts which exist between the different parts of his character. He must also develop a harmonious approach to his life experiences as a whole, so that it makes no difference to him whether things are seemingly good or bad: he will always find God in everything. It is through Torah and the Tzaddikim that we can achieve this harmony. Both are called "peace," and through them each person can feel his love for God regardless of his situation — whether things are good or seemingly bad. He will also feel his love for his fellow Jew. This way peace will spread throughout the Jewish people (33).

7) To spread peace, give charity (57:6).

8) Divisiveness leads to atheism, and prevents people from praying with genuine devotion. But when men are at peace and open with each other, people can be guided away from their illusions and free themselves of their doubts and atheistic inclinations. When there is strife between people, they are not open with one another and it is impossible to speak to other people and draw them towards the truth. Even if people do talk to each other, their main concern is to win the argument, which means that neither side is open to the words of the other. Therefore true faith depends on peace (62:2).

9) The way to attain peace is through studying Torah law as set

forth in the legal codes. Then you will be able to pray with all your heart (*Ibid.*).

10) The real meaning of peace is to fit together two opposites. So you shouldn't be disturbed when you come across someone who is the exact opposite of yourself and thinks the exact opposite.

Do not assume you will never be able to live amicably with him. And similarly if you see two people who are completely opposite types, you should not decide it is impossible to make peace between them. Quite the contrary! Perfect peace is achieved through the effort to make peace between two opposites, just as God makes peace in His high places between Fire and Water, which are two opposites. The way to achieve peace is through complete self-sacrifice to sanctify the name of God. Then it is possible to pray with genuine devotion (80).

11) God always takes into account the good that people do. It may be that something not so good was mixed up with it, but God pays no attention to this. If this is God's way, how much more so should we attempt to do the same. Never look for the bad side of other people or hunt out their shortcomings and weak points when it comes to religion. Look only for the good and always search out the merit and worth in them. You will then be at peace with everybody (II, 17).

TORAH STUDY תלמוד תורה

1) Through studying Torah all our prayers and requests are accepted and the favor and standing of the Jewish people are enhanced in the eyes of whoever they have need for, materially and spiritually (1:1).

2) Studying Torah with all your might gives power to the forces of holiness and strengthens the good inclination against the evil inclination (*Ibid.*).

3) If you labor in the study of Torah you will be able to understand the hints and meanings contained in all the different things in the world and use them as a means of coming closer to God. Even if you find yourself in a place of darkness where you might think it hard to draw close to God, true wisdom will radiate to you and you will be able to draw close to God even from there (*Ibid.*).

4) Nobody sins unless he is overcome by the "spirit of folly" (*Sotah* 3a). The sins and damage a person may have done literally make him mad. This is why the majority of people suffer from all kinds of quirks and idiosyncrasies. The remedy is to study Torah intensively. The Torah consists entirely of the names of the Holy One, blessed-be-He, and it has the power to crush the evil inclination and banish all the madness and folly which cling to a person because of his sins (*Ibid.*).

5) One of the most subtle devices of the evil inclination is that rather than starting off by trying to persuade a person to do a blatant sin, it dresses itself up as if it wanted to persuade him to do an actual mitzvah. But Torah study develops the sharpness and intelligence which will help you escape these devices (*Ibid.*).

6) Torah and prayer give strength to one another and illuminate each other (2:6).

7) When a person studies the *gemara* by night, a thread of lovingkindness is drawn down over him and he can free himself of all his impure motives for Torah learning — desire for recognition, etc. *Gemara* study by night is a protection against the spiritual harm caused by unholy music, which can otherwise make it very difficult to serve God. But with this protection he will discover the power of holy music and be able to attach himself to God through music and song. This strengthens the forces of holiness and gives him the power to control whatever he wants. He will be able to achieve the level of prophecy (3).

8) Studying the codes of Torah law gives us the ability to distinguish between good and evil and separate them from one another (This is because the essence of the *halachah* is to distinguish between pure and impure, *kasher* and *passul* etc...) Thus the evil contained in the four cosmic elements which are the source of the various human character traits is banished. This is the way one can achieve perfection, and then whatever one prays for will emerge from potentiality to actuality and one's request will be fulfilled. Those who oppose him with obstacles and barriers will be cast down to the ground (8:6,7).

9) Reaching the correct legal decision depends upon prayer (*Ibid.*).

10) When studying Torah it is necessary to articulate the words and say them aloud. Then the words themselves will illumine all the places where we have to repent, and in the end we will be able to achieve perfect repentance, which will outbalance all our sins. This is a continuous process: with each act of repentance we advance from level to level until we emerge from our own low level and are able to comprehend the true depths of Torah (11:1).

11) But it is only possible to receive this illumination from the words of the Torah if we first break our pride and pretensions, which give us false motives for Torah study — to acquire prestige or be able to boast or attain rabbinic office etc. The

degree to which we succeed in this depends on our moral purity (*Ibid.* 2,3).

12) When people study Torah for extraneous motives, especially the Oral Torah — the *gemara* and the legal codes — it gives them an opening to speak disparagingly about the true Tzaddikim. This is why there is opposition to the Tzaddikim from certain scholars (12:1).

13) Before a person sits down to study he should understand that at the very moment he is learning, the Tzaddik in the Garden of Eden will be listening to his voice. He must therefore bind himself to the *Tanna* — Mishnaic teacher — or Tzaddik who first revealed the Torah teaching which he is studying in order that their two souls may "kiss" and be attached to one another. This brings great joy to the *Tanna*, and through this the student sitting learning will be able to return to God and put fresh life into all the days of his life that were spent in darkness. But this can only come about when he studies Torah for its own sake with the intention of fulfilling God's commandment to *study* Torah — which is equal to all the other commandments put together — and to *fulfill* the Torah he learns. But when someone learns because he wants to be considered clever, etc.., he is worse than a carcass of a dead animal (which is forbidden to be eaten unless it was ritually slaughtered) and he will certainly not be able to attach himself to the spirit of the *Tanna*. He will never see the truth. He will turn into an enemy of the true Tzaddik and cause the exile of the Shechinah, because the oral Torah is in exile on the lips of this so-called Torah scholar (*Ibid.*).

14) When one learns for the right motives and studies the words of a *Tanna*, one restores the soul of the *Tanna* to his [the *Tanna's*] body (*Ibid.*).

15) It is a good practice to study legal rulings in conjunction with the *B'er HaGolah*, the commentary which gives the Talmudic source of each ruling, in order to mention the name of the *Tanna* or legal authority who originated the ruling in question and so attach oneself to his spirit (*Ibid.*).

16) The study of Torah in holiness and purity makes it possible to arouse the sinners of Israel and converts to return to God. But it is only possible to achieve this when one is absolutely humble (14:3-5).

17) Whenever a person learns Torah — and this applies especially to a Torah scholar — he must aim to send light into the root of their souls. Then he will be able to arouse even those who are far from God — the wicked and the proselytes — and draw them closer to Him. He will be worthy of having a son who is learned in Torah. But when a person's learning is not on such a level, his son will not be learned in Torah (*Ibid.* 3,4).

18) Through meditation and self-examination, in which one judges oneself and all one's actions, it is possible to attain fear of God, which is the means to understand the revealed aspects of Torah and attain true humility. This is the foundation of genuine prayer, where one nullifies one's very being and material existence. Then he can understand the hidden aspects of Torah, which is the light treasured up to be revealed in the future. Happy is he that attains this. (15).

19) It is only possible to understand the secrets of Torah if you "make your face black as a raven's" (*Erubin* 54)and act just like the raven to its young. You must nullify your materialistic aspects completely, as if you were simply not in the world (*Ibid.*).

20) The secret aspects of Torah are called "holy" and "no common man shall eat thereof" (Leviticus 22:13) — only His holy ones and those who are close to Him (*Ibid.*).

21) When Torah is drawn into the world, God's providence is drawn over us. The closer a person is to Torah the more completely God's providence is drawn over him (13:4).

22) There are times when the way to observe the Torah is by *bittul Torah*, neglect of Torah. It is impossible to be constantly occupied with Torah and devotion without interruption. There are times when one has to make a break and "neglect" the Torah in order to go out and deal with everyday matters. This stops the forces of the Other Side from rising up with disturbances and distractions and destroying one's mind

completely, God forbid. Periodic neglect of Torah is an inescapable necessity. Only when Mashiach comes will there never be any need to interrupt one's devotions (16).

23) When a person wants to receive new insights into Torah he must first arouse himself with words hot as flaming coals: he must pour out his prayer before God, and then God's love will be aroused for him and the Supreme Heart will be opened and a stream of words will pour forth. By means of these words, new insights will come from this same source (20:2).

24) In the prayer a person makes before discoursing on Torah, he must plead with God and beg Him to open His hand out of generosity alone. He should never demand anything as of right, as if he were entitled to something in virtue of his own merits. He should stand before God like a poor beggar. He should also bind himself with the souls of his listeners. Then his prayer will be a joint prayer, and "the prayer of the community is never spurned." (*Berachot* 8a) It will surely be accepted, and each of those present will then have a share in the Torah he reveals (*Ibid.*).

25) Through the merit of the Torah which is drawn into the world in this way you can succeed in coming to the Land of Israel (*Ibid.* 6).

26) When a person studies Torah without gaining new insights it is because the wisdom of the Torah is concealed from him like an embryo in the womb. He should cry out in his prayers and as he learns. Then he will give birth to wisdom (21:7,8).

27) When someone studies Torah without understanding what he is learning or gaining any new insights, God Himself has great joy from his learning, but even so, he should make no attempt to teach publicly. But when God bestows understanding on a person and grants him original ideas, it is right and fitting that he should reveal what he has learned to others and bestow his understanding upon the Chosen People. He should share his own good with others (*Ibid.*).

28) Be very careful not to listen to Torah lectures from scholars lacking in integrity. They are "Jewish demons" (cf. *Zohar* III,

253) who receive their Torah from the demons who are in possession of the fallen Torah. Their discussions may seem very remarkable and they are usually well received by the mass of people. Their style is florid and ornate: they give elaborate examples and seemingly profound explanations. But there is nothing to be gained from them. Their Torah has no power to direct men on a good path. On the contrary, it leads people into doubts and disbelief and they end up despising those who are truly religious (28:1).

29) The remedy for this is to open the doors of your house to genuine Torah scholars and offer them hospitality. This is the way to develop true faith and lovingkindness and to nullify yourself before God, as it is written: "I am a worm and not a man" (Psalms 22:7). This will give you the strength to confront the opposition and banish the doubts and disbelief they foment. Then you will be able to sift out the good that is in their Torah and elevate it (*Ibid.* 3).

30) You have to be assertive and determined if you want to acquire Torah. You must be "bold as a leopard" (*Avoth* 5:24) in the service of God. Pay no attention whatsoever to those who put obstacles in your way or try to ridicule you. The quality of your boldness and determination will be reflected in the Torah you learn. One whose boldness expresses a determination to acquire genuine holiness will gain new insights and find new horizons in the Torah. But someone whose boldness is really a form of pride and arrogance stemming from the Other Side and who lacks genuine respect for men of piety will not gain true insights into Torah. The Torah he will acquire will be from the forces of the Other Side. And the quality of his prayer will reflect the quality of the Torah he learns (30:8).

31) To achieve complete fulfillment one must be developed in one's character and learned in Torah at one and the same time. Our Sages said that "an ignoramus will never be a saint" (*Avoth* 2:6). On the other hand, to be learned by itself is useless. It is possible to be learned and completely wicked, and when a person is unworthy the Torah becomes an elixir of death for

him. But when a person is both learned in Torah and saintly in his actions he is like an angel of the Lord of Hosts. He shapes the letters of Torah for good and brings life and goodness into the world. One who mistakenly believes that the main thing is to be learned alone is like "Acher" (R. Elisha ben Abuya, the notorious scholar-turned-disbeliever of the Talmud) who "uprooted the saplings" (*Chagiga* 14b) (31).

32) There are times when even a perfect Tzaddik who is both learned and saintly falls from his level — because it is impossible to remain on the same level constantly. When this happens, it is no good for him to try to fortify himself with the thought of the great learning he still retains. He must work on his character and behavior, not his Torah intellect. He should strengthen himself in the fear of Heaven and work on the good points which are still within him (*Ibid.*).

33) The Torah and the Tzaddikim are the source of peace: peace within the Jewish people as a whole and peace in each individual. It is no good for a person to be at war with himself. There must be a harmony between his various traits, and he must also develop a harmonious approach to life so that it will make no difference to him whether things are good or seemingly bad: in everything he will find only God (33:2).

34) Extraneous ideologies are darkness and folly compared to the wisdom of Torah. Through fasting and giving charity to causes in the Land of Israel we become worthy of the wisdom of Torah, which elevates the soul and fills it with love, light and life, and the harsh judgements are sweetened (35:1).

35) The world cannot endure nor can the harsh judgements be sweetened except through the merit of the breath of little children studying Torah. Every person has a duty to search out a good, upright, God-fearing teacher — and beg God to help him find one — in order not to let the holy breath of the children be corrupted by a bad teacher (37:4).

36) When a person studies Torah in spite of all the pressures of hardship and poverty, the Torah he learns draws a thread of love over him and banishes all his opponents and all the forces

of impurity. Speech is cleansed and elevated to its source, and he becomes worthy of expressing himself before God with words of heat and fire which flow from the heart in truth (38:4).

37) When a person sharpens his mind by studying Torah, his intellect is sharpened and his awareness of the greatness of the Creator is expanded. This will make him even more ashamed of his sins — and shame is the essence of repentance. He will be worthy of the light of *tefilin*, which is a ray of the light of God's inner countenance and a "tree of life" (*Ibid.* 5).

38) Deficient faith brings neglect of Torah, resulting in exile and wandering (40).

39) Even in learning Torah there has to be a certain limit, a level of sufficiency and contentment. One can easily become confused by wanting to learn more than one is able to. He sees how much there is to learn and wants to learn the entire Torah while standing on one leg. He may end up being so bewildered that he actually learns nothing at all. You must be content for your learning to be within the limits of what is possible for you, because "it is not for you to complete the task" (*Avoth* 2:21) (54:3).

40) Heaven and earth are recreated afresh when new innovations of Torah are born. This is the source of all the blessings in the world. But there are certain original conceptions which are purely a product of the imagination. The Torah student is more at risk from the deceptions of the imagination than anyone else. His misconceptions may appear very attractive and convincing — because the whole power of the imagination is to make one thing seem like another, and therefore these misconceptions have a strong semblance of truth. Inasmuch as they are Torah they do contain some good, but this is outweighed by the bad which is in them, and original concepts like these cause famine in the world and have an adverse effect on one's livelihood. One must pray to God to be saved from them. The remedy is to be very careful neither to speak nor listen to *lashon hara*, malicious slander. Also be sure that you are always happy, because the main reason for the fantasies and temptations created by the imagination is

depression. Therefore the way to overcome them is by being happy (*Ibid.* 6).

41) Devotion to Torah brings vitality and length of days. The Torah is made up of the names of the Holy One, blessed-be-He. When we speak words of Torah we are calling upon the Life of Life, blessed be His name, and thus we draw long life and vitality from him. This is why we have to study Torah aloud and actually form the words on our lips. This is how we call upon God and draw long life and vitality from Him (56:3).

42) A person who devotes himself to Torah can give guidance even to those who are far from him, despite the fact that he does not know exactly what they need and that they may not even be physically present. His learning and devotion to Torah cause those who are distant to hear the voice of Torah clearly. For the Torah cries out constantly and declares: "How long, ye thoughtless, will ye love thoughtlessness?" It is only that her voice is not heard because Godliness has been so heavily concealed as a result of our many sins. Today God is hidden from us in a "concealment within the concealment" — the double hiding referred to in the prophecy of *haster astir panai*, "I shall surely hide My face" (Deut. 31:18). But devotion to Torah causes that which is concealed to be revealed, and even those who are distant can then hear the voice of Torah raised in warning, and they can all return to God (*Ibid.*).

43) Certain kinds of people are very far indeed from God and have virtually *leapt* away from the One who is the place of the whole world. There are other cases of people who once had a period of closeness to God but now they have forgotten about it. And then there are those who still remember God but whose strength has become too weak for them to be able to conquer their evil inclination. But the power of the Torah is so great that those who study it in truth can cause its warning voice to be heard by all these different kinds of people (*Ibid.*).

44) When you study Torah you must draw out "judgements of truth" from what you learn. That is, you should try to derive practical directives as to how to live, both for yourself and for

those who are under your influence, regardless of whether they are few or many. You will be able to do this if you have faith in the Sages (61:1).

45) There are many holy books in existence today, and many more are destined to be printed in the future. The world needs all of them, and it is wrong to cast aspersions on any of them. They are all firmly based upon the Written and Oral Law. It is philosophical works based on speculation and false ideology that you should keep away from, no matter who they might be written by. But all books which are in accordance with the Holy Torah that we received on Mt. Sinai are very precious, and they are all necessary for the world. One who scoffs at them will be subject to the judgement of boiling excrement, and he will never succeed in gaining any practical guidance from the Torah he studies. He will never be sure about anything. He will constantly be afflicted with doubts in whatever he does until he repents and revises his view of these holy books. And when he does, the harsh judgements in the world will be sweetened by means of the Holy Torah. The very perfection of the Torah depends upon the abundance of books concerned with the oral Law (*Ibid.* 5).

46) A person who introduces new and original Torah concepts and whose intention is for the sake of Heaven must have faith in *himself*. He needs to have faith that God has great joy from his innovations. He should never be dispirited. He should always be diligent in his studies and see to it that he is constantly developing new ideas. He should note them down and write books about them. Then all the harsh judgements in the world will be sweetened (*Ibid.*).

47) Studying the legal codes has the power to strike at the very roots of strife and contention. (A legal decision represents the resolution of all the arguments on the subject between the Sages.) By striking at the roots of strife, the divisiveness manifested in the lower worlds is dissipated, and so also is the turmoil which the evil inclination stirs up in the heart. This turmoil expresses itself in the form of all the doubts and problems about faith which rise persistently in a person's heart

and divide him from God to the point that he finds it impossible to pray as he should. The main reason why people find it hard to pray with the proper devotion is that their faith is not perfect. If a person knew and believed with all his heart that the entire world is full of God's glory and that God stands over him while he is praying and listens to his every word, he would certainly pray with tremendous fervor and would make sure that he concentrated on every word he was saying. It is only because people are not entirely firm in their faith that they are not as enthusiastic as they should be about their prayers. This is because of the turmoil stirred up in the heart by the evil inclination. The remedy is to study the legal codes, which puts this turmoil to rest and brings peace. The heart is no longer divided, and one can serve God with all one's heart — with both inclinations. The gates of wisdom will be opened to him and he will know how to reply to the atheist in his heart. He will be worthy of praying with all his heart (62:2).

48) When a person labors in Torah until he succeeds in knowing and understanding it, his soul will be healed and elevated to its source, all the harsh judgements will be sweetened, and a "tree of life" will be planted in the worlds above that has the power to heal everything. Through his labors all the worlds are sustained and renewed and the glory of God is revealed in the world. This is the goal of man's work, that the glory of God should be magnified (74).

49) If a person labors in Torah even without understanding what he is studying, it is still very good. All the words rise up to the higher worlds, and God takes joy in them and makes them into "willows of the brook" (*Ibid.*).

50) Without Torah it is impossible to live. At times a person burns with a fiery passion for God, but the passion is excessive and could engulf him completely. But Torah study has the power to cool the flames and allow him to survive. There are other times when a person burns with desire for the temptations of this world. The fire of his passions could burn his entire body. But learning Torah protects him against this. The fire within him

is extinguished and he can live. Torah is therefore the source of all true life (78).

51) True repentance depends on Torah. A person must labor in the study of Torah until he is able to understand one thing from another and make original contributions for the sake of Heaven. This is perfect repentance, and then all the letters had combinations which fall within this person's portion in all the worlds will be restored to their true root and brought back from the scattered places to which they were banished. He will become a new person. His mind will become settled, and he will arouse God's love for him to the point that God Himself will "pray" for him — in His pure compassion He will stir up His abundant love and send complete salvation (105).

52) When a person studies Torah it is a good thing to paraphrase what he is learning in the language he understands. This is a benefit to the whole world (118).

53) No matter what a person is learning he should find himself in it: he should derive a personal lesson from what he is learning and recognize his own insignificance and lowliness. This is a sign that he wants to perform the will of God (121).

54) When someone unworthy discourses on Torah he may be subjected to sexual temptations. It is a grave sin for one who is unworthy to discourse on Torah even to one other person, let alone a group (134).

55) When a person is studying a Torah concept originally introduced by a *Tanna* or a Tzaddik, he should imagine the form of the Tzaddik or the *Tanna* standing before him. This can protect him from forgetfulness (192).

56) One who feels the sweetness of Torah will be saved from becoming a widower (199).

57) A person who wants to gain new insights and introduce new concepts in Torah, must weep profusely beforehand to prevent the forces of the Other Side and the husks from having any share in these innovations (262).

58) There are people whose Torah teachings are broad below but narrow above. They are broad below because these people

expound at great length. But above they are narrow — because in the upper worlds nothing remains except a mere spark. On the other hand the Torah discourses of the true Tzaddikim may seem very slim and narrow below, but in the worlds above they are very broad. Happy are they. The same applies to their power to arouse men to repentance (279).

59) Even a simple person who sits with a book and examines the letters of the Torah carefully can perceive new concepts and real wonders. But don't make a test out of this (281).

60) One has to literally steal time from one's business and other activities in order to study Torah. Even someone who is burdened with many obligations and duties cannot be so pressed that it is impossible for him to snatch some period each day to devote to Torah (284).

61) Every Jew must spend a portion of his time every day studying the law codes. This applies under all circumstances. It is a very serious matter, and no one should ever miss his daily session. Even in an emergency, when he has no time — for example, if he is traveling — he should still learn at least one paragraph of the *Shulchan Aruch,* even from somewhere other than the place he has reached in his regular daily study routine. Do not let a single day of your life go by wihtout studying something from the *Shulchan Aruch*. Under normal circumstances when you are not under pressure, go through each of the four sections of the *Shulchan Aruch* in turn until you have finished them all. Then go back to the beginning and start again. Follow this practice all your life. It is a great remedy for all the damage caused by sin. The study of the legal codes sifts the good from the bad. It is the ultimate remedy (Rabbi Nachman's Wisdom 29).

62) Through the study of the *Shulchan Aruch* you will be worthy of becoming "master of the house" and ruler over all the earth. The gates of the Garden of Eden will be raised up and you will attain to the Upper Wisdom and the Lower Wisdom, which make up the delight of the Garden of Eden (286).

63) When little children first go to school and commence the

study of Torah, they start with the first words of Leviticus. It is from here that they receive the holy breath of their lips — which is untainted by sin — with the help of the Tzaddikim of the generation (282).

64) The study of *halachot*, legal rulings — and especially making original contributions — is the "joy of the World to Come." Giving birth is made easy and people are saved from all their troubles (*Likutey Moharan* II, 2).

65) One who prevents scholars from studying will be stricken with diseases of the feet (*Ibid.* 3).

66) When a person teaches Torah in public and his words are heard by unworthy students it can cause drought and imprisonment (60).

67) Honor of the Torah is the source of the blessing of rain (*Ibid.*).

68) If you want to devote yourself to Torah study unflaggingly, be careful never to speak against a single Jew. Do your best to seek out merit and worth in every Jew. A particular individual may seem to you to be wicked. But you should still make an effort to find some good points in him, and then he will no longer be wicked! When every Jew is lovely and pleasant in your eyes you will be able to apply yourself to Torah continuously (Rabbi Nachman's Wisdom 91).

69) The study of the Zohar can give you enthusiasm for all your sacred studies. The very language of the Zohar is precious and can arouse you to serve God (Rabbi Nachman's Wisdom 108).

70) Rabbi Shimon bar Yochai, who wrote the Zohar, invested the Aramaic language with such sanctity that even other things written in Aramaic have the power to arouse you to God (*Ibid.* 109).

71) The Torah possesses a unique pleasantness. The main thing is to be worthy of tasting this pleasantness and sweetness. You can attain this if you break your pride completely. Never take credit for yourself, give all the credit to God alone. Also through giving charity, especially charity for causes in the Land of Israel, you can draw from the "mentality of the Land of Israel" and

thereby taste the sweet pleasantness of the wisdom of the Torah (*Likutey Moharan* II, 71).

72) One who is truly devoted to the Torah can learn the future from it (35).

73) When one studies the books of the true Tzaddikim he must concentrate hard in order to understand the remarkable originality of their teachings and to find their true depth and sweetness. For as soon as their words are put into the form of a book it causes a great concealment of their light. Even the highest and most remarkable Torah teachings become obscured and hidden as soon as they are put into a book, and the purity of their light is covered over. The book cover alone sets up a great barrier against the light. When you study from a book you must pay extra attention to discovering the greatness of the original ideas contained in it (36).

74) Those who study Torah should be sure always to produce original ideas. Torah thoughts are a great remedy for immoral fantasies. When a man has union with his wife he should meditate on the words of the Torah (*Likutey Moharan* II, 105, 106).

75) When you study subjects connected with tragedy, such as the laws of mourning etc. go through these sections very rapidly (Rabbi Nachman's Wisdom 8).

76) The power of the Torah is very great. Someone who labors in Torah continuously will have the power to bring about miracles. It is possible to achieve this even without being familiar with mystical devotions. The main thing is to study the legal codes until you know how to make legal rulings. In previous eras there were many leading sages who were able to bring about miracles merely by virtue of the fact that they devoted themselves to Torah study day and night (*Likutey Moharan* II, 41).

77) The power of the Torah is strong enough to release one from one's sins. No matter how trapped a person might be, if he simply makes it his business to set a regular time for Torah study every day without fail then he will be able to emerge from

the hold of his evil past through the great strength which comes from the Holy Torah (Rabbi Nachman's Wisdom 19).

78) Even if a person learns and later forgets, it is still very good. In the future world everyone will be reminded of everything he learned, even if he forgot it. Still, it is certainly better if one can remember all the words of the Holy Torah (*Ibid.* 26).

79) It is good for a person to visit all the different places in the Torah during his lifetime. He should learn all the holy books of the Torah: the Five Books of Moses themselves, the writings of the prophets and the rest of the *Tanach*, the Talmud and all the legal authorities, all the holy books of the Zohar, all the Midrashim, the writings of the *ARI HaKadosh* and all the other holy books. Then when he reaches the World to Come he will be able to boast that he visited all parts of the Torah. Don't be put off and say it is too difficult to cover all this. You don't have to finish everything in a single day. If your soul loves the Torah and you make a regular habit of studying you will be able to finish everything we have mentioned and more and even go back over them several times. This has been proved by the many Torah scholars of past ages who were authorities on the Talmud and knew all the other holy books virtually by heart. They achieved everything through their unflagging application to study. Every person of learning can achieve this if he wants. But he should still take the time to pour out his prayers before God and converse with Him each day. There is time for everything — for Torah, prayer and all the other devotions. The most important thing is to be sure to learn all the legal codes and finish them several times over (*Ibid.* 28).

80) When a person is thinking about a Torah idea and wants to find a new angle he must go over the verse or the subject in question again and again. He must knock on the door persistently until it opens for him (*Ibid.* 58).

PRAYER תפילה

1) The main reason why prayers are not accepted is that the words lack grace and beauty. It is through studying Torah that the words of the prayers are invested with grace. One should always try to pray with words that have grace and beauty, and then one's prayers will be accepted (1:1).

2) Prayer is the Jew's main weapon. Whatever battles a person has to fight, whether against his evil inclination, or against those who put barriers and obstacles in his path, they should all be fought with prayer. Prayer is the source of our very life. If you want to attain the true holiness of Israel you must pray profusely. Speak to God and beg Him to help you in every way. Prayer is the weapon with which to win the battle (2:1).

3) A person may have prayed profusely and secluded himself with God day after day for years and years and still feel that he is very far from God. He may even start to think that God is hiding His countenance from hm. But it is a mistake if he thinks that God does not hear his prayers. He must believe with perfect faith that God pays attention to each and every word of every single prayer, petition and conversation. Not a single word is lost, God forbid. Each one leaves its mark in the worlds above, however faintly. Little by little they awaken God's love. If there seems to be no response, the reason is that as yet the holy edifice he is destined to enter is not yet complete. The main thing is not to give up and fall into despair. This would be foolish. Be firm and continue with your prayers with new determination. In the end God's love will be aroused and He will turn to you and shine His radiance upon you and fulfill your wishes and desires through the strength of the true Tzaddikim. He will draw you

towards Himself in love and abundant mercy (*Ibid.* 6).
4) It is impossible to achieve perfect prayer except through observing the Covenant with perfect purity. Therefore each Jew must bind his prayers to the Tzaddikim of the age, because they know how to raise every single prayer to its proper place, and out of all the prayers they build the structure of the Shechinah, which brings the coming of Mashiach closer (*Ibid.* 2:6).
5) You must give charity before you pray. Charity is a protection against the distracting thoughts which come while praying (*Ibid.* 4).
6) Never feel that you are entitled to a reward for anything. All the good deeds we do are sent to us by God. At times God may help a person in a certain way, or he may achieve a certain spiritual success. But he should not think that this is a reward for his Torah study, prayers, or good deeds, or anything else. Everything is sent by God, and if it were not for His great mercy, he would have been sunk in failure long ago, God forbid (*Ibid.*).
7) Torah study and prayer reinforce one another and throw light on each other. Both of them are necessary (*Ibid* 6).
8) The greatest of the Tzaddikim draw down sparks of the light of the Infinite over all who are close to them and joined to their name. At times it happens that a person is in the middle of his prayers when suddenly he takes fire and says a number of words with tremendous passion. The reason is that God in His mercy unveils the light of the Infinite and shines it down upon him. Consciously, perhaps, he does not see these sparks, but his guardian angel sees it (cf. *Megillah* 3a) and his soul is immediately kindled with a fiery passion to be bound with the light of the Infinite. As long as the revelation lasts he says all the words which shine their light to him with tremendous intensity and absolute self-surrender. It is only with the help of the great Tzaddikim that it is possible to have experiences like this, because they alone have some apprehension of the light of the Infinite and only they have the power to radiate the sweet pleasantness of this illumination to each person in accordance

with the capacity of his heart (4:9).
9) Each person should say to himself: "The whole world was created only for my sake," One should therefore constantly be looking for ways of improving the world in order to make up for any deficiencies, and one should constantly pray for the world (5:1).
10) You must pray with all your strength. The sound of your voice will then penetrate your mind and you will be able to concentrate on your prayers. Your heart will hear the words your lips are saying, and you will be able to straighten the crookedness of the heart and attain true joy. Your joy will be so great that you will be able to carry out all the mitzvot with a great joy derived from the mitzvah itself and you will be able to clothe your prayers even in story form. You will have the power to annul all harsh decrees even after the decree has already been made (*Ibid.* 3).
11) It is absolutely vital to empty your mind of all foreign ideologies and extraneous ideas. You must never allow your Divinely-given intellect to be infected in the least by the *chametz* — yeast — of these fallacious beliefs or by physical appetites and desires. They distort and sully the mind, making it impossible to concentrate while praying or to experience real joy. You should never be afraid of anything except God. All other fears are simply an obstacle to concentration on prayer and joy. The main thing is to guard the mind against "yeast" by avoiding all bad thoughts and physical appetites. This "yeast" is rooted in the domain of death. You must do battle against these loathsome thoughts and expel them completely from your mind. Don't let them enter your mind at all. As regards fear of Heaven, you should aim to combine it with love. Then you will be able to purify your mind and pray with all your might and with intense concentration — to the point where your prayer will be like "thunder." Then you will attain true joy (*Ibid.* 4).
12) Prayer is "faith." It has the power to improve the memory and banish forgetfulness, which is caused by an absence of faith (7).

13) The fountain of the wisdom of the Torah flows from prayer. To reach a clear decision in matters of Torah law therefore depends on prayer. A legal decision in Torah is tantamount to renewing the world. Torah law concerns the distinction between what is permitted and what is forbidden, what is pure and what is impure. Therefore the clarification of the law is a vital part of the process of sifting the good from the bad in the four elements of the universe. Through this the opponents of truth are cast down to the earth and humiliated (8:6-7).

14) Our very life-force comes from prayer. You must pray with all your strength and put your strength into the very letters of the words or the prayers in order to renew it there. Through this you will attain true faith (9:1).

15) The quality of a person's prayer has an influence on his marital union and his livelihood (*Ibid.* 2).

16) Perfect prayer brings a flow of life into the three divisions of the universe: the terrestrial world, the world of the stars and the world of the angels (*Ibid.*).

17) As soon as a person stands up to pray, he is immediately surrounded by extraneous thoughts and *kelipot*, "husks," which leave him in darkness and make it impossible for him to pray. The best remedy for this is to make sure that the words emerge from your lips in truth. Every word which comes from your mouth in truth and sincerity will provide you with an exit from the darkness which is trapping you, and then you will be able to pray properly. This is a fundamental principle whenever you are praying or meditating. You may feel unable to say a single word because of the intense darkness and confusion which hedge you in on every side. But see that whatever you do say, you say truthfully as far as you possibly can. For example you could at least say the words "God, send help" truthfully. You may not be able to put much enthusiasm into the words, but you can still make yourself say them sincerely and mean what you say quite literally. The very truth of your words will send you light and you will be able to pray with the help of God. When you do this it sustains and perfects all the worlds (*Ibid.* 3).

18) You will also be able to break open the way for others and free them from the traps they are caught in and help them return to God (*Ibid.*).

19) It requires great merit to be able to offer up a person's prayers so that they ascend to the gate of his tribe. Each person must therefore bind his prayers to the Tzaddik of the generation, because the Tzaddik understands how to reach the different gates and cause each prayer to ascend to the proper gate (*Ibid.*).

20) You must pray so intensely that you pour your heart out like water before God. This will help to bring the Mashiach (*Ibid.* 9).

21) The secret of true prayer is known only to the Tzaddikim of the generation. Anyone who has a problem in his household should go to the Sage to appeal for mercy. God yearns for the prayers of the Tzaddikim. Those self-important people who refuse to go to ask the Tzaddik to pray for them and who try to stop others from going as well are preventing God from satisfying His yearning (10:4).

22) One should have no wish to occupy oneself with worldly pursuits at all. His whole concern should be with his soul. When he prays, his only thought should be for his spiritual welfare. Even when it comes to the prayers which seem to deal explicitly with material matters, such as the prayer for healing ("Heal us!") and prosperity ("Bless this year!") one should have in mind not the needs of the body but of the soul. The thought should be that the soul should be blessed and healed, etc. As a person perfects himself spiritually all his material problems are straightened out too. But his only thought should be for his spiritual welfare (14:9).

23) One should get into the habit of always praying for whatever one needs, be it livelihood, children or healing for someone who is sick at home, etc. The main recourse should always be to prayer, in the faith that God is good to all. One should always put one's main effort into searching for God and not go running after all kinds of other solutions. Most of them are no help at all, and the few that could be he probably isn't aware of and won't find in any case. But God is always to be found. If we call

on Him it will help for everything (*Ibid.* 11).

24) When you pray, it should be with a sense of complete self-sacrifice. You must nullify your body and your whole sense of self and let no motive of personal gain enter your thoughts at all. Indeed you should not think of yourself at all. You should nullify yourself as if you simply did not exist. The way to achieve this is through "judgement" — secluded meditation in which you speak to God and examine and judge yourself with regard to all your actions. Through this the faculty of fear is elevated to its root which is *Da'at*, the knowledge of God. This is the gateway to the revealed aspect of Torah, through which one can come to pray with true devotion and surrender. When your prayer is on such a level you will be worthy of uncovering the secrets of Torah, the "light stored up for the Tzaddikim." Happy is the man who is worthy of this (15:2-4).

25) There is a serpent which induces people to pray for their own benefit: "Give us life! Give us food!" and so on. You must be firm and try to pray without any intention of gaining something for yourself. Simply pray as if you did not exist in this world at all. Then you will be worthy of the light stored up for the Tzaddikim (*Ibid.* 5).

26) The Holy One, blessed-be-He, yearns for the prayers of Israel. When we pray we are satisfying His desire, and He has great joy from us (*Ibid.*).

27) It is a great kindness of God to permit us to address Him in human terms in our prayers and blessings and to answer our appeals and requests when we do so. If it were not for His kindness, it would be completely inappropriate to call upon God with names and praises made up of mere words and letters. This thought alone should move you to pray with fire and passion: when you consider the true greatness of the Creator — to the extent that you can form any conception of it at all — and how He is exalted beyond all our human praises and titles, it is a wonderful sign of His love and tender mercy that He has given us permission to address Him in human terms and to pray to Him in order that we should be able to bind ourselves to Him.

Therefore we should at least be sincere when we address Him in this way, since it is only through His love and mercy that we are able to do so at all (*Ibid.*).

28) When a Sage is about to give an exposition on Torah he must first pour out his prayers before God in order to arouse the Supreme Heart to send him words hot as coals of fire. Only then should he begin his discourse. For then illumination will flow down in abundance from the Supreme Heart (20:2).

29) When he prays before his discourse, he should plead with God and beg Him for a gift — a free present which he knows he has not earned. He should not rely on his own merits. He should stand before God like a poor beggar and beg for His help. Whenever a person prays, he should never try to force matters and insist that God should to exactly what *he* wants Him to do. He should make his request and entreat God's love. If God grants it, well and good. And if not, then not (*Ibid.* 5).

30) When the Torah teacher prays before his discourse he should bind his soul with the souls of all his listeners. This will make his prayer into a "communal prayer" which "God never spurns," and it will surely be accepted. The bond between all these souls will cause a great concentration of holiness in the worlds above (*Ibid.* 4).

31) No matter what level a person is standing on, it always has two aspects: the revealed and the concealed. These correspond to Torah and Prayer respectively. Each individual must constantly climb from level to level and thereby transform what was previously concealed from him into something revealed. The way to achieve this is through devotion to Torah and praying intently. A person must study intensively and pray to God again and again until He reveals what was hidden from him until now. Then it will be revealed, leaving a new level of concealment even more exalted than before. He must now pray again until this in turn is revealed. In the same way he must climb from level to level, constantly pleading with God to grant an even higher perception. He must go on until he is merged with the first point of the world of Emanation — the highest of the four worlds —

and thereafter he will be merged with the Infinite. Then he will be worthy of the "Torah of God" and the "Prayer of God." This is the way to attain joy, and it is joy that gives us the strength and determination necessary to enter the gates of holiness and draw close to the genuine Tzaddikim. With their help we can attain complete faith. The basis for all these attainments is prayer. Prayer encompasses everything. In essence prayer stems from awe — the awe which fills one with such a deep sense of shame before God that one could never think of transgressing, God forbid. One who reaches the levels we have mentioned will have "hands" with which to receive the guidance of the true spiritual leaders. Then the world will be free of persecution and divisiveness and peace will spread everywhere. Peace will reign between Israel and their Father in Heaven, and the forces of Holiness will be secure under the "seal within the seal" (22:10).

32) When a person prays with such intensity that he sacrifices himself completely and "kills" himself in his prayers, he should understand that wherever he finds extraneous thoughts entering his mind which need to be elevated, this is where he needs to put in the fiercest efforts in order to elevate the sparks of holiness (26).

33) It takes great determination to deal with the extraneous thoughts which come while praying. The whole medley of thoughts and ideas which are with a person all day suddenly marshal themselves and demand attention precisely at the moment he is trying to pray. This is why we have to be so firm in dealing with them when we are praying (30:7).

34) The secret of prayer is to be bold. We have to have the audacity to ask God for everything we need — even if we need to ask Him to work miracles for us. The only way to stand up and pray to God is with boldness and daring. When we consider the utter greatness of the Creator — to the extent we can form any conception of it at all — and think of our own smallness and worthlessness, how can we stand up and pray before him? When we are praying we have to cast aside our timidity and

boldly ask God for whatever we need. This boldness and assertiveness are necessary in order to thwart the opposition which tries to prevent us from serving God (*Ibid.* 8).

35) Prayer must be spoken out loud — literally. It is not enough to *think* the prayers. It is true that God knows what we are thinking. But the words have to be *spoken*, because speech is a vessel with which to receive the influx of blessing. The blessing we receive is in accordance with the words we speak. When we articulate the words on our lips and our speech is well-ordered and dignified we are then able to receive rich blessings. This is the reason why one should pray for whatever one needs, whether spiritual or material, in *words*: then one will be able to receive the influx of blessing (34:3).

36) The reason for clapping our hands while praying is that it has the power to purify the place we are praying so that it becomes like the "air of the Land of Israel." The "air of the Land of Israel" is the remedy for the extraneous thoughts which come while praying. All idolatrous thoughts are cast aside and murder and destruction cease from the world (44).

37) Even if a person stands up and prays in the place where a Tzaddik has prayed it is still very hard for him to pray there because he is not accustomed to the air of that place. All the more so when a Tzaddik prays where an ordinary person has prayed. This is why one must set a fixed place for one's prayers, as the Rabbis taught (*Ibid.*).

38) Through prayer the secrets of the Torah are revealed (*Ibid.*).

39) A remedy for the confusing thoughts which flood in and disturb us when we are trying to pray is to give charity for causes in the Land of Israel. In this way we become merged with the pure air of the Land and we are freed from distracting thoughts. The mind becomes clear and we achieve *tikkun habrit* (*Ibid.*).

40) When a person who is praying feels such excitement in his very hands that he claps them together, speech is brought into being thereby and the mouth can then receive the words within it (45).

41) Clapping our hands while praying sweetens the harsh judgements, thus protecting us against forgetfulness and putting strife and conflict to rest (46).

42) When we pray with such fervor that we put all our strength into the letters of the prayers and "all my bones will say, Lord, who is like unto Thee?" (Psalm 35:10) the words of the prayer are themselves the words of the Holy One, blessed-be-He. The power of these letters gives fresh strength to the Ten Utterances through which the world was created (48).

43) Intense prayer is a *segulah* for having children. It saves us from conflict and opposition, and strengthens the power of truth in the world. The whole world is brought to serve God with one accord, and the true teacher of the generation is revealed (*Ibid.*).

44) Intense prayer, the Land of Israel and the mitzvah of succah are interrelated concepts (*Ibid.*).

45) In essence, prayer depends on the heart. One must concentrate one's whole heart upon one's prayers, binding the thoughts in the heart to the words of the prayers. It is no good if the heart is far from the words the mouth is speaking. You must listen carefully to what you are saying. Then the kingship of God is revealed and exalted and the sovereignty of evil collapses. The Jewish people is blessed with a flow of life and riches and goodness without end. The upper unification and the lower unification are completed and the mystical Torah of the Ancient One is revealed (49).

46) When a person observes the Covenant in purity and binds himself to the true Tzaddikim, who are the embodiment of the Covenant, he is able to taste the sweetness in the words of the prayers and a lion waits to consume his "sacrifice" — his prayer. But one who abuses the Covenant and tastes the "bitter waters" will be unable to taste the sweetness of the words of the prayers, and a dog will come and snatch his "sacrifice" (50).

47) The "dogs" are the brash and arrogant people who stand round waiting to divide up the spoils of the prayer of the Jew who has not taken care to observe the Covenant faithfully in all its details. Not that his own failures are any excuse for the sin of

these people in trying to distract and confuse him. It is true that it is his own shortcomings which have brought this opposition against him in the form of these "dogs" who stand about waiting to snatch his "offering." But the crime of these "dogs" themselves is that they have torn their own souls away from their roots in the realm of holiness and sunk to the level of dogs. Their victim, on the other hand, must put all his efforts into concentrating on his prayers and praying with devotion. It may be that he still doesn't taste the sweetness of the words of the prayers. But the efforts he puts in are themselves very precious. As for his opponents, they are literally like dogs and their sin is "too great to bear" (cf. Genesis 4:13) (*Ibid.*).

48) When the innocent person tries to judge the evil-doer in the scale of merit, his eyes will be enlightened and he will begin to perceive the righteousness of the Holy One, blessed-be-He. He will understand that even though the guilty party has won his case, God is still perfectly righteous. The innocent one will thereby be able to straighten himself out of the crooked thinking which he suffered from previously. His faith will be strengthened and now he will be able to pray (45:3).

49) Prayer is a battle against evil — specific evil and evil in general. Specifically, the person who is praying must nullify his own coarse body and materialistic impulses, just like the saintly men of old, who divorced themselves completely from all physicality when they prayed. The general evil is the prayers of the "sinners of Israel" with whom he is praying. He must nullify this evil completely and transform it into a throne of holiness (*Ibid.* 5).

50) He must also bind himself both in general and in particular with the *nefesh, ruach* and *neshama* of the souls of those who "lie in the dust." He must stir them up through his prayers until they are praying with him. The particular case refers to the *nefesh, ruach* and *neshama* of his own soul which have already come into the world in previous incarnations and attained perfection. The general case refers to the *nefesh, ruach* and *neshama* of all the others who "lie in the dust." He must stir them up as well so

that they too will pray with him (*Ibid.*).

51) There are three other things which a person must also try to achieve through his prayers. Firstly he must fortify those who have fallen victim to alien belief systems and seek to plant true faith in their hearts. Secondly he must aim to achieve intense concentration when he prays, because when his own heart is concentrated on his prayers it is a cure for the hearts of all the speculative philosophers who would otherwise be led astray by their "wisdom." Thirdly, the more perfect his own prayer becomes, the more immune he is to the insults and abuse which his enemies hurl against him, because he can turn them all to his own credit (*Ibid.* 6).

52) When a person prays he stands in the palace of the King. At that moment he must nullify himself completely so that he sees nothing except the King Himself, blessed-be-He. He should feel no sense of self at all while praying. When he attains this, the insults and abuse will simply disappear (*Ibid.* 7).

53) When we pray with true intensity, the light of the merit of the patriarchs shines, and then we can have the experience of the holiness of the Land of Israel even in our present exile. Through this we become worthy of witnessing the fall of the wicked. The main thing is to judge the wicked in the scale of merit. Doing this can enable us to pray (*Ibid.*).

54) Not everyone is able to achieve the three things mentioned above and to humble the wicked and crush his enemies through his prayers. Only the Tzaddik on the highest of levels — the "Moses" — can do so, and even he needs tremendous strength in order to stand up against the most powerful amongst the wicked and destroy and nullify them (*Ibid.* 9).

55) It is through studying the codes of Torah law that one can achieve true prayer which emerges from the heart with complete sincerity. If a person really knew and believed wholeheartedly that the entire world is filled with God's glory and that God stands over him while he is praying and hears every word of his prayers, he would be scrupulous about saying them in the correct way and praying with total concentration and devotion.

But people's hearts are divided, and they do not *feel* this reality with all their heart. Instead their hearts are filled with questions and doubts — because it is in the heart that the Evil Inclination fights his battle. Now the legal codes set forth the final decision of the law after all the arguments between the Sages. These arguments are really the source of the turmoil stirred up by the Evil Inclination, because even that which is unholy derives its vitality from the realms of the holy. The legal codes represent the resolution of conflict, and therefore studying them resolves the turmoil in the heart at its root. Then one can pray as one should — wholeheartedly and truthfully (62:2).

56) The ultimate goal of prayer is to make the whole prayer into a single unity. When a person stands up to pray, as soon as he starts on the first word — *Baruch,* "Blessed..." — and the first letter of the word — the letter *bet* — emerges, the letter immediately begins to plead with the soul and beg her not to leave her. The letter tries to stop the soul from moving on and saying more. She holds on to the soul and clings to her in an effort not to be parted from her. And when he completes the whole word, the word as a whole clings to the soul and holds on to her, trying to stop her going on and saying the other words of the prayer. When a person is saying the words of the prayers, he is collecting beautiful flowers and blossoms. He gathers them one after the other and makes them into a first bunch. Then he goes on and gathers more, until he makes a second bunch and puts it together with the first. So he goes on, gathering more and more beautiful garlands. Thus it is when he prays: he goes from letter to letter until he joins several letters together and makes up a word. Then he goes on and joins more letters together and makes a second word. The two words are joined together. Then he collects more, until he finishes the first blessing. He continues and passes from the first blessing of the *Amidah* — the blessing of the fathers Abraham, Isaac and Jacob — to the second, which speaks about the power of God. Then on to the third, which speaks of His holiness, and so on. Who can describe the beauty of these precious garlands which a person gathers as he goes

through the words of the prayer? When the words emerge from his lips they come from his very soul and are heard by his ears. The words plead with the soul not to be parted from her. As soon as the first letter comes from his lips it clings to him, refusing to allow him to go further. All the more so when he finishes a whole word — the word grasps firmly onto the soul, embracing her and trying to stop her from continuing: "How can you go on and leave me? Do you not see the preciousness of my beauty, my radiance and glory? Am I not the word *Baruch*? Listen, please listen to what you are saying. Let your ears hear what your mouth is saying. How can you go on and be parted from me?" But you must go on. You have to continue and gather more precious treasures. Yet still, "how can you separate yourself from me and forget me? Well if you must, at least see to it that wherever you get to, you still never forget *me*. Do not be parted from me." True prayer is when we make one whole out of the entire prayer. When we reach the last word of the prayer we are still at the very first. Even at the end of the prayer we are still not parted from the very first letter. And then the prayer is complete and perfect. But the only way to attain this is with the help of the true Tzaddik, who is the "Master of the Supernal Field." He alone can bring each one of us to the ultimate goal, which is truly good and truly One. Through his help we can make a unity of the whole prayer and achieve perfect prayer (65:2).

57) When a person genuinely prays for the sake of God alone with no ulterior motives of gaining anything from flesh and blood, he is able to bring the World to Come into this world, and by means of this the wicked are cast down. The greatness of the true Tzaddikim and the righteous is then revealed, just as it is destined to be revealed in time to come. Speech attains perfection as the vessel for holiness, and through this the potential can be made actual and it is possible to accomplish all the holy tasks one yearns to complete (66:3).

58) It is hard for someone who is dependent on other people to pray. It may be that he depends on them for his livelihood, or it

could be for something else — for example if he wants their respect and admiration. Anyone who depends on other people in any of these ways can easily start lying when he prays. For example, he may start swaying or clapping his hands, etc. in order to give the impression that he is praying with great devotion, because he wants to attract the attention of certain people he depends upon for his livelihood or his sense of importance. There are other cases of people who are somewhat more honest than this and cannot bring themselves to lie so blatantly. But because they are still dependent on other people it is very hard for them to pray with perfect honesty and sincerity. They would be ashamed to try to deceive people with a show of great devotion, and indeed they may even genuinely want to pray sincerely. But they are over-sincere, so to speak, because they deceive themselves with their own sincerity. They want to make some movement like swaying or clapping their hands in order to impress someone they depend on. And so they manufacture a rationalization, telling themselves they genuinely *need* to make this movement as part of their devotions.They hide the basic lie with a veneer of truth. But the Searcher of Hearts knows that this is not the truth. There is only one truth — devotion to God alone with no other motive. If a person is in any way dependent on flesh and blood he will find it very hard to pray with the community, because as soon as he is among other people all sorts of extraneous motives immediately start crowding in on him — false motives which he covers with a veneer of truth. At the time he is praying, at least, one should see to it that one has a sense of complete independence of other men. He should place all his hopes and trust in God alone. Then he will be able to stand up even among thousands of people and pray with perfect sincerity to God alone (*Ibid.*).

59) You should pray with all your heart. You must feel the words of your prayers in every bone. When a person doesn't put his heart into his prayers, his soul is separated from her source. She becomes weak and his bones begin to shake. His soul and his bones lose their vitality. Prayer without the heart causes the

wisdom of the elders and the wise to depart (67:8).

60) With the help of the true Tzaddikim we can draw the "cooling waters" which have the power to revive the soul when she is faint. Then a person can pray with his whole heart, and all his bones hear the words of the prayer. "All my bones will say: Lord, who is like unto Thee?" (Psalms 35:10). He prays with all his strength, and his whole mind and very essence are concentrated on his prayer. This is true prayer (*Ibid.*).

61) When a person prays intensely and binds his thoughts tightly to the words of the prayers he can come to understand the inner secrets of the Torah and his prayers will bring rich blessings into the world. God yearns for his prayers (73).

62) When a person speaks words of Torah and prayer, all the fallen sparks are elevated and restored and the fallen worlds are renewed. It is accounted to him as if he had created heaven and earth and all the worlds afresh. This is why we must speak only words of holiness and nothing else, in order to elevate the sparks and restore all the worlds. This will bring the coming of Mashiach closer (75).

63) Someone who is prepared to sacrifice himself for the sanctification of God's Name can attain peace. Through this he will be able to speak words of holiness — Torah and prayer — with full concentration, binding the thought and the words together so strongly that he truly hears and understands what he is saying. His speech becomes sanctified, and God has great joy from this (80).

64) When you find it hard to concentrate on your prayers properly because of irrelevant thoughts and distractions, remind yourself that you would be prepared to die for the sanctification of God's Name — and even the sinners of Israel are willing to sacrifice themselves for this, as has been proved on many occasions. This sense of self-sacrifice will enable you to bind your thoughts to the words of the prayers and pray with total concentration. You should always pray in this spirit of self-sacrifice (*Ibid.*).

65) Every Jew has the power to achieve absolute mastery

through his prayer and accomplish whatever he wants. The main obstacles are arrogance, praying for ulterior motives, and being distracted by irrelevant thoughts. There are some people who are filled with a sense of pride whether because of their family connections or because they feel they have labored hard in the service of God, etc. But such a state of mind will make it impossible for them to achieve this mastery. They should simply forget about their pedigree or their spiritual achievements and imagine to themselves that they were created today and that they are alone in the world with no family connections whatsoever. In the same way they must banish all the other improper or irrelevant thoughts which creep in while they are praying. Then they will experience the true power which prayer confers. God's desire will be fulfilled, and He will have great joy from this person's prayer. Abundant blessings will be drawn into the world (97).

66) If someone is in trouble, those who pray on his behalf should avoid mentioning his name, in case the harsh judgements are stirred up with even greater force, God forbid (174).

67) Everybody offers up bad prayers at times. As the Rabbis said: "The thief at the entrance of the breach calls on the Lord for help" (*Berachot* 63a). These prayers confuse him when he stands up to pray good prayers. The remedy is to offer hospitality to a Torah scholar (209).

68) Clapping our hands while praying makes it possible to express the praises and titles with which we address and depict God in a fitting manner, and "gaze upon the similitude of the Lord" (Numbers 12:8). The idea of clapping hands is also contained in Ezekiel 10:21: "And the likeness of the hands of a man was under their wings." Through clapping one's hands, the prayers are merged with the written Torah and the oral Torah (212).

69) Prayer has the power to change nature and to humble and crush the atheists and disbelievers (216).

70) When you are saying the passage in the morning prayers which describes how "the host of Heaven prostrate themselves

before You" you should pray for anything you need. At that moment the entire host of Heaven come to worship and praise God. This is the time to ask God to command them to send you whatever you need. If you are not well and you need healing, have in mind that God should instruct them to channel the necessary powers of healing into the bread you eat and the water you drink. The same applies to everything you need (231).

71) When you reach the words "Praise the Lord from the Heavens, praise Him all His messengers" (Psalm 148:1-2) you should rouse yourself and pray with real life and fire. You are calling on all the angels, the *seraphim*, the *ophanim* and the *chayot hakodesh* and all the worlds to offer praises to God (232).

72) Hearing another person praying with fervor can inspire you to pray with passion yourself. In exactly the same way you can be aroused simply by hearing the words you yourself are saying (270).

73) You may feel totally unable to open your mouth to pray or meditate because of the materialism you are sunk in or because of your troubles, physical or spiritual. This is precisely when you should make a special effort to stir yourself and call upon God from the very midst of all these pressures. The truest inspiration comes when a person makes the effort to arouse himself amidst troubles and difficulties. In almost every case you will find that the relief God sends will be so intense that you will be able to pray and meditate with true devotion and perhaps even reach the level of *ruach hakodesh,* the spirit of holiness (279).

74) Usually people find it impossible to pray with real involvement and vitality and with a sense of yearning for God because of a sense of inadequacy and dissatisfaction with themselves. They are aware that their actions are far from good. Before you start praying you should therefore put new life into yourself by searching until you find the good points in yourself. No matter who you are, you must have done many mitzvot in the past. Maybe there was an admixture of questionable motives, extraneous thoughts, etc. But there are still good points for you to be happy about. When you gather them all together it will

give you a new vitality and you will be able to pray as you should (282).

75) Whoever leads the prayers of the community has to have the ability to gather together all the good points which are to be found in each member of the congregation. All these good points will be merged together in the prayer leader, so that when he stands up to pray it will be with all this goodness. A community which finds such a prayer leader is fortunate indeed (*Ibid.*).

76) At the present time prayer itself is in exile because of our many sins. Prayer is really something very exalted, but people treat it lightly. When they stand up to pray all they want is to be through with it. Only when the three basic character flaws are corrected — the appetite for food, money and sex — is prayer released from its exile, and then it is possible to attain true prayer. The need for doctors and medicines disappears because prayer can channel healing powers into our very food and drink, and then we can be healed with bread and water alone. Prayer such as this has the radiance of Mashiach, and it brings under its sway the entire host of Heaven: the planets, the constellations and the highest of the angels. All are sustained by this prayer; all of them are captivated by its grace and charm. Prayer such as this can bind one with the roots of the souls of Israel — with the most renowned of the true spiritual leaders and all the souls that come under their wing. In the face of such prayer, the false leaders, whose whole influence comes from arrogantly pushing themselves forward, lose all their power. A Jew who attains this level of prayer has dominion over the very angels themselves — and this is the ultimate destiny of the Jew and the reason why he was created (II, 1:8-9).

77) There are three things which spoil our prayers. Firstly, an attitude of contempt for other people. Secondly inadequate faith — which is tantamount to idolatry. And thirdly, lack of moral purity. Only when we rid ourselves of these shortcomings can we achieve genuine prayer (*Ibid.* 10).

78) There are illnesses which do not manifest themselves openly.

They remain hidden, and no doctor can ever cure them. But a person who attains true prayer can be cured, even if the disease is not manifest. He need never fall sick at all (*Ibid.* 11).

79) Perfect prayer depends on the quality of truth. This we achieve through praise and acknowledgement of God and the study of Torah law. This is the main delight of the World to Come (2).

80) The prayers of Israel give them strength and power. They cause all the harsh decrees of God to be revoked, and then Israel are called by the name of the Lord (*Ibid.*).

81) True prayer must be filled with the quality of love. Prayer is a plea for God's grace and kindness. The ability to love depends upon understanding. When the forces of the Other Side sap the strength of love, God forbid, it becomes flawed. Anger and cruelty come in its place and understanding diminishes. Immoral desires become rampant. At a time like this, prayer comes under the shadow of God's somber judgement, and the forces of the Other Side sap its strength. It takes a leader of tremendous strength to pray at such a time. The task is to release the vitality which has been captured by the forces of the Other Side in order to restore things to their pristine state. When this happens, it causes large numbers of people to convert, and the glory of God is exalted and magnified. The power of prophecy comes into the world. Man's creative and imaginative faculty is cleansed and he is able to attain perfect faith. Then he is worthy of singing the song which is destined to be sung in time to come (8).

82) When one newcomer is added to a community of Jews — for example when a number of Jews are praying and one more soul is added to them — the whole house of prayer is enhanced beyond measure. The forces of holiness are multiplied and whole new edifices are built in the highest realms of holiness. Awesome joy spreads over the worlds above. The mouth cannot declare it nor the heart conceive it. Sin is forgiven and healing comes into the world (*Ibid.* 6).

83) When irrelevant thoughts come into your mind while you are praying, you should simply ignore them. In the end they will go

away by themselves. Even if the same thought comes again and again, simply remain firm and refuse to pay any attention. Just concentrate your mind on the words of the prayer you are saying at the time. In the end the irrelevant thought will simply go away (51).

84) When a person prays he must be so tightly bound to God that he does not notice anybody else at all. He should think that there is nothing in the world except God, and that he himself is the only creature in the world. All he should hear is what he himself is saying before God. It is true that the ultimate goal is to surrender yourself so much that you do not even hear yourself. But even if you have not attained this level, you should at least not hear anybody else (103).

85) It is through prayer that we become attached to God. Prayer is the gate through which we enter the path to God and it is through prayer that we can know Him (84).

86) It often happens that when a person is praying he begins to have feelings of grandeur and pride. This is the "exile of the Shechinah." But intense prayer has the power to overcome these thoughts and false motives, and the Shechinah is released from her exile and restored. The Holy One, blessed-be-He and the Shechinah are unified through this. Intense prayer also causes God's oath to the patriarchs to be renewed. It is as if He had made the oath just now (*Ibid.*).

87) Prayer helps for everything. Even if a person is unable to study Torah he will be able to do so if he prays for it. Everything good can be attained through prayer: Torah, devotion, holiness... everything good in all the worlds. Amen (111).

88) You must really force yourself to concentrate on your prayers. I disagree with the people who say one should not try to force it. It is very hard to pray, and people are usually not able to pray more than a portion of the prayers. But even if you sometimes cannot pray at all, the *effort* you put into forcing yourself to pray is also very precious to God, even if you don't actually succeed in praying as you should. These efforts are accounted as sacrifices, and this is the meaning of the verse:

"But for Your sake we are killed all the day; we are accounted as sheep for the slaughter" (Psalms 44:23). This refers to the effort we put into our prayers even if we find it impossible to pray. This is a general principle in serving God. Even if we do not manage to serve Him in a way that is fitting, the effort we put in is still very precious, and in the worlds above it is accounted as a sacrifice (Rabbi Nachman's Wisdom 12).

89) You should be very careful to get up and pray early in the morning. As soon as the first light of day begins to appear you should start praying without delay. You shouldn't learn, and you certainly shouldn't do anything else — work or business or the like — before you pray. And don't make the mistake of those who are overly concerned with evacuating their bowels and waste a lot of time on this. How much Torah and prayer are lost because of this! They can also harm themselves physically and even become ill. It is all very foolish and futile. It is one of the deceptions of the Evil One, who appears in the guise of "extra strict devotions." In actual fact, as long as a person does not actually feel the need to relieve himself it is permissible for him to pray. Pay no attention to the arguments of those who are overly strict in this. They have made a big mistake. Even if there is a legal source for the stricter view the majority opinion is not to be strict. And you can be sure that the Sage who takes the stricter view had no intention of legitimizing mere foolishness. All too often the people who are unnecessarily strict in this miss the time limit for reciting the *Shema* and the *Amidah*, and even afterwards they suffer from a lot of distractions while trying to pray. Pay no attention to any of it. You can rely on the majority ruling. Most of the Tzaddikim in our times have advised us to pay no attention to it at all (*Ibid.* 30,31).

90) Sometimes you may feel absolutely no enthusiasm at all for your prayers. When this happens you have to manufacture the enthusiasm as it were. It is the same as when a person works himself up into a temper until he becomes genuinely angry. The same applies to praying. You must work yourself up until you are warm and your heart begins to burn with enthusiasm for the

words of the prayers. In the end you will feel this fire genuinely. The same applies to being happy. Even if you find it impossible to be truly happy through following the advice we have given about joy (See *Simcha*), you should *pretend* to be happy and eventually you will come to genuine joy. This applies especially to being happy when you are praying. You must be very careful about this, and if necessary you should follow this idea of pretending until you feel the real thing. It is a good thing to make it a habit to sing the words of the prayers to a joyous melody (74).

91) What is true prayer? Simply to say "Blessed art Thou, O God..." according to the simple meaning of the words. Just concentrate on the plain meaning of the words and listen to what you are saying. You should not try to follow the Kabbalistic devotions of the ARI even if you have started to study his writings. The only people to whom these devotions apply are those who have already attained such a level that for them these devotions *are* the plain meaning of the words! This is the level of the truly great Tzaddikim. But all other people should simply concentrate on the straightforward meaning of the prayers (*Likutey Moharan* II, 120; Rabbi Nachman's Wisdom 75).

92) Even if you find it totally impossible to pray you should still force yourself to say the words with absolute simplicity — as if you were a little child at school. You should say the words just like this, without any sophistication. Say a few words and simply try and listen to what you are saying and pay attention to the words. You should concentrate your thoughts intently so that you are not distracted by anything outside. All your thoughts should be concentrated on the words of the prayer. You should go through the prayers in order until in the end you will most likely be inspired and you will be able to pray with great passion and yearning. Only you should not make a test out of this (*Ibid.*).

93) As a general rule, to achieve anything holy you must throw all your strength into it and use whatever ingenuity you can to

succeed. This applies especially to prayer, which is on a supremely high level. Even if you don't succeed, don't be put off. You can still try to say some psalms or one of the other prayers with sincerity. If you can't manage this either, what then? You must hope for God's help — perhaps in the fullness of time you will attain sincere prayer. Follow this path confidently and you will achieve everything good (*Ibid.*).

94) You should be able to feel another person's troubles in your own heart. This is especially true when many are suffering. Cry out to God and pray for them (*Ibid.* 39).

95) Good news can enable you to say psalms (*Ibid.* 97).

MORAL GUIDANCE תוכחה

(Including discussions between friends on spiritual matters)

1) The Sages who offer guidance and criticism to their contemporaries in order to improve them sweeten the harsh judgements and cause peace to spread throughout the world. But when people's wickedness is so great that it spoils the very guidance and criticism themselves, the cause of peace is ruined and instability and strife become rampant throughout the world (22:1).

2) It is impossible to learn from the guidance and criticism of the Sages without having faith. Faith is a pair of "hands" held out to receive guidance. When a person is lacking in faith he can easily come to atheism and believe in false ideologies. Because of his attitude of scorn and derision, he will not listen to criticism and guidance from the true moralists at all. One must guard one's faith and see that it is not deficient in any way. Faith is the key to holiness. When people have faith they listen to the guidance of the Sages and then they can return to God, and He will take pity (*Ibid.* 2).

3) When you act on criticism and improve yourself you can come to perform acts of charity and kindness and in this way overcome the influence of false beliefs. Your divine intelligence will be strengthened and you will be worthy of a new perception of Godliness (30:7).

4) You should always talk to your friends about spiritual matters. Each Jew has a "good point" unique to himself. When two friends have a discussion, each one can benefit from the "good point" of the other. Sometimes the "good point" of one of the friends is communicated to the other in a veiled form in a conversation which to outward appearances is about secular

topics. Because at times even a secular conversation can give you ideas and inspire you spiritually. Indeed sometimes the "good point" *needs* to be veiled — and the words of the conversation become a kind of clothing for it. The main thing is that you should discuss spiritual matters with your friends all the time. Then you will all be able to gain from each one's "good points." You will be able to break the "foreskin of the heart" — the lusts and desires which break a person's heart — and be filled with the holy desire for God (34:4).

5) The efforts a person makes to draw others to God enhance his own understanding of Godliness and bring it to perfection: he can come to understand everything which it is in man's power to apprehend and reach the very limits of human understanding. He will be worthy of children and cause the barren to give birth (53).

6) Each Jew has a certain authority — a power to dominate and influence. There are some whose authority extends over their own household. Others have a wider influence — each according to his level. A person must always take care to use his authority and influence not for his own personal benefit but for the sake of God alone: he should use it to guide whoever comes under his influence to draw closer to God. For example, if his authority extends only as far as his own household, he must make sure that he guides all the members of the household along the path of serving God. If his influence spreads wider, then he is under an obligation to use it to draw *all* the people who fall into his province towards God. A person who is negligent about guiding those who are under his influence will be punished because of them and his days will be shortened, God forbid. This is what the Sages meant when they said: "Authority buries those who possess it" (*Pesachim* 87). But those who use their authority to offer guidance and moral criticism and draw people closer to God will be blessed with long life and vitality (56:1-3).

7) The only way to give the right guidance and criticism is through devotion to Torah. This gives you the power to guide even those who are very far from you, even if you have no idea

what they need. When a person devotes himself to Torah, even those who are distant from the Torah hear its voice crying out: "How long, ye thoughtless, will ye love thoughtlessness?" (Proverbs 1:22). This cry of the Torah will bring everyone to return to God (*Ibid.*).

8) Someone who tries to draw others closer to God must be careful not to get caught up in the "husks" and wickedness of the people he works with. The way to protect himself is with "judgement," to see to it that he examines and judges himself concerning everything he does to see if it is right or not. He must criticize himself and feel contrition for anything he may have done that is not right. This self-examination will kindle a fire in his heart which will burn all the "husks" and prevent them from clinging to him. They will even be stripped from the people he is trying to draw closer to God (59:1).

9) A person who works hard to draw people closer to God and make souls builds a holy sanctuary. It may be that some of those souls will fall away from the holiness they attained. Nevertheless if at least some of the people who were brought to the fear of Heaven through his efforts remain devoted, "he that is left in Zion and he that remaineth in Jerusalem shall be called 'holy' " (Isaiah 4:3). The glory of God is exalted when those who were far are brought close to His service (*Ibid.*).

10) The self-examination and judgement which a person makes when he tries to bring people closer to God enable him to celebrate Shabbat. For the concept of Shabbat includes the destruction of evil and the impure husks (*Ibid.* 3).

11) You must watch over your name and your soul. You do this by keeping well away from anger. If you feel yourself getting angry, you must be "slow to anger" and suppress it. Then you will become rich and your name and soul will be enhanced. You will be worthy of a good name. All the souls will yearn to be merged with yours and you will be able to draw many souls closer to God and have many disciples (*Ibid.* 5).

12) When a person draws many souls closer to God it is better than having children. It is not possible to have more than a few

children — but here there are many souls: they draw all their life from the one who brought them closer and it is as if he himself gave birth to them (*Ibid.*).

13) You should realize that there are certain people who are so wicked that it is not permitted to draw them beneath the wings of God's service. They can cause the person who brought them close to fall from his level, and the self-examination and judgement mentioned earlier are powerless to nullify their evil. This can cause terrible damage. Anyone who tries to bring people closer to God must pray profusely for guidance so as to understand whom he should reject and whom he should draw closer (*Ibid.* 6).

14) It is good to discuss spiritual matters with your friends. Discussions like this create "direct" and "reflected" light. Even if your friend gains nothing from the discussion, it can still be a great benefit to you yourself. Someone who tries to encourage a friend can actually be greatly inspired himself. If he had merely said what he told his friend to himself, it could be that the words would not have inspired him at all. But by virtue of saying them out loud to his friend he himself can be inspired even if the words have little or no effect on his friend (184).

15) We must judge everyone in the scale of merit. Even if someone appears to be totally wicked, we still have to search and find even a modicum of good — by virtue of which he will no longer be wicked! By finding this modicum of good and judging him in the scale of merit he really *is* elevated to the scale of merit, and it is possible to bring him to return to God through this (282).

16) There is no love greater than the love one has for Israel when they sin. Sin is the most terrible burden for Israel — it is the worst scourge in the world. The root of the soul of the Jewish people is so holy and exalted that they are completely detached from sin. The Jewish people has no connection whatsoever with sin, so great is the subtle spirituality of their inner essence. This is why sin is such a heavy burden, God forbid. The greatest love one can show for Israel is to draw them from beneath the

burden of their sins. One should always discuss spiritual matters with one's friends and show one's love for them by trying to draw them away from sin. This is something which can be done by everyone, even the simplest of people. When a person speaks to his friend about spiritual concerns and radiates his own wisdom in words which will penetrate his friend's very heart so as to draw him away from sin, then his friend is counted as his pupil. (It is the same the other way around, when his friend radiates his wisdom to him, he is counted as his friend's disciple.) Even when the time comes for him to leave this world, he will still be clothed in these words which radiate in his friend, and it will be as if he himself is still alive in the world. The essence of the soul's perfection after its passing from this world depends on leaving a son and a pupil behind in whom the holy wisdom they received from their teacher still radiates. Everyone has a duty to try and draw other people closer to God. The true well-being of the world depends on its being filled with men of understanding who *know* of God and serve Him. Anyone who lacks the knowledge of God does not come into the category of "man" at all: he is a beast with the appearance of a man. Every individual must be constantly aware himself and make known at all times to others that it is God who rules over the earth and there is no other purpose in this world except to do His will. Nothing is left of a person in this world after his death except the knowledge of God that he communicates to his friends and pupils (II, 7:3,4).

17) Someone who wants to influence another person to fear God must himself have the fear of God. Otherwise his words will not be heard and they will not stay with his friend: they will simply pass right through him immediately (*Ibid.* 5).

18) When a person tries to discuss spiritual matters with his friends he can gain a perception of the "encircling lights" — which means that he can apprehend and understand what he was not able to previously. He will constantly rise to higher and higher perceptions until he reaches the perception of the most

transcendent levels — which is the joy and delight of the World to Come (*Ibid.* 6).

19) It is true that giving moral guidance and criticism is of the utmost importance and every Jew has an obligation to guide his fellow Jew if he sees him acting incorrectly. But nevertheless not everyone is fit to offer such guidance. When guidance and criticism are given by someone unfit to give them, not only do they fail in their purpose, worse still, they cause the fragrance of the souls which hear them to become putrid. The strength of those souls is weakened and blessing is withheld from all the worlds which are dependent upon them. Only those who can add to the fragrance of the souls they guide are fit to criticize and rebuke Israel for their sins. The voice that rebukes must be the "voice which waters the Garden of Eden." It is there that all the fragrances grow and holy awe takes root. This is the voice of the song that is destined to be sung in the future (II, 8).

There is no contradiction between what was said earlier about the obligation which every Jew has to discuss spiritual matters with his friends and the statement here that not everyone is fitted to give criticism. If you examine the different passages carefully you will see that the idea that is applicable to everyone is having discussions with friends about spiritual matters: what is the purpose of life? What will remain of us in the end? and so on. Even the simplest of people should discuss these things. The kind of moral criticism which is referred to in the last passage is a completely different matter. It means making explicit reference to another person's sins and saying to him: "Why did you do such and such?" One should be very careful not to discuss people's sins and bad behavior with them because one can weaken their soul through arousing this bad smell. The distinction between moral guidance and rebuke is implicit in Rashi's comment on the opening words of Deuteronomy, where he says that Moses did not *rebuke* the Children of Israel until immediately prior to his death. The comment seems surprising, because surely Moses had spoken to them in a critical vein many times before and had given them many warnings to observe the

Torah. The meaning of the term "rebuke" is that he made mention of their sins, as it says in the opening verses in Deuteronomy: "In the wilderness, in the Arabah, over against Suph..." (Deut. 1:3). As Rashi (*loc. cit.*) explains, Moses mentioned all the places where the Children of Israel had made God angry. It is noteworthy that he did not administer his rebuke until immediately prior to his death, and this in spite of the fact that in his case the rebuke was spoken with the "voice which waters the Garden of Eden" (*Ibid.*).

TEFILIN תפילין

1) The straps of the *tefilin* are a protection for faith against the parasitic forces of evil. They protect the mind and the soul, and fresh wisdom and a fresh soul are drawn from the inner light of God's countenance (35:9).

2) A person should constantly search himself to see if he is attached to God. The *tefilin* are the sign of attachment (38:1).

3) The way to experience the true sanctity of *tefilin* is by sanctifying and purifying speech, which is achieved by learning Torah even when one is poor or under great pressure. When a person is overwhelmed with darkness and suffering and still makes an effort to study Torah, he elevates the faculty of speech and he will be able to speak to his Maker with strength and fire and pour out his words in truth. He will understand his own insignificance and the utter greatness of the Creator, and he will be filled with shame at the greatness of his sins against the Master and Ruler of the Universe, the Root of all the worlds. His shame will show on his very face, and then he will be worthy of the light of *tefilin*, which are the sign of attachment to God (*Ibid.* 2,4,5).

4) *Tefilin* are the "radiance of God's countenance." They are the true glory of Israel. They are "life" and "truth," the source of wealth and all blessings. Abuse of the *tefilin* brings poverty, contempt and shame and puts one in mortal danger, God forbid (47).

5) The *tefilin* strengthen the memory — the awareness that the goal of this world is the World to Come and that one must constantly expand one's intellect so as to understand the

messages God sends every day in order to draw men closer to Him (54:3).

6) The more efforts a person makes to break his immoral desires, the more receptive he becomes to the holiness of *tefilin*. It is those who are truly righteous and God-fearing, the "guardians of the earth" who fulfill the mitzvah of *tefilin* to perfection. The full force of immoral temptations is unleashed against them with a fury and could even bring them to waste their seed and be stamped with the seal of the forces of the Other Side, God forbid. But they steel themselves against them, totally separating themselves from any such thoughts, and they elevate the seal of the evil husk until it becomes transformed into the seal of holiness — the *tefilin*, which embody the radiance of the sparks of wisdom, whereby one knows and acknowledges the Divinity and Kingship of God. The light of the seven faithful shepherds shines, corresponding to the seven heads of the two *shin*s' on the *tefilin* (one with four heads, the other with three). Thus the significance of the *tefilin* is that we have to draw down the radiance of God and strive for ever-deeper understanding of Godliness. But there are necessary limits to the human intellect, and these must also be observed. The *tefilin* are the *tikkun* for this, enabling us to deepen our understanding while remaining within the bounds of holiness. Even in our striving to draw close to the radiance of Godliness, it is forbidden to go beyond the boundaries and "break through" (cf. Exodus 19:21).

FASTING תענית

1) Each person has a duty to subdue his physical aspect. The way to achieve this is through fasting. Fasting weakens the four basic elements of which man is composed and which are the source of all his lusts and impulses. This is the way to humble and nullify the coarse materialism of the body, which is the source of folly and darkness, animality and death. The finer side of man is thereby strengthened and his Divine intellect — the form as opposed to the substance — is elevated. The Divine intellect is the soul — "wisdom," "light" and "life." The power of forgetfulness is broken and man remembers his mission in the world. The darkness and harsh judgements are nullified and lovingkindness and blessing are drawn into the world. The main effect of the fast is accomplished through the charity one gives while fasting. (It is customary to give the value of the food one would otherwise have eaten to charity). Through fasting the influence of alien ideologies is thwarted and the wisdom of Torah reigns supreme. Fasting is also a help for one's livelihood (77).

2) In times of danger, God forbid, it is usual to decree a fast. Fasting brings about an illumination of God's favor, and this in itself sweetens and nullifies the harsh judgements, thereby averting the danger. Fasting protects against poverty, degradation and shame and leads to wealth. It also makes us worthy of experiencing miracles (47).

3) When a Tzaddik eats, it is something very precious, because the Tzaddik eats to satisfy his holy soul. Therefore the Tzaddik is forbidden to fast. But one who has to fast should certainly do so. For him it is a mitzvah to fast (50).

4) Fasting is a means of conquering one's anger. In fact this is the main value of a fast. Because of this, the Evil One attacks people with extra force during a fast and tries to make them angry in order to spoil it, God forbid. One must be especially careful to avoid the fire of anger on a fast day. The main value of fasting lies in breaking the force of anger (57:6).

5) Fasting brings a new radiance to the face and restores a person's wisdom — the very image of God — and makes it shine on his face. He will be held in awe and respect by those around him and his enemies will fall before him. But in order to spread peace, it is necessary to give charity plentifully (*Ibid.*).

6) Through fasting it is possible to perfect our speech, and then we can speak before God and pray with devotion. Through perfecting our speech we can draw closer those who were far from God, and this will deepen our faith until it is perfect. It is through faith that we refine the food we eat, and then our eating brings about the unification of the Holy One and the Shechinah face to face (62).

7) Fasting has the power to resolve conflict, both physical and spiritual. When a person is unable to pray or do what he should to serve God, this is "conflict." Fasting helps to subdue the heart and devote one's will to God alone and make peace (179).

8) Fasting revives the dead. The fast gives life to all the days that were spent in darkness without true vitality. When a person wastes a day by doing no mitzvot or good deeds — or far worse, by doing actual evil, God forbid — then that day has no life. It has been "killed." But all these dead days are brought back to life by fasting. The more a person fasts, the greater the number of dead days he can revive (*Ibid.*).

9) Fasting brings joy. The more times you fast, the greater the joy (*Ibid.*).

10) The reason we fast after a bad dream is to draw joy over ourselves by means of the fast. This is the *tikkun* for the dream. This is why when a person does not want to fast over such a dream, the prayer that is recited says: "Go eat your bread in

joy." Because the main *tikkun* for the dream is through joy (II, 5:10).

11) On fast days it is a good practice to recite the sections in Leviticus dealing with the sacrifices (*Ibid.*).

REPENTANCE תשובה

1) To make amends for one's sins and rebuild what was damaged, the role of the Tzaddik is of paramount importance. Anyone who wants to attain the ultimate good must make every conceivable effort to draw close to the true Tzaddik and his followers. He must pour out his heart before the Tzaddik and confess his past actions. Then all his sins will be forgiven. The sins one commits are engraved on one's bones. Each sin corresponds to a certain combination of letters. When a person commits a particular sin, an evil combination is inscribed on his bones corresponding to the letters of the negative commandment of the Torah he has transgressed. Because of this the words of that commandment are cast into *tum'ah*, the realm of impurity. The powers of holiness are sent into exile among the forces of the Other Side, and the evil combination inscribed on his bones exacts vengeance from him. But when he confesses before a Sage, the letters inscribed on his bones are released, and what was damaged can be completely restored (4:5).

2) When a Jew is moved to repent through a feeling that a small hint of impurity is spoiling his prayers and devotions, his repentance has an effect even on those who are totally wicked and who have become completely alienated from their Jewish roots because of their evil deeds. They, too, become part of the Holy Throne and return to God, helping His servants to construct their holy edifice (*Ibid.*).

3) The true sign of a person who has returned to God is that he can hear himself insulted and remain silent. He can endure even the most murderous abuse with patience. Through this he reduces the blood in the left side of his heart (the seat of the

animal soul) and slaughters his evil inclination. He will be worthy of partaking of the glory of God (6:2).

4) Before a person returns to God, he has no being. It is as if he has not yet been created. Because it would have been better for him not to have been created at all. But when he comes and purifies himself in order to return to God, he puts himself in order and prepares *to become* a being. This element of preparation for *becoming* — coming into being, as it were — explains why the Divine Name which is associated with repentance is *Ehyeh*, "I shall be" (*Ibid.*).

5) When someone wants to purify himself and return to God, they tell him "Wait!" (*Yoma* 38b-39a). It is true that he should hurry to release his soul and flee from the darkness. But he shouldn't be discouraged and depressed when he sees how far he is from true prayer and other holy devotions. It is a necessary part of the process that he should wait. In the end he will be worthy of making amends completely, and all will be restored. Understand this well (*Ibid.*).

6) Repentance never stops. It is a continuing process. Even at the very moment that a person is saying "I have sinned, I have transgressed, I have rebelled, etc." it is still impossible for him to say the words with complete sincerity without a single extraneous motive. Thus he must repent for his earlier repentance — namely the flaw in his previous confession (*Ibid.* 3).

7) Even when a person knows that he has achieved perfect repentance he must still make amends for his earlier repentance. For what he achieved then was good only in proportion to the perception of Godliness he had at the time. But now, after his repentance, his perception has undoubtedly been heightened. Compared with his present perception, the earlier perception turns out to have been grossly materialistic. Therefore he must repent for the levels he achieved earlier — because he degraded the true exaltedness of the Creator to the level of materialism. Happy is the man who achieves true repentance (*Ibid.*).

8) There are three aspects to repentance: seeing with the eyes,

hearing with the ears and understanding in the heart (cf. Isaiah 6:10). Repentance involves all of them. One must use one's eyes to look towards the ultimate goal and purpose of this world, and concentrate on it with all one's heart. He must set himself to travel there and nowhere else. And he must use his ears to listen carefully to everything that our holy Rabbis said. Then he will be able to return to God (7).

9) The essence of *teshuva,* repentance, is achieved through humility. One has to make oneself into nothing — like a wasteland which people trample over. He must pay no attention whatsoever to opposition or to the contempt with which people may treat him. He should train himself to be silent and to be able to hear himself insulted without replying. One such as this is worthy of the name "wise" and he will attain perfect repentance — the "Crown," which is the summit of the *Sefirot*. This is the way to true and enduring glory, the glory of God (6).

10) When a person wants to return to God he must become an expert in the *halachah,* the law (*halachah* literally means "going"). Two kinds of skill are needed: in the "running" and the "returning" (cf. Ezekiel 1:14). These two expressions correspond to the rising and falling which King David speaks of in the Psalms: "If I ascend to Heaven, You are there, and if I make hell my bed, behold there You are (Psalms 139:8). This means that a person who wants to return to God must gird his loins and keep firmly to the pathway of God regardless of whether he makes progress ("if I ascend to Heaven") or suffers reverses ("if I make hell my bed"). If he makes progress and reaches a particular level of spirituality — be it high or not so high — he should still not stop here and content himself with his achievement so far. In his case the skill he needs is to know and believe that he must still advance further. This is the skill of the "running." On the other hand, even if he falls to a lower level — and even if he falls into the lowest pit of Hell, God forbid — he must still not despair in any way, regardless of his condition. He should remain firm and search for God, pleading with Him and begging Him to help in whatever way he can. Even in the lowest

pit of hell God is present, and even from there it is possible to be attached to Him. As King David said: "If I make hell my bed, behold, there You are". The skill he needs now is in the "returning." The only way to achieve true repentance is with these two skills. Indeed, it takes extraordinary skill to understand that it is necessary to struggle all the time in order to serve God. One has to aim constantly for a higher level while at the same time never allowing oneself to fall in any way or become despondent and discouraged. Someone who acquires these skills will be able to walk the path of true repentance, and God's right hand will be open wide to receive his repentance. He will attain to the glory of God, and Man will be placed upon the throne. Happy is he (*Ibid.* 4).

11) There are certain Torah scholars who are highly learned but have not begun to repent, and on the contrary, they resist the Tzaddikim and take issue with them. The reason for this is that their motives for learning Torah are not pure. They want prestige and influence, and they like to feel important and take issue with everything. Their learning simply develops their subtlety, making them more and more insidious. The Torah is double-edged, "For the ways of the Lord are just, the righteous walk in them, and sinners stumble in them" (Hosea 14:10). Their expertise in the oral Law merely opens their mouths to speak arrogantly and contemptuously against the Tzaddik. However there exist certain great Tzaddikim who understand the Torah concepts which are the source of the ideas they are using against the Tzaddikim. These great Tzaddikim have the power to elevate these ideas and make out of them *halachot*, legal rulings (12:1).

12) When those who were far from holiness draw closer — whether they are proselytes who convert, or Jews returning to their roots, for they too were "outside" — God's glory is exalted through their drawing closer, and His Name is glorified in the upper and the lower worlds. Glory is raised to its root and through this peace spreads over the whole world (14:2).

13) When a person is completely humble and lowly he can reach such a level of attainment in Torah that his very learning can

bring radiance to the roots of the souls of Israel, which are to be found in the Torah. He has the power to radiate even to those who are very distant, even to the sinners and those who are farthest removed from Torah. He can arouse them and encourage them to return to God. No matter how greatly a person may have sinned, as long as he is still called by the name of Israel he is still a Jew in spite of his sins, and the radiance of the root of his soul can be transmitted to him wherever he may be by means of the study of Torah. Then he will return to God (*Ibid.* 3-5).

14) Even when those who were distant from holiness are roused to return to the light of Torah, they are still very far away and they may experience tremendous obstacles. It takes enormous effort for them to strip themselves of their "filthy garments" (Zechariah 3:4). These "filthy garments" are as difficult a barrier as a river which it is impossible to cross. If you want to draw closer, do not be discouraged if you find yourself confronted by all kinds of obstacles. This is inevitable, because all these obstacles stem from the "filthy garments" — the sins of the past. It takes great efforts to strip off these "filthy garments" and throw them aside. At times the experience is very bitter. But in the end all the obstacles and barriers which separate you from holiness will disappear (*Ibid.* 5).

15) We have to make amends even for the sins we committed unwittingly. Through this we attain perfection in the Holy Tongue, which is *tikkun habrit* (*Ibid.* 19).

16) *Teshuva* means to return a thing to the place from which it was taken — to restore it and return it to its root. Now wisdom is the root of everything. This is why you must guard your mind and your wisdom against alien ideologies and extraneous thoughts, not to speak of evil temptations. The reason for all the sins and transgressions which people commit and all their shortcomings is that their thoughts are impure. They are not careful to guard their thoughts and avoid overstepping the bounds of holiness. When a person protects his thoughts and his wisdom, he can remedy everything and return to God (35).

17) *Teshuva* depends upon the heart — more specifically, the thoughts in the heart. You must be firm and avoid all evil thoughts. Think only good thoughts. Focus your heart on the purpose of life. Think up plans and strategies for coming closer to God. Then you will be worthy of attaining the Hidden Torah of the Ancient One — the inner secrets of Torah, which are the essence of the joy of the World to Come (49).

18) More than any other times of the year, the months of Tishrei and Nissan are the times for *teshuva*. The Redemption is destined to take place in Nissan, and it will come about only through *teshuva* (*Ibid.* 6).

19) You must be "like a strong man running his course" (Psalms 19:6) because even if you have succeeded in repenting and making amends for the damage you did, you must still make up for all the good deeds which you could have done but didn't all the time you were rebelling against God. You must be *extra* enthusiastic and run *extra* fast in order to make up for what you failed to do then (*Ibid.*).

20) An action is not an action until it is carried through from the realm of possibility to that of actuality. This applies equally to mitzvot and good deeds and to sins. A mitzvah is not complete until it has been brought from potentiality to actuality. It must be realized in actual fact. When a potential mitzvah is made actual, this is literally the "creation of the universe" — because the mitzvah sustains the entire universe. Conversely in the case of sin, when a person merely contemplates the possibility of sinning in his mind, the sin is still potential. If he then makes the potential actual and commits the sin in practice, God forbid, he is totally wicked and might as well be dead. He destroys himself and the whole world. Because the entire creation of the world is brought about through the process of emerging from potentiality to actuality by the hand of God. Every single sin therefore spoils the totality of all the worlds and all the holy names of God. The only remedy is *teshuva* — because when one experiences genuine regret for one's sins and abandons them, the damage that was done can be repaired and the repair of all the worlds is carried

through from potentiality to actuality (66:2).

21) Repentance out of love has the power to efface every trace of sin, and then one can pray and learn with a clear mind in a state of expanded consciousness. He can pray as he should and learn and understand rapidly and expand and refresh his mind every day (74).

22) Each individual must see to it that he is not responsible for holding up the coming of Mashiach. He must make amends for what he did in the past and return to God with all his heart, and this way he will make sure that Mashiach is not prevented from coming because of his sins (79).

23) True repentance depends on Torah: when a person labors so hard in his studies that he reaches the level where he can understand one thing from another and produce original ideas for the sake of Heaven alone, this is perfect repentance (74).

24) If a person feels genuine pain for having sinned — if he "circumcises the foreskin of his heart" and feels true contrition for what he did and returns to God with all his heart — then the hearts of all the drops that left him — his actual children and the drops that went elsewhere, God forbid — will also be circumcised in the "foreskins of their hearts." They too will feel the pain of their degradation. They will all be aroused and rise with a thunderous noise and return to God (141).

25) The difference between being alive and dead only has any meaning for someone caught up in his appetite for food and drink. For him death is a reality. It is different for the Tzaddik who has conquered his inclination and is always in complete control of himself, even in things which are permitted to him. The Tzaddik is always alive, even after his death. For him there is no difference between death and life (144).

26) A person should take pity on his soul while he is young and hurry to return to God before he becomes old. In his youth he still hears the voice of Torah crying out every day and calling on men to return. This "voice of Torah" is all the thoughts of *teshuva* which rise in a person's mind continually. But once he becomes old it is harder for him to return (205).

27) There is such a thing as *words* of *teshuva*, as it is written: "take with you *words* and return to the Lord" (Hosea 14:3). We must talk and talk before God until we pour out our words like water and attain true repentance. The way to achieve this is with the three "lines of truth": prayer (to pray in truth and with sincerity), true Torah and true partnerships and marriage bonds. It is through praise and thanks to God and the study of Torah law that we can attain this: they are the essence of the joy of the World to Come (*Likutey Moharan* II:2).
28) You must understand that the Jew is completely remote from sin. He has no connection with sin at all, so exalted is the subtle spirituality of his inner essence. This is why sin is such a heavy burden for the Jew. It is impossible to bear it even for a single day. It is worse than any other suffering in the world. A person must take pity on himself and try to repent of his sins and pray to God to help him find a leader who will show him true love, enlighten him with wisdom and draw him from his sins. There is no love greater than this (7:3).
29) The only way to attain complete *teshuva* is by passing through all the places one had been before *teshuva* — and obviously this will vary for each individual, depending on what he went through in the earlier part of his life. When he passes through them and encounters the very same temptations that he experienced before, he must turn his head aside and control his inclination without repeating what he did in the past. This is the essence of perfect *teshuva*. There is no other way (49).
30) An essential element in *teshuva* is shame. We must feel a deep sense of shame before God. We can come to this through seeing ourselves with the true Tzaddik (72).
31) If you want to accomplish complete *teshuva* you should make a habit of reciting the psalms. They are a great help to *teshuva*. There are many obstacles to *teshuva*. Sometimes people feel no inclination to return to God at all — they are simply not interested. There are certain people for whom the gate of *teshuva* is closed. There are others who simply do not know how to reach the gate that is right for them — the path *they* need in

order to return to God. There are also other barriers which prevent people from accomplishing *teshuva*. One can waste away one's whole life and die without *teshuva*, God forbid. But reciting the psalms is a great help. Even a person who feels no enthusiasm at all for *teshuva* can experience an awakening if he recites the psalms. No matter who you are, you can always find yourself in the psalms you are reciting. This will arouse you and help you find the gate of repentance which is appropriate for your soul. You will be able to open the gate and attain perfect repentance, and then God will return to you and show you love. This is why during the month of Elul and the Ten Days of Repentance all Jews recite the psalms. But this is something one should do throughout the year in order to accomplish *teshuva* (73).

32) Repentance helps for every conceivable sin, even the most serious sin of all — the deliberate emission of seed in vain, or other forms of grave immorality. When the Zohar says that *teshuva* does not help in the case of a person who wastes his seed, the meaning is not what it appears on the surface. The truth is that as our Sages said, "there is nothing which stands in the way of *teshuva*." (*Yerushalmi Peah* 1:1; *Yerushalmi Sanhedrin* 10:1; *Rambam, Mishnah Torah, Hilchot Teshuva* 3:14; *Zohar* II, 106a; *Tosefot* on *Baba Metzia* 58b). But perfect *teshuva* can only be attained with the help of the true Tzaddikim (Rabbi Nachman's Wisdom 71).

SIMPLICITY תמימות

1) To take on the yoke of Heaven we must abandon all of our own sophisticated ideas and walk in the path of purity and simplicity. The Holy Torah is the only true wisdom. All other ideas are nothing in comparison (Rabbi Nachman's Wisdom 5; 308).

2) People should throw aside all their sophisticated ideas and serve God with purity and simplicity. Action is the main thing, not study, and you should see to it that your practical achievements are greater than your intellectual development. It is obvious that this applies to the "wisdom" of the average person, which is nothing but foolishness. Without doubt this has to be thrown out completely. But it even applies to genuine wisdom. When it comes to serving God, even someone whose head is filled with genuine wisdom should put it all aside and serve God with purity and simplicity. At times it may even be necessary to behave in a way that seems mad in order to serve God. We may have to do things which seem crazy for the sake of carrying out His will. We may have to roll about in all kinds of mud and mire in order to serve God and fulfill His commandments. This does not apply only to things which are explicitly mitzvot. *Anything* which God desires to be done is called a mitzvah. It may be necessary to throw oneself into the mud and mire to carry out a certain action that will be pleasing to God. When one's love of God is strong enough, he becomes a "precious and beloved son," and God will show him abundant love and compassion and permit him to investigate the hidden store-chambers of the King, until he will learn the deepest secrets of all — why the righteous suffer and the wicked prosper, and so

on. He will be worthy of the secrets of Torah and he will be able to raise up "judgement" out of the deep and restore it (*Likutey Moharan* II, 5:15).

3) Someone who follows his own ideas can easily fall into all kinds of traps and get into serious trouble, God forbid. Too many people have been led astray by their own wisdom. They themselves have sinned, and they have caused many others to sin as well. All because of their fallacious "wisdom." The essence of the Jewish religion is to follow the path of purity and simplicity without sophistication: simply to make sure that God is present in everything one does. Have no thought at all for your own honor and glory. The only question is whether *God's* glory will be enhanced. If so, do it; if not, then don't. This way you will never stumble (*Ibid.* 12).

4) Besides simplicity and purity, you should understand that there is no need to search for specially strict practices to take upon yourself. To think that you should is an illusion: it is simply one of the devices of the Evil One to deter you from serving God. Such practices are not part of serving God. As our Sages said: "The Torah was not given to the ministering angels" (*Kiddushin* 54a). It was given to men of flesh and blood. These exaggerated practices can put you off completely. The greatest wisdom of all is not to be wise at all. It is simply to be pure and straightforward (*Ibid.* 44).

5) Sophistication can be very harmful. Thinkers are easily trapped in their own wisdom. Keep well away from the wisdom of those self-important people who believe they know great truths about serving God. Their wisdom is nothing but foolishness. All their sophistication is quite unnecessary in serving God. The main thing is to be pure and simple and to have pure faith in God and His Tzaddikim. True, you have to be careful that you are being pure and simple as opposed to idiotic. But sophistication is entirely unnecessary. Simplicity, purity and faith can bring you to great joy (*Ibid.*).

6) The greatest sophistication is to work out how to avoid sophistication (*Ibid.* 83).

7) You should be careful to follow the simple devotions and customs of Israel: singing songs on Shabbat and at the conclusion of Shabbat, and similar practices. It is good to recite many prayers and supplications — such as those printed in the large prayer books. People think it is clever to ridicule these practices. But they are wrong. The essence of Judaism is simplicity and purity, without sophistication at all (Rabbi Nachman's Wisdom 155).

ברוך הנותן ליעף כח, ולאין אונים עצמה ירבה

Blessed be He who gives strength to the weary,
power and courage to the weak.

POSTSCRIPTS

LIKUTEY HALACHOT

At Rabbi Nachman's request, Rabbi Nathan used the ideas in the Likutey Moharan *and Rabbi Nachman's other teachings, to throw light on the* practical *meaning of the laws in the* Shulchan Arukh *— the standard legal compendium governing all aspects of the life of the Jew. The eight volumes of* Likutey Halachot *follow the exact order of subject-headings of the* Shulchan Arukh, *with one or more discourses on each subject. The discourses in* Likutey Halachot *are very elaborate, with extensive essays on themes drawn from the Torah, Talmud, Midrash, Zohar and Kabbalah, while serving as the basic commentary on the* Likutey Moharan *itself. We have included in this work a few excerpts of Rabbi Nathan's own* chidushim *on the subject of Advice.*

Guidance in a World of Uncertainty

Why are people superstitious? Why do they try to use magic and sorcery to find out what course of action they ought to follow? The reason is because by themselves they have no idea at all what they should do. They find themselves faced by a situation which demands that they make a choice — to do this or that. And because of their uncertainty they resort to superstition. "a deer stopped me!" "The piece of bread I was eating dropped from my mouth!" "A bad sign," they say. "Better not go through with the business deal!" "Will such-and-such a day be a lucky day to start on a certain venture?" (*Sanhedrin* 65b; Rashi on Leviticus 20:8). This kind of mentality is sheer folly. No one will ever find genuine guidance this way.

The anguish of choice and doubt is an inescapable feature of this world, filled as it is with all the diversity of the lights and shades and seeming contradictions that God has created in it. But there is a realm which transcends Creation. Here all is unity, and all is good. In this realm, guidance and advice have no relevance. They are only needed when there are two paths and we do not know, *which one to choose, how to behave, what to do*. It is only in the realm of the created that guidance and advice are necessary, because here we are never clear where each thing leads to. If we were, we would never have any doubts at all what to do. For example: a businessman is in doubt whether to invest in one kind of merchandise or another. His whole reason for trading is because he has a particular aim in view: to make a profit, and this in order to make a living for himself. Any doubts he has about which kind of merchandise he should buy come only because he does not know which of them will give him the best profit. The merchandise itself is of no interest to him. He has no need for the yarn, the wax, or whatever it may be in themselves. All his doubts and uncertainties are concerned, only, with how to make the most money. That is his goal. Our ignorance of where things will lead is what makes for all the doubts and uncertaintics in this world. No one knows what advice he should follow for the sake of his soul.

But if you look to the ultimate purpose of things, if you are truthful and honest and your only aim in whatever you encounter is to achieve this ultimate goal, then you will find perfect counsel. Indeed your path will become increasingly clear, because the ultimate goal is one. It is a unity which is wholly good. Here there is no need for doubts or guidance at all. The goal is the joy of the World to Come: to acknowledge God and to know Him. It is true that there are many different paths of devotion which can lead a person to God. Many times King David pleaded with God to "guide me to walk Your path in truth," "lead me with Your counsel," "guide me in truth and teach me," and so on. But the main thing is that your intentions should be pure, because "God desires the heart." If your intentions are truly directed towards God in everything that you do, then no matter what you do or what path you follow, it will bring you to the ultimate goal. The only condition is that you must never turn aside from the words of the Torah. "In all your ways acknowledge Him and He will direct your paths." (Proverbs 3:6). "In all your ways acknowledge Him" — whatever you do, let your intention be directed towards God, who is the ultimate goal. And then "He will direct your paths" — God will guide you along the paths of righteousness and send you counsel, and then you will know how you should behave.

The only way to find genuine guidance is by turning to the ultimate goal, which is to know and perceive God. God is, as it were, the fountain and source of all the guidance in the world. In the sphere of the ultimate goal of unity and goodness there is only one counsel. All individual pieces of genuine advice and guidance derive the truth they possess from this realm. In the created world in which we live, the only way to find the right path is to bind the world, with all its diversity and uncertainty, to the realm which transcends Creation. Bind every detail and situation in this world to God. Let your only purpose be to achieve the ultimate goal. Let all your actions be for the sake of Heaven. In the sphere of the ultimate goal on which you set your eyes you will find the counsel you need to guide you through this world.

But someone who fails to bind this world to the World to Come and pays no attention to the ultimate goal will never know what he should do. Having cut this world off from the only purpose which gives it any sense, he must always be divided in his mind and he will never know how to act. Ours is a world of separation and plurality. Nothing is ever really clear in this world. Someone who ignores the ultimate goal will never have any sense of direction. There is nothing at all to guide him because his aim is not to achieve the ultimate goal for the sake of Heaven. No matter which way he goes, it will be no good for him. Take the example of the businessman who doesn't know which merchandise will be the more profitable. If his purpose is not in some way for the sake of Heaven, be it to use the profits for charity, to sustain himself while studying Torah, or to devote them to other mitzvoth...if his purpose is purely material, then even if he *does* make a profit it will still be no good for him. His days will be filled with worry, tension and anxiety. And in the end he will go naked to the grave, just as he came into the world. What pleasure will he have then from all the profits he labored for? Neither silver nor gold nor jewels nor pearls accompany man in the grave (*Avoth* 6). Only his Torah and good deeds go with him. Regardless of the course this person follows in his lifetime nothing will help him. But when a person's whole aim is centered on the ultimate goal, then it makes no difference what path he follows, because everything will always be for the best. As the Sages said: "Whether one does a lot or a little, what counts is that one's heart should be directed towards Heaven" (*Berachot* 17a). By binding this created world to the realm beyond Creation, one will find guidance from the fountain of all counsel. For the essence of all guidance is to lead us to attain the ultimate goal. This ultimate goal is therefore the source and the root of all true guidance. Each one of the six hundred and thirteen commandments of the Torah is called "counsel". Moses bound himself to God so completely that he was worthy of apprehending the ultimate goal. Through this he could receive the entire Torah with its six hundred and thirteen rules of holy counsel. But of the heathen nations, who were not worthy of receiving the Torah, it is said: "Take counsel together and it shall be brought to naught" (Isaiah 8:10). "The Lord bringeth the counsel of the nations to naught" (Psalms 33:10). They are bereft of guidance or direction because they are bound up with *this* world and they have no regard for the ultimate goal.

This is why they are entangled in the foolishness of their superstitions and divination. Being tied to this world they try to find guidance in signs and signals from material objects. "A deer crossed my path," "The bread fell from my mouth," "It's a lucky day to start". They rely upon things bound by space, time and physicality because they are absorbed in the material desires of this world. They have severed this world of diversity and doubt from the transcendent realm which alone gives it meaning. Therefore they must seek advice from their idols. This was precisely what the cunning serpent in the Garden of Eden suggested. He tricked man into eating from the Tree of Knowledge because "the tree was good for food... and was to be desired to make one wise" (Genesis 3:6). He said to them "Eat from this tree and create the world" (*Bereshith Rabbah loc. cit.*). He thereby turned things upside down. The real task is to bind this created world to the realm beyond Creation, and this we do through faith, which is the foundation of the whole Torah. By believing that God Almighty created everything, we bind the whole Creation to that which is beyond Creation, namely God. But on the advice of the serpent who said "Eat from this tree and create," the heathen nations have turned things upside down. They have made the created, material world the foundation of everything. The sorcerer and the diviner try to find guidance by using material objects. But the truth is that there is no guidance to be found from this physical world, only through binding it to the ultimate goal, which is beyond Creation.

This explains why the Torah concludes its warnings against sorcery and divination with the words: "Be whole with the Lord your God." Unless one binds the created world with the realm which transcends Creation, one can never attain wholeness or perfection. The only perfection is with God. Without Him, everything is incomplete. When one binds everything to God, then one is "whole with the Lord." You must bind everything — yourself and the entire creation — to God. Then you will be whole and perfect, and then you will find perfect counsel.

This is why genuine guidance and advice comes only from the Tzaddik. Ordinary people are far from the ultimate goal, and therefore they have no true guidance to offer. But the Tzaddikim can perceive the radiant light of the ultimate goal, and they are therefore able to give perfect advice to each individual, because the goal they perceive is the source of all true counsel.

(*Yoreh De'ah, Hilchot M'onen U'Menachesh* 3)

Excerpts from Likutey Halachot

1) Intelligence and sophistication alone are not worthy of the name "wisdom" unless they give one guidance as to the best way to lead his life and serve God. The only true wisdom is that which guides a person in his spiritual advancement and awareness of God. This is the very essence of our holy Torah, which the Sages called "advice". The world in which we live — the world of *asiya*, action — is called the "feet" in relation to all the other worlds, because with its gross physicality it is on the lowest level of all in the universal order. For this very reason we in this world require guidance stemming from the most profound source. Only thus can we extricate ourselves from the filth of this lowly world and attach ourselves to God. The only genuine intelligence is that which enables a person to find the right way to serve God in all the different situations which confront him. (*Hilchot Techumin* 5:10).

2) The entire Torah and all of the six hundred and thirteen mitzvot consist entirely of *advice* — guidance as to how to live. But we need something more as well: advice about how to follow this guidance. It takes considerable determination to follow the guidance of the Torah in the face of all the obstacles. Each individual mitzvah consists of many many details. The task of turning from evil and doing good is very great. Giving advice as to *how* to follow the guidance of the Torah has been the task of all the tzaddikim throughout the generations, and this indeed *is* the Oral Torah. It is written in the Torah (Deuteronomy 17:11), that we should follow the guidance of the Sages unswervingly — and this applies to the sages in every generation. The reason for this is that God in His wisdom knew that it was not possible to convey all the different aspects of Torah guidance adequately in writing.

Ultimately the guidance we have to follow involves hints and allusions. These we can only receive from the true tzaddikim who exist in every generation and who play the role of Moses in relation to the Jewish people.

In the past there were many tzaddikim who instituted all kinds of rules and hedges whose purpose was to guide people as to how to observe the Torah. But every day the forces of the Other Side continue to rise up and seek to distort or even conceal the guidance which the Torah offers us. And in any case the Torah's advice is hard enough to follow as it is. For this reason we constantly need to make fresh efforts in our fight against the forces of evil. But for all that, "You, O Lord, are on high for evermore"— (Psalm 92:9), and "the counsel of the Lord stands for ever" (Psalm 33:11). The main *tikkun* will be achieved by the Mashiach, who will give counsel so profound that it will be drawn from the sublimest level of all: the innermost unification, which is called "the Ancient One". The Mashiach is called *pele yoetz*, "the one who gives extraordinary counsel" (Isaiah 9:5), because the counsel which will then be revealed will be so profound and extraordinary that the forces of the Other Side will be totally powerless to subvert it. This is the meaning of the concept of the "new Torah" which will be revealed in the time of the Mashiach (see Isaiah 51:4). It is clearly unthinkable that even the smallest dot in our present Torah will become obsolete. On the contrary, Mashiach's whole purpose will be to ensure the observance of the Torah as we have it. The new dimensions of Torah which will be revealed in the time of the Mashiach will enable every single individual, no matter what his level, to find suitable guidance to enable him to observe the Torah perfectly. (*Ibid.* 16:25).

3) Anyone who thinks about his life and his ultimate purpose knows full well that every single day brings with it the need for all kinds of practical guidance — deep and profound guidance — as to how to free himself from the problems which face him and finish the day in peace. Within each person the evil inclination

rises up against him relentlessly. And on the outside he is confronted by all kinds of difficulties. Every day he is beset by bands of murderers and cruel plotters — the evil inclination and its forces. Every day he must cry from the very depths of his heart: "Out of the depths have I called You, O Lord!" (Psalm 130:1). "Their heart cried out to God" (Lamentations 2:19). This is the only way to draw upon the deep guidance given by the true tzaddik, as it is written: "Deep waters are the counsel in a man's heart, and a man of understanding will draw it up" (Proverbs 20:5). In this way one can find the right course to follow in all the different situations which face him and then he will be able to succeed in life — to succeed in the true sense, which means gaining the eternal life of the World to Come. King David himself cried out like this: "How long shall I take counsel in my heart?" (Psalm 13:2): "Lead me with Your counsel" (Psalm 73:24); "I will bless the Lord who hath given me counsel" (Psalm 16:7). And it was for this reason that the Sages introduced the prayer for guidance in the evening service: "....direct us aright through Your own good counsel". (*Hilchot Rosh Chodesh* 6:7)

4) The worst torment of all is when a person is divided in his own mind and cannot decide which course of action he should follow. There is no problem in the world which does not have a solution. The cause of the pain is that we do not know what the right approach should be, and as a result we do not know how to escape from the problem. There are times when a person does have some idea about what he should do, but at the same time his thoughts are divided and he is afraid he might do more damage if he follows his idea than if he does the very opposite. Everyone is familiar with these kinds of dilemmas in business, with medical problems and so on. Worst of all are the conflicts people have in their efforts to draw closer to God and extricate themselves from the places to which they have been exiled because of their sins. The remedy is to believe in the Sages. In practical terms this means having respect for the entire range of Torah literature without exception. One should never look down on a particular

work. The very abundance of holy books is what brings about the sweetening of all the harsh judgements and constrictions which are the source of life's problems, and then one can find the guidance he truly needs. (*Ibid.* 7:3,7).

5) It is not always possible to achieve everything one would like to in life. There are times when the best thing to do is to use what could be called the "divided approach" — a course of action which provides one with a "surviving camp to serve as a refuge" (Genesis 32:9). This is the way to ensure that one will not lose everything. For example in matters of religious observance a person might ideally like to try to study Torah for long hours, pray with intense devotion, meditate in the right way and strive to be utterly clean of sins both in thought and in action. But it is hard to achieve this in practice. Therefore it is best to use the "divided approach" and ensure that if one does not achieve the maximum he will at all events achieve a minimum and not loose everything just because he did not succeed in the fullest sense. He should leave himself a "surviving camp to serve as a refuge". No matter what he has to do in life — even if it is not what he would like to be doing ideally — he should make sure to search for God at all times. He should see to it that he snatches at least the little good he *is* able to achieve each day. He may find that he has failed to pray with the necessary devotion. But he should at least make sure that after finishing the fixed prayers he tries to say a few words of private prayer with sincerity. If this too is denied him, let him at least see to it that he studies some Torah — a lot or a little — and cries out to God from his very heart, "Master of the World, help!" There may be times when he is uncertain as to whether he should undertake a particular journey or stay at home. He may find himself totally unable to decide what is best. But at all events, whether he ends up staying at home or goes out travelling, one thing he should be unyielding about: to do something good wherever he is (*Ibid.* 52).

6) The ultimate value of any form of intellectual endeavor lies in

the practical guidance to which it leads. How can it be called wise to apply one's intelligence to making military weapons? In the end the weapons will be the undoing of those who made them. It is a well known fact that many inventors have been killed by their own inventions. The only true wisdom is that which provides one with the guidance he needs to succeed in life. A person may be successful in terms of this world as a result of the wisdom he has acquired. But wisdom which leads to worldly success alone cannot be called "perfect counsel," because this world is a passing shadow. "Perfect counsel" is that which gives one success in the eternal world. Such counsel can be attained only through having faith in the Sages and drawing close to them, to their followers and their holy works, which are filled with guidance as to how to serve God. Even in the realm of religious devotion there are many paths where the forces of evil have positioned themselves and made them crooked. The Torah itself possesses two powers: for those who are worthy it is the herb of life, but for those who are not it is the potion of death. "The righteous will walk in them but the wicked will stumble in them" (Hosea 14:10). For this reason it is vital to draw close to the true tzaddikim in order to find the counsel he needs each day and in every situation. (*Ta'anit* 4:1).

7) The path a man wishes to travel is the path he is led along" (*Makhot* 10b). This is the cause of all the misconceived ideas which come to a person. He may like to think that the ideas which come to him are heaven-sent or based upon the guidance of the tzaddik. But in actual fact he himself is the source of them, as it is written: "A man's folly perverts his way" (Proverbs 19:3). For the tzaddik answers according to the way he is asked. Because of this a person who really wants to take pity on himself must beg and plead with God and with the true tzaddikim to look carefully at what is going on in his life and to show him true love by giving him sound guidance to enable him to succeed in his life — the life eternal. (*Ibid.* 8).

8) The ultimate redemption depends upon counsel so deep and

profound that no prophet or seer can grasp it. Of this it is written: "For the Lord of Hosts gave counsel, who will break it?" (Isaiah 14:27). Jacob wanted to reveal to his sons the deep counsel through which the redemption will come about, but the Shechina left him and he was unable to continue. (cf. Rashi on Genesis 49:1). It is impossible for it to be revealed — and it was especially so at that time, before the start of the first exile in Egypt and before the giving of the Torah, the source of all true spiritual guidance. Accordingly, all Jacob said to his sons was "Gather yourselves together" (Genesis 49:2). But these words were a revelation in themselves — a revelation of the very foundation of all true spiritual guidance, namely that there must be love, unity and peace within the Jewish people. We should gather ourselves together to speak to each other about the ultimate purpose of life and the world. In the end we will thereby be worthy of perfect guidance. (*Ibid.* 13:14).

9) In kabbalistic literature advice and guidance are referred to as "the feet". This is because more than anywhere else advice is needed for "the feet" — namely this low world in which we live, "the earth, My footstool" (Isaiah 66:1). In the world of truth — the World to Come — there will be no need for advice. But the lower the level the more profound and far—reaching the advice which is needed to be able to rise out of it. In what does the greatness of man lie as compared with the angels, and of "ba'ale teshuva" — literally, masters of repentance — compared with perfect tzaddikim? The answer is that being so much more remote from God they need the profoundest advice of all in order to emerge from their degraded condition. When they succeed in freeing themselves from it God has the highest regard for them and they are very dear to Him (*Ibid.* 14).

10) The main path to *teshuva* is by following the right advice. Deep inside every person there is a latent fear of God and a longing to return to Him. The problem is that people are simply unaware of the means by which they can emerge from their

darkness. Each person is caught in his own individual trap. It is in spiritual matters more than any other area of life that a person requires guidance. All the knowledge and wisdom in the world are worth nothing if they do not help one draw closer to God and earn the eternal life of the World to Come. Systems of knowledge which do not do this are worthless. And if one actually becomes distanced from God because of such ideas, this is worse than anything. It is to intellectual approaches like these that the Torah refers when it says, "For they are a nation void of counsel" (Deuteronomy 32:28). It is written: "There is no wisdom, no understanding and no counsel in the face of God" (Proverbs 21:30). This means that any body of wisdom or knowledge, any form of guidance which carries implications contrary to the will of God, cannot be called wisdom or counsel at all. Anyone with even a minimum of understanding should be able to see that the main concern which should occupy his thoughts is how he can emerge from the hell which threatens to engulf him. One has only to consider the nature of this world: it is a place full of troubles. People's days are spent in anger and pain. In the end one returns to the dust. What does he gain from all his toil?! If only all the sages in the world — including even the wise men of the gentile nations — were to sit down together and devote themselves to the task of thinking out what the purpose of this world is and why man was created, and develop ideas about how to live life as it really should be lived, they could spend years on this task quite profitabley — as did Abraham and the other Patriarchs. Today this task is more vital than ever. We already have the Torah in our hands together with the six hundred and thirteen mitzvot which constitute the practical advice it has to offer us. If we would only put all our energy into thinking out how we can simply observe the Torah just as it is, with simplicity and purity! This is the greatest wisdom of all. Sound advice is advice which leads to Torah observance. That is why King David started the book of Psalms with the words, "Happy is the man who has not followed the advice of the wicked" (Psalm 1:1). The main thing is to have absolutely nothing to do with the ideas offered by the wicked but to concentrate only on thinking which guidance one should follow in order to serve God and observe the Torah (*Hilchot Succah* 7:2).

11) Only from the true tzaddikim is it possible to obtain sound advice as to how to come close to God. All too often a person is divided in his own mind about what he should do. This is particularly true in questions concerning spiritual life. The root of these conflicts is the "flaming sword which turns every way" (Genesis 3:24) which was sent into the world because of Adam's sin of eating from the fruit of the Tree of Knowledge. As a result of his sin he was expelled from the Garden of Eden, where the Tree of Life is to be found, and God placed the "inflaming sword... to keep the way." This "flaming sword which turns every way" is the root of the constant mental twisting and turning which man has to endure in this life. He constantly shifts from thought to thought and from one idea to another about what he ought to do. He is never sure which is the path that will lead to the Tree of Life and the life eternal.

In everyone's inner heart, everyone in the world fears God and wants to draw closer. But every day man's evil inclination rises up against him, and people are caught like birds in a net. No matter where a person might be or what his situation is, there is always a way for him to get free and return to God. The problem is that he usually does not know exactly which path to follow in order to save his soul from the destruction which threatens him. The consequences of Adam's sin exercise their grip over the entire human race, and this is why people are never able to know which path will prove to be good in the end and which not. At times a person is faced with a path which seems to be straight, but "its end is the ways of death" (Proverbs 14:12). Thus people are constantly confused about the best course of action to take in order to serve God. However the true Tzaddik is the "Holy of Holies", and within him dwells the Supernal Wisdom. This is the source of all things, and there, all the harsh judgements and "contractions" are sweetened. The Tzaddik thus knows all the different routes and paths which exist even in the very depths of the darkness. At the very root of all things there are no divisions or conflicts at all. Everything is a unity. Thus the advice and guidance which are drawn from this source are perfect, and the Tzaddik has the power to draw guidance from here and offer each individual the advice he needs in his unique place and time (*Ibid.* 3).

12) The only test of whether advice is good or not is if it leads to success in the ultimate sense — success in gaining the eternal life. There are many ideas which at first sight seem good but which can never lead to success in the true sense of the word. They cannot therefore be called "good advice". One must pray intently to God to be given good, sound advice which will enable him to fulfill his ultimate destiny. We can understand this point by a simple analogy from the world of business. There have been many cases of terrible commercial failures brought about by so—called "good advice". People were advised to buy a particular commodity and were so successful that they borrowed heavily in order to buy very large stocks. Then suddenly the price of the commodity slumped and they were unable to make back their investment. They ended up with tremendous debts and sometimes even had to flee from where they had been living. The "good advice" they had been given proved completely worthless in the end! A person may be "successful" all his life, but if the success in question does not lead him to the eternal life what profit was there from all his efforts! A person should therefore pray again and again for God to grant him the true counsel which will lead to genuine — and enduring — success (*Hilchot Shechitah* 5:3).

13) The reason why true spiritual enlightenment is so heavily concealed in this world is that people lack the guidance necessary in order to find it. In their hearts everyone knows that this world is a fleeting shadow. Who can deny the fact that man is here today

and in the grave tomorrow? But because of the strength of people's physical cravings they are unable to find a way to free theselves and save their souls from destruction. They prefer to turn a blind eye to the realities of the human situation and follow the vanities of this world instead. "What else can we do?" they say, "we're caught in a trap!" People use every kind of excuse to justify their complacency. The only true solution lies with the Tzaddik. He alone has the power to draw from the Supernal Wisdom and illumine the world with true counsel. He is even able to radiate the light to those who stand outside the bounds of holiness. The power of the concealment is broken and enlightenment spreads (*Ibid.*)

14) True advice is "the light of day". It is only through the darkness of night that this light can be revealed. For when a person truly desires to serve God and is constantly searching for guidance as to how to draw closer to Him, the very darkness he experiences when he is bereft of guidance is actually beneficial to him. It is when he feels least able to decide what he ought to do in order to draw closer that he digs and searches the most. He craves for assistance and presses God with every kind of prayer and entreaty to send him radiant counsel within his darkness. Then God takes pity on him and sends him the deepest guidance out of the very darkness itself. Each time this happens the counsel is entirely new, and in this way his faith is renewed and he acquires new vigor. This is the essence of man's service of God. (*Ibid.*).

15) To be deprived of true guidance is to be subjected to the darkness of night. When the right advice is revealed it is like the light of day. The guidance of the true tzaddik sheds the radiance of light into the hearts of men even when they are trapped in the thickest darkness — a darkness so intense that it threatens to overwhelm them completely. The same pattern of light emerging from darkness is embodied in the very act of God's creation of the world, where first all was darkness and then there was light. This same pattern is repeated every single day. Each day of a person's

life he needs the deepest guidance in order to escape the forces that threaten to engulf him and destroy the vitality of that day. Every day the evil inclination renews itself in its battle against him, and accordingly each day he needs fresh advice as how to escape from it. The purpose of this repeated cycle is that the faith within him should be revealed and grow. Faith is renewed every day, and the main source of its renewal and growth is the new guidance which is revealed each day in accordance with the needs of the day. This explains why when night falls we have to engage in the task of renewing the day to come. With the onset of darkness the light of the guidance which illumined the passing day is withdrawn. The time has come to work again to dig and uncover new guidance from out of the darkness — because before the light of day there is always darkness. It is through the evening prayers, the recital of Sh'ma and the study of Torah by night that we uncover the guidance we need for the day to come. That is why the request that God should "...direct us aright through Your own good counsel" was included in the evening service. (*Hilchot Nezikin* 5:39,40).

16) Sometimes a person falls into such a state of mental confusion and inner conflict that he is totally powerless to decide what to do. The more he tries to work out what he ought to do the more confused he becomes. One moment everything seems to point perfectly clearly and convincingly in one direction. Then all of a sudden a totally opposite approach opens up in his mind and his first idea seems totally wrong. At times the inner conflict becomes so intense that he simply has no idea how to decide what he should do. When a person sees that he has been sunk in his darkness for so long and still has no idea how he can extricate himself from it, what he should do is to cry out to God about the very agony of uncertainly itself. He should explain to God that he has fallen so far that he has no idea how to get out of the darkness and find the light. There is no such thing as despair. Even in such a plight there must exist some means of escaping from the darkness. The only reason for the darkness is that his sins have

caused the guidance he needs to be concealed from him. The solution is that he should at least acknowledge the reality of his situation — that he has fallen so far and become so distanced from God that he does not have any idea what he should do. When this is the situation, he should cry out to God to help him with. He should plead with God to show him the way to conduct himself. The truth of the matter is that even the greatest tzaddikim also undergo inner conflicts about their activities and behavior — as we can see from King David's cry: "How long shall I take counsel in my soul?" Clearly he went through many conflicts as to what he should do. How much more so is this the case with people on a lower level — especially those who are trapped in the net of their desires and fantasies. They must know and believe that no matter how grave their situation, there is always *some* means by which they can emerge and return to God — if only they have the correct *advice*. And if they are riddled with conflicts, they should acknowledge the truth — that they *are* in conflict. This is precisely what they should pray to God about. In the end their very fall will be transformed into a great spiritual advance, and they will find that the whole purpose of the fall was precisely that they should thereby rise higher. (*Hilchot Gittin* 3, 25).

LIKUTEY TEFILOT

Rabbi Nachman instructed his followers to make "prayers out of their studies." His prescription was an expression of the integral relationship between prayer and study in the spiritual life of the Jew — a relationship which is one of the recurrent themes of Rabbi Nachman's writings. With the Rebbe's encouragement, Rabbi Nathan wrote extensive prayers based on the discourses in the Likutey Moharan. *The diction of the prayers is simple, flowing, eloquent and poetic. In content, they range over all concerns of man in this life. Their approach is one of frankness, sincerity and soul-searching. The following prayers have been included to provide the reader an insight into Rabbi Nathan's personal quest for* advice.

Prayer by Rabbi Nathan (from *Likutey Tefilot* 61)

You are the Source of counsel, the Master of mighty deeds. Your eyes behold all the ways of mankind. You know and understand their thoughts and secrets. You have the power to release them and save them from the hand of all who oppress them. Take pity on me for Your Name's sake and help me to do Your will. Send me salvation speedily and direct me aright with Your own good counsel. Endow me with knowledge, understanding and wisdom, in order that I may always know how to decide what to do in every situation in the world. Grant me perfect counsel in order that I may never suffer the torment of doubts and uncertainty, dilemmas and inner conflicts. Endow me with the spirit of wisdom and understanding and grant me good counsel, strength, the spirit of knowledge and the fear of God. Take pity on me and save me. Let me have faith in all the true sages — complete, genuine, heartfelt faith. Let me never diverge from their words to the right or the left. Let this be my path to holy judgement: that I may examine myself and judge myself truthfully, and see the truth of my situation. Let me learn the holy Torah for its own sake at all times — learn it in order to teach, to observe, to do and to fulfill all the words of Your Torah in love. Lighten my eyes with Your Torah and give me wisdom, understanding and knowledge so that I may derive understanding and wisdom from all my studies. Let me be worthy of learning from the entire range of Torah teachings and of understanding all the different works, and let me derive from all of them sound guidance as to how to conduct my life in uprightness and justice. Let me not swerve from the truth either to the right or the left. Let me always understand correctly what You desire and what is Your will — in order to know how to conduct myself in all matters according to the teachings of the holy Torah.

״גְּדֹל הָעֵצָה וְרַב הָעֲלִילִיָּה אֲשֶׁר עֵינֶיךָ פְּקֻחוֹת עַל כָּל דַּרְכֵי בְּנֵי אָדָם״ וְיוֹדֵעַ וּמֵבִין מַחְשְׁבוֹתָם וְסוֹדָם, וּמִיַּד כָּל לוֹחֲצֵיהֶם אַתָּה גוֹאֲלָם וּפוֹדָם. רַחֵם עָלַי לְמַעַן שְׁמֶךָ. וְעָזְרֵנִי לַעֲשׂוֹת רְצוֹנְךָ וְהוֹשִׁיעֵנִי מְהֵרָה, וְתַקְּנֵנִי בְּעֵצָה טוֹבָה מִלְּפָנֶיךָ. וְחָנֵּנִי מֵאִתְּךָ דֵּעָה בִּינָה וְהַשְׂכֵּל, שֶׁאֶזְכֶּה לָדַעַת לָתֵת עֵצָה לְנַפְשִׁי עַל־כָּל דָּבָר שֶׁבָּעוֹלָם, וּתְזַכֵּנִי לְעֵצָה שְׁלֵמָה תָּמִיד, וְלֹא אֶהְיֶה מְסֻפָּק לְעוֹלָם עַל שׁוּם דָּבָר, וְלֹא תִתְחַלֵּק עֲצָתִי לִשְׁתַּיִם, חַס וְשָׁלוֹם, וְתַשְׁפִּיעַ עָלַי ״רוּחַ חָכְמָה וּבִינָה רוּחַ עֵצָה וּגְבוּרָה רוּחַ דַּעַת וְיִרְאַת יְיָ״ וּתְרַחֵם עָלַי וְתוֹשִׁיעֵנִי וּתְזַכֵּנִי לֶאֱמוּנַת חֲכָמִים בֶּאֱמֶת כִּרְצוֹנְךָ הַטּוֹב. וְאֶזְכֶּה לְהַאֲמִין בְּכָל הַחֲכָמִים הָאֲמִתִּיִּים בֶּאֱמוּנָה שְׁלֵמָה בֶּאֱמֶת וּבְלֵב שָׁלֵם. וְלֹא אָסוּר מִדִּבְרֵיהֶם יָמִין וּשְׂמֹאל. וְעַל־יְדֵי־זֶה תְּזַכֵּנִי לְמִשְׁפָּט דִּקְדֻשָּׁה שֶׁאֶזְכֶּה לִשְׁפֹּט עַצְמִי בֶּאֱמֶת. וְתוֹצִיא מִשְׁפָּטִי לָאוֹר. וְאֶזְכֶּה לִלְמֹד תּוֹרָתְךָ הַקְּדוֹשָׁה לִשְׁמָהּ תָּמִיד, לִלְמֹד וּלְלַמֵּד לִשְׁמֹר וְלַעֲשׂוֹת וּלְקַיֵּם אֶת כָּל דִּבְרֵי תוֹרָתְךָ בְּאַהֲבָה, וְתָאִיר עֵינַי בְּתוֹרָתֶךָ, וְתִתֶּן לִי חָכְמָה וּבִינָה וָדַעַת דִּקְדֻשָּׁה לְהָבִין וּלְהַשְׂכִּיל מִכָּל הַלִּמּוּדִים שֶׁאֶזְכֶּה לִלְמֹד בְּכָל סִפְרֵי תוֹרָתְךָ הַקְּדוֹשָׁה, לְהָבִין וּלְהוֹצִיא מִכֻּלָּם מִשְׁפְּטֵי הַנְהָגוֹת יְשָׁרוֹת בֶּאֱמֶת. וְלֹא אַטֶּה וְלֹא אָסוּר מִן הָאֱמֶת יָמִין וּשְׂמֹאל, רַק אֶזְכֶּה לְכַוֵּן תָּמִיד רְצוֹנְךָ בֶּאֱמֶת. וְלֵידַע תָּמִיד אֵיךְ לְהִתְנַהֵג בְּכָל דָּבָר עַל־יְדֵי לִמּוּדֵי הַתּוֹרָה הַקְּדוֹשָׁה.

(ליקוטי תפילות ח״א ס״א)

Prayer of Rabbi Nathan (*Likutey Tefilot* 117)

Guide me with Your counsel and take me towards Your glory. Master of the World, my King and my God. To You I pray, to You, O God, I cry out and plead: how long must I search my soul for counsel and suffer the burden of anguish in my heart? How long will my enemy rise up against me? Take pity upon me for the sake of Your Name and direct me with Your own good counsel. Free me from my troubles quickly for the sake of Your name. You know how desperate my situation is. I have no idea what I should do. My heart is riddled with doubts about all the things I am involved with. Almost all the time I have conflicts within myself about what I should do. No matter what I have to think about, large or small, I do not know what I should do. I am in a turmoil. It is keeping me back from serving You and cleansing myself and returning to You as I should. Take pity on me, for You are the Fountain of lovingkindness, the Source of counsel, the Master of mighty deeds. At all times let me follow the advice of the tzaddikim and those who are truly God-fearing, because all their advice is drawn from the holy Torah teachings which they received from their teachers, the holy tzaddikim of the previous generations. Let me be close to them and follow their advice in every single aspect of life, be it my religious devotions or my working life or anything else that I may be involved in — in all things let me ask for their guidance. Let me have the benefit of their advice and counsel, so that their wisdom may shine within me. Through this the holy influence of Your lovingkindness will be drawn over me and all the harsh judgements which threaten me will be sweetened and removed. I will be worthy of complete salvation at all times, as it is written: "Salvation comes from abundant counsel."

Guard me at all times from tripping and stumbling because of

״בַּעֲצָתְךָ תַנְחֵנִי וְאַחַר כָּבוֹד תִּקָּחֵנִי״. רִבּוֹנוֹ שֶׁל עוֹלָם, מַלְכִּי וֵאלֹהַי אֵלֶיךָ אֶתְפַּלָּל, ״אֵלֶיךָ יְיָ אֶקְרָא וְאֶל יְיָ אֶתְחַנָּן. עַד אָנָה אָשִׁית עֵצוֹת בְּנַפְשִׁי יָגוֹן בִּלְבָבִי יוֹמָם עַד אָנָה יָרוּם אוֹיְבִי עָלָי״. רַחֵם עָלַי לְמַעַן שְׁמֶךָ, וְתַקְּנֵנוּ בְּעֵצָה טוֹבָה מִלְּפָנֶיךָ וְהוֹשִׁיעֵנוּ מְהֵרָה לְמַעַן שְׁמֶךָ, כִּי אַתָּה יוֹדֵעַ גֹּדֶל חֶסְרוֹן הָעֵצָה וְעֹצֶם רִבּוּי הַסְּפֵקוֹת שֶׁיֵּשׁ בְּלִבִּי בְּכָל הַדְּבָרִים, אֲשֶׁר עַל־פִּי־רֹב כָּל עֲצָתִי חֲלוּקָה לִשְׁתַּיִם, וְאֵינִי יָכוֹל לָתֵת עֵצוֹת בְּנַפְשִׁי בְּשׁוּם דָּבָר ״לְמִגָּדוֹל וְעַד קָטָן״, אֲשֶׁר זֶה הַדָּבָר הָיָה בְּעוֹכְרַי, וּמוֹנֵעַ אוֹתִי הַרְבֵּה מֵעֲבוֹדַת יְיָ וּמִתְּשׁוּבָה אֲמִתִּיִּית. רַחֵם עָלַי, בַּעַל הָרַחֲמִים. ״גְּדוֹל הָעֵצָה וְרַב הָעֲלִילִיָּה״ וְזַכֵּנִי לְקַבֵּל תָּמִיד כָּל הָעֵצוֹת מִצַּדִּיקֵי וּכְשֵׁרֵי הַדּוֹר הָאֲמִתִּיִּים, אֲשֶׁר כָּל עֲצוֹתֵיהֶם נִמְשָׁכוֹת מֵהַתּוֹרָה הַקְּדוֹשָׁה, שֶׁקִּבְּלוּ מֵרַבּוֹתֵיהֶם הַצַּדִּיקִים, הַקְּדוֹשִׁים, הָאֲמִתִּיִּים. זַכֵּנוּ לְהִתְקָרֵב אֲלֵיהֶם בֶּאֱמֶת וּלְקַבֵּל מֵהֶם כָּל הָעֵצוֹת בְּכָל הַדְּבָרִים שֶׁבָּעוֹלָם הֵן בַּעֲבוֹדוֹת יְיָ, וְהֵן בַּעֲבוֹדוֹת מַשָּׂא וּמַתָּן וּפַרְנָסָה, וְהֵן בִּשְׁאַר עֲסָקִים, בְּכֻלָּם אֶשְׁאוֹל אֶת פִּיהֶם וְאֶזְכֶּה לֵהָנוֹת מֵהֶם עֵצָה וְתוּשִׁיָּה. וְיָאִירוּ בִּי חָכְמָתָם הַקְּדוֹשָׁה. וְעַל־יְדֵי־זֶה יִהְיֶה נִמְשָׁךְ עָלַי חֶסֶד גָּדוֹל. וְיַמְתִּיקוּ וִיבַטְּלוּ מִמֶּנִּי כָּל הַדִּינִים שֶׁבָּעוֹלָם. וְאֶזְכֶּה לִישׁוּעָה שְׁלֵמָה בְּכָל עֵת, כְּמוֹ שֶׁכָּתוּב: וּתְשׁוּעָה בְּרֹב יוֹעֵץ. וְתִשְׁמְרֵנִי וְתַצִּילֵנִי תָמִיד שֶׁלֹּא אֶכָּשֵׁל לְעוֹלָם בְּעֵצָה שֶׁאֵינָהּ טוֹבָה, חַס

faulty advice, and protect me from causing myself injury, pain and suffering because of worthless counsel. Let me constantly take only the advice of the tzaddikim and those who are truly God-fearing, so that their wisdom will shine within me. And then You will stir up Your tender mercy and abundant love and always free me and save me from any situation where I am in need of help, whether in material or spiritual matters. Draw down over me the love of God all the day, and fulfill in my life the words of the verse: "God breaks the counsel of nations and brings to nought the calculations of the peoples. Many are the thoughts in the heart of a man, but the counsel of God — this is what will endure. The counsel of God will stand for ever and the thoughts of his heart from generation to generation. "The Lord of Hosts has given counsel, who will break it?" "He will grant you according to your own heart and fulfill all your counsel. We will shout for joy at Your salvation, and in the name of our God we will set up our standards. The Lord will fulfill all our requests... Save, O Lord, let the King answer us on the day that we call." "Let the words of my lips and the meditation of my heart be acceptable before you O Lord, my rock and my redeemer." Blessed be the Lord for ever, Amen.

וְשָׁלוֹם, וְלֹא אַמְשִׁיךְ עָלַי שׁוּם צַעַר וְיִסּוּרִים וְהֶזֵּק, חַס וְשָׁלוֹם, עַל־יְדֵי עֵצוֹת נִבְעָרוֹת, חַס וְשָׁלוֹם, רַק אֶשְׁתַּדֵּל תָּמִיד לְקַבֵּל כָּל הָעֵצוֹת מִצַּדִּיקֵי וּכְשֵׁרֵי הַדּוֹר הָאֲמִתִּיִּים, בְּאֹפֶן שֶׁיָּאִירוּ בִּי חָכְמָתָם הַקְּדוֹשָׁה. וּתְעוֹרֵר רַחֲמֶיךָ וַחֲסָדֶיךָ הַגְּדוֹלִים עָלַי בְּכָל עֵת, וְתוֹשִׁיעֵנִי תָמִיד בְּכָל מַה שֶּׁאֲנִי צָרִיךְ לְהִוָּשֵׁעַ בְּגַשְׁמִיּוּת וְרוּחָנִיּוּת, וִיהְיֶה נִמְשָׁךְ עָלַי "חֶסֶד אֵל כָּל הַיּוֹם" וִיקֻיַּם בִּי מִקְרָא שֶׁכָּתוּב: יְיָ הֵפִיר עֲצַת גּוֹיִם הֵנִיא מַחְשְׁבוֹת עַמִּים. רַבּוֹת מַחֲשָׁבוֹת בְּלֶב אִישׁ וַעֲצַת יְיָ הִיא תָקוּם. עֲצַת יְיָ לְעוֹלָם תַּעֲמֹד מַחְשְׁבוֹת לִבּוֹ לְדוֹר וָדוֹר. וְנֶאֱמַר: יְיָ צְבָאוֹת יָעָץ וּמִי יָפֵר. וְנֶאֱמַר: יִתֶּן לְךָ כִלְבָבֶךָ וְכָל עֲצָתְךָ יְמַלֵּא. נְרַנְּנָה בִּישׁוּעָתֶךָ וּבְשֵׁם אֱלֹהֵינוּ נִדְגּוֹל יְמַלֵּא יְיָ כָּל מִשְׁאֲלוֹתֶיךָ. יְיָ הוֹשִׁיעָה הַמֶּלֶךְ יַעֲנֵנוּ בְיוֹם קָרְאֵנוּ. יִהְיוּ לְרָצוֹן אִמְרֵי־פִי וְהֶגְיוֹן לִבִּי לְפָנֶיךָ יְיָ צוּרִי וְגוֹאֲלִי. בָּרוּךְ יְיָ לְעוֹלָם אָמֵן וְאָמֵן:

(ליקוטי תפילות ח"א קי"ז)

THE LIFE OF RABBI NATHAN

The Life of Rabbi Nathan

"Without you, I am nothing; and without me, you are nothing."
(Rabbi Nachman to Rabbi Nathan)

Rabbi Nathan was born in the town of Nemirov on 15 Shevat, 5540 (1780). His father, Rabbi Naftali Hertz, was a scholar of great distinction and also a wealthy businessman. He was a partner in three stores in Odessa, Berdichov and Nemirov. Rabbi Nathan was brought up in his father's house in an atmosphere of Torah and learning. and was particularly close to his mother's father, R. Yitzchak Danziger. He was given a traditional Torah education, and had the opportunity to learn the various facets of his father's business.

In 5553 (1793), R. Nathan married Esther Shaindel, the daughter of the well known scholar Rabbi David Zvi Orbach, who was the Rav and leading rabbinical authority of Mohilov, Sharograd and Kremenetz. The wedding took place (as was the custom) when R. Nathan was thirteen years old. The next two years he lived in his father-in-law's house, and there he continued with his Torah studies at an advanced level and became familiar with the complete range of Talmudic and *halachic* literature. The opposition of the *misnagdim* to the Chassidic movement was then at its height. Both R. Nathan's father and father-in-law were staunch opponents of Chassidism, and the latter in particular made efforts to inculcate Rabbi Nathan with his own attitudes.

After Succot 5556 (Autumn 1795), R. Nathan returned to Nemirov — and there met R. Naftali, who was to be his lifelong friend. R. Naftali belonged to the Chassidic movement and introduced R. Nathan to Chassiduth. Rabbi Nathan tried hard to find spiritual guidance, but did not feel that he had found what he was searching for.

Towards the end of 5562 (1802), Rabbi Nachman moved to

Breslov, which is situated nine miles to the south of Nemirov. R. Lipa, who was a good friend of R Nathan's, witnessed Rabbi Nachman's first Sabbath in Breslov. On his return to Nemirov after the Sabbath he told Rabbi Nathan about his experience. Rabbi Nathan felt that now he might find what he was searching for, and the very next morning he set off with R. Naftali for Breslov. It was on Sunday, 22 Elul, 5562 (September 18th, 1802), that Rabbi Nathan had his first meeting with Rabbi Nachman. Rabbi Nachman was thirty years old and Rabbi Nathan just twenty-two. Rabbi Nachman said to him: "We've known each other a long time, but it's been very long since we've seen each other face to face."

Rabbi Nathan was immediately drawn to Rabbi Nachman, and returned to Breslov the following week to spend Rosh Hashanah of 5563 (1802), with the Rebbe — this in the face of great opposition from his wife and father. R. Nathan began writing Rabbi Nachman's lessons. At first he recorded the Rebbe's teachings informally, but by Chanukah he was systematizing his notes and had begun reviewing them with Rabbi Nachman.

All this time Rabbi Nathan was living in his father's house, and he was unable to conceal either his visits to Breslov or the spiritual practices that he was following on Rabbi Nachman's recommendations. His father became so incensed that R. Nathan was chased out of the house and had to go to the house of his grandfather, R. Yitzchak Danziger.

During the winter of 5563 (1802), Rabbi Nathan's wife gave birth to a son, Shachna.

On Rosh Chodesh Nissan, 5563 (1803), Rabbi Nachman made a wedding for his daughter, Sarah, in the town of Medvedevka. Despite the opposition of his wife and family, R. Nathan set out on the long journey to Medvedevka, and overcame many barriers in order to be with the Rebbe for the wedding. He stayed for several weeks, from Purim until after Pesach. This was the only time that Rabbi Nathan was able to celebrate Pesach with Rabbi Nachman.

That summer, Rabbi Nathan's father's business partners prevailed upon him to assist R. Nathan. "How can you act so harshly against such a fine and precious son?" they argued. His father relented and made arrangements for Rabbi Nathan to share in his business activities, providing an honorable livelihood.

On 2 Kislev, 5564 (1803), Rabbi Nathan's mother died. Later that year Rabbi Nachman advised Rabbi Nathan to undertake a special, intensive study of halachic literature.

During this same year many of Rabbi Nachman's writings were arranged in order. The Rebbe asked R. Nathan to draw up an abridged version of the main points of each of his lessons, and this formed the basis of the *Kitzur Likutey Moharan*. Later that year, R. Nathan started copying all of Rabbi Nachman's lessons. It took three months to complete the task, and shortly after Shavuot, 5565 (1805), the manuscript was given to be bound. This volume contained what is now the first part of Rabbi Nachman's main work, *Likutey Moharan*. Rabbi Nachman told R. Nathan that the whole work was his, and that if it were not for him not a single page of his writings would survive. The same year, he also began work on his *magnum opus*, the *Likutey Halachot*.

After Succot 5566 (1805), a son, Meir, was born to R. Nathan. He passed away very young. In the winter of the same year Rabbi Nachman dictated to R. Nathan another work, which was known as the *Sefer HaNisraf*. (Some years later Rabbi Nachman gave instructions for both the original and the copy to be burned.) In the summer of 5566 (1806), Rabbi Nachman revealed to Rabbi Nathan and Rabbi Naftali the course of events which would lead to the coming of the Messiah.

In the summer of 5566 (1806), Rabbi Nachman began telling his stories, and they were written down by Rabbi Nathan. During Succot of 5567, Rabbi Nathan was obliged to move to his father-in-law's house in Mohilev, which was sixty miles from Breslov. Because of the distance he was only able to visit the Rebbe on the regular occasions which the Rebbe had instituted for his followers to gather.

Immediately after Yom Kippur, 5568 (1808), R. Nachman told Rabbi Nathan to write a table of contents for the manuscript of *Likutey Moharan*. Later on that year Rabbi Nachman decided to publish the book and it was printed in Ostrog at the end of the year.

In the course of the same year another son was born to R. Nathan — Yitzchak — to whom most of the letters in *Alim LeTerufa* (collected letters of Rabbi Nathan) were written. Esther Shaindel subsequently bore Rabbi Nathan two more children — Chana Tzirel in 1820, and David Tzvi in 1822.

During the month of Av, after an absence of two years, Rabbi Nathan returned to Nemirov, where he could be close to R. Nachman. Following the publication of *Likutey Moharan*, Rabbi Nathan began working on Rabbi Nachman's more recent lessons, which were published after the Rebbe's death as *Likutey Moharan Tinyana.*

On Tuesday 3 Iyar, 5570 (May 7th, 1810), Rabbi Nathan traveled with Rabbi Nachman from Breslov to Uman, where the Rebbe stayed until his death on 18 Tishrei, 5571 (October 16th 1810). Rabbi Nathan was appointed the executor of Rabbi Nachman's will, and he immediately assumed a position of authority among the Rebbe's followers. Before leaving Uman Rabbi Nathan explained that it had been Rabbi Nachman's intention that his followers should gather in Uman each Rosh Hashanah. At the same time Rabbi Nathan spoke about the need to print the second part of *Likutey Moharan.* He himself raised the money for the printing.

In the winter of 5571, Rabbi Nathan made his first pilgrimage to Uman. After Shavuot the same year most of the houses in Nemirov, including Rabbi Nathan's, were consumed in a fire and he decided to move to Breslov. That summer, besides the publication of *Likutey Moharan Tinyana*, Rabbi Nathan also published the *Sefer HaMidot* and the *Kitzur Likutey Moharan.* All three volumes were brought to Uman when Rabbi Nathan went there for Rosh Hashanah, 5572 (1811).

That year R. Nathan started spreading Rabbi Nachman's teachings more widely and drawing people closer. In 5573 (1813), Rabbi Nachman's house in Breslov, which had been burned in a fire just prior to the Rebbe's move to Uman, was rebuilt. The following year, (5574) Rabbi Nathan began the building of a new and enlarged synagogue in Breslov.

In 5575 (1814-1815), Rabbi Nathan began writing his collection of prayers, *Likutey Tefilot*. The following year he had Rabbi Nachman's stories, the *Sippurey Ma'asiot*, printed. In 5577 (1817), his son R. Shachna was married. The same year Rabbi Nathan wrote the prayer to be recited after the *Tikkun HaKlali*.

In 5579 (1818-19), Rabbi Nathan set up a printing press in his own house to facilitate the printing of Rabbi Nachman's writings. Between 5579 and 5581 (1818-1820), both the first and second parts of *Likutey Moharan* were reprinted; the *Sefer HaMidot* was reprinted together with the *Shemot HaTzaddikim*, a collection of the names of all the tzaddikim compiled by Rabbi Nathan; and the *Tikkun HaKlali* was also reissued.

In the winter of 5582 (1822), Rabbi Nathan, accompanied by his student R. Yehuda Eliezer, left for the Holy Land, sailing from Odessa to Istanbul. There they had difficulty in finding a ship, but eventually they were able to reach Egypt, and spent Shavuot in Alexandria. In the summer of 1822, Rabbi Nathan first set foot on the soil of the Holy Land, when he disembarked at the port of Sidon. He visited Safed, Meron and Tiberias, and left Israel just before Rosh Hashanah 5583. He spent Rosh Hashanah on the ship near Sakis and was in Istanbul for Yom Kippur, returning to his home after Succot.

Likutey Tefilot was printed in 5584 (1824). During this period Rabbi Nathan had to endure fierce opposition from the opponents of Breslover Chassidim. Later in 5584, they succeeded in having his printing press closed down. It was only in 5586 (1825), that R. Nathan received official permission from the authorities in Vilna to reopen the press. Rabbi Nathan then began the task of rearranging and expanding the *Kitzur Likutey Moharan* in order to produce *Likutey Etzot*.

On the eve of Elul, 5586, Rabbi Nathan's first wife died. In 5587 he remarried, and at the end of the year, his wife Dishel bore a son, Nachman. A second son, Yoseph Yonah, was born in 5589 (1829).

So many people came to Uman on Rosh Hashanah 5590 (1829), that it was apparent that the local synagogue was too small. Rabbi

Nathan began collecting funds for a new building and the foundation stone was laid in 5593 (1822). The building was completed in 5594. Rabbi Nathan was then stricken with an intestinal disease from which he ultimately passed away.

In 5595 (1834-5) the opposition to Rabbi Nathan and the Breslover Chassidim reached its peak. It was led by R. Moshe Tzvi of Savran. The printing press was closed down a second time and Rabbi Nathan — having been slandered by his opponents that his activities were against the Czar — was arrested by the authorities. Many of his writings were seized and were lost. In 5596 (1835-6) Rabbi Nathan was expelled from his home in Breslov and forced to move to Nemirov, where he was confined for three years until the beginning of 5599 (1838). His leading opponents subsequently died during these years, and the opposition quieted down.

Though he suffered greatly, he nevertheless devoted himself to spreading Rabbi Nachman's teachings and working to draw people closer to Torah. He was also engaged in the writing of the eight volume *Likutey Halachot*, of which only the first volume of *Orach Chaim* was published in his lifetime — in 5603 (1843).

Rabbi Nathan passed away on Friday afternoon, the 10th of Tevet, 5605 (1844), one hour before the Sabbath. On his last morning, the first two stories of the *Sippurey Ma'asiot* were read to him. On hearing the closing words of the second story — "Let us go home" — Rabbi Nathan nodded as if to say: "It is *my* time to return home." As he recited the grace after meals he added the following prayer: "May the All Merciful draw the holiness of the Land of Israel upon us."

He was buried in Breslov after the departure of the Sabbath on 12 Tevet, 5605, in the presence of a large assembly which included Chassidim and *misnagdim* alike.

The following is a list of additional translations and publications available or due to be published by The Breslov Research Institute within the coming year in English, French and Russian.

ENGLISH:

Rabbi Nachman's Stories (*Sippurey Ma'asioth*), by Rabbi Aryeh Kaplan (with commentary and index) - 550p.
Rabbi Nachman's Wisdom (*Shevachey v'Sichoth HaRan*), by Rabbi Aryeh Kaplan (with notes and index) - 510p.
Restore My Soul *(Meshivat Nefesh)*, by Avraham Greenbaum - 128p.
Outpouring of the Soul *(Hishtaphkhut HaNefesh)*, by Rabbi Aryeh Kaplan - 96p.
Gems of Rabbi Nachman (drawn from Rabbi Nachman's Wisdom with additions), by Rabbi Aryeh Kaplan - 180p.
Rabbi Nachman's Tikun (*Tikun HaKellali*), by Avraham Greenbaum - 160p.
Rabbi Nachman's Biography by Rabbi Aryeh Kaplan (July 1983).

French:

Les Contes (*Sippurey Ma'asioth*), by Shlomo Regnot - 180p.
Hithbodedouth ou La Porte du Ciel, by Ithzchak Besançon - 128p.
Rabbi Nachman de Breslev (a collection of major teachings and stories), by Ithzchak Besançon - (June, 1983).
La Sagesse de Rabbi Nachman (*Shevachey v'Sichoth HaRan*), by Shlomo Regnot - (September, 1983).
Courage, by Ithzchak Besançon - (March, 1983).

Russian:

Sippurey Ma'asioth, by Gershon Berman (September, 1983).
Likutim, by Natan Feingold (April, 1983).

These publications are an outcome of many years of research by the Breslov Research Institute, *Zvi La'tzadik in memory of Rabbi Zvi Aryeh Rosenfeld zal*, within the framework of Yeshivat Chasidei Breslov, in Jerusalem. The institute is devoted to the translation and publication of all the major works of Rabbi Nachman into different languages, making them accessible to the various Jewish communities throughout the world.

Established in 1937 in the old city of Jerusalem, Yeshivat Chasidei Breslov has more than 100 students, involved in rabbinical and *baalei teshuvah* programs. Forums are held regularly by our students in various towns, kibbutzim and settlements throughout the land of Israel, working with wayward youth. A work-study program, with the latest computer technology, provides job-training. A free loan fund, sick fund and a fund for needy families is maintained to assist the members of our community.

Understandably, the costs are enormous, reaching hundreds of thousands of dollars per annum. This, in addition to plans for building and expansion,which are presently estimated at four and one-half million dollars.

To those who enjoyed this and other books of Rabbi Nachman, and are looking forward to future publications, we urge you to take part in this great mitzvah. Please contact us, at any of our offices listed below:

Israel:
Zvi La'Tzadik
36 Salant Street
POB 5370
Jerusalem, Israel
11-3256

Canada:
Canadian Friends of
Chasidei Breslov
152 Strathearn Road
Toronto, Ontario M6C 1S1
0547430-09-13

United States:
American Friends of
Zvi La'Tzadik
3100 Brighton 3rd Street
Brooklyn, New York 11235
11-2524542

England:
Rabbi Nachman of Breslov
Charitable Foundation
43, Manchester Street
London, England W1M 5PE
280174